To my
soulmate
Michael
Christmases
2010
Miriam Cuddles
New update
Dec 2012

(2.50

For Audrey
My wife of Golden Years
With Love and Gratitude

For Miriam

with best wishes

Kipling's Sussex

By Michael Smith

Michael Smith

Printed by Croft Litho
© Published by Brownleaf
ISBN *978-0-9515107-1-1*

H.M.S. *Kipling* was launched in 1939, and The Kipling Society gained permission from the Admiralty
to present a plaque to her. It was a bas-relief sculpted by A. Lowental, which
with other gifts for ward-room and mess decks were delivered in July 1940.
In May 1941, having rescued survivors from *Kashmir* and *Kelly,* she was herself sunk. Having re-established
contact with *Kipling's* survivors association in the 1990s a replica was presented to the group by the Society.
It was moulded from a second bronze held by the society by sculptress Janet Leech of Rottingdean.

A more detailed account of the courageous life of the ship can be seen on www.kipling.org.uk

INTRODUCTION

Rudyard Kipling lived in Sussex for half of his life and he made the county his own. As with everywhere else he had lived, his acute observation enabled him to show a real understanding of the landscape in which each story was set, whether it was in India, or South Africa or the United States. Sussex was, for him, a home in which he experienced both greatest joy and deepest sorrow. There has been another book with the same title, by Robert Thurston Hopkins, *Kipling's Sussex* and its sequel, *Kipling's Sussex Revisited*. He wrote a number of other books including *The Kipling Country*, about his fascination with the landscape and people of Sussex, as well as a trio of biographies of Kipling. Thurston Hopkins was wholly dedicated to protecting the county and wrote extensively about it in the 1920s. As he was an interpreter of Sussex locations, he tended to use his knowledge of Kipling as a framework for commentaries on the places near which he lived or which he introduced into his stories and poems. Thurston Hopkins was only one among a legion of authors who have created an almost unsurpassed literary heritage for the county whose varied landscapes form the south-eastern bulwark of England. Writers of international stature, Kipling himself, A. E. W. Mason, Hilaire Belloc and G. K. Chesterton, and those with a national reputation such as E. V. Lucas, Richard Jefferies, A. S. Cooke, W. H. Hudson, Esther Meynell, Arthur Mee, Norman Wymer, Donald Maxwell and Dirk Bogarde. There are also a host of local authorities, Hadrian Allcroft, Louis Jennings, Barclay Wills, Arthur Beckett, Tickner Edwardes, A. A. Evans and most recently Bob Copper and Peter Brandon, all of whom were clearly enthralled by their special interests or areas and had expert knowledge of them. The list could be extended amazingly. Each had a particular enthusiasm and we can classify them accordingly. The very first were the guides who catered for an increasing number drawn from the capital by the beauty of the countryside and the inspiration of seaside air. Trains brought early passenger contingents on the London, Brighton and South Coast Railway, which itself featured amusingly in Kipling's Arabian Nights' pastiche entitled *Railway Reform in Great Britain*. To the railway explorers were added legions of intrepid cyclists and pioneer motorists. The guides offered tempting tranches of countryside, often centred on a specific railway station or accessible town. They were followed by those who wanted to delve more deeply, and to explain what lay behind the immediate visual impression. These could be called the interpreters. Then there were naturalists and countrymen who focused on plant or animal habitats and on rural life. Archaeologists, historians and geographers all added to the quilt. Biographers of Sussex folk and the autobiographies of those who loved living here fleshed-out the bare outlines, each in his or her own time. Poets and philosophers added yet another dimension. A host of novelists, including Sheila Kaye-Smith, A. E. W. Mason, Jeffrey Farnol, E. F. Benson, William Black, Warwick Deeping, H. G. Wells and George Moore set their tales in the county, and their perspectives often enhanced reality and gave an historical insight to times often more gentle and less frenetic than now.

Ruyard Kipling, in many short stories, painted exquisite word-pictures of time and place in which his characters acted out they lives. As a dedicated letter-writer he left a bequest of great importance, and as a poet his deep understanding of the subtleties of landscape and people are so crafted as to be virtually perfect. In preparing for a series of lectures related to those who wrote about the Sussex landscape I was drawn, inevitably, to the conclusion that he was undoubtedly the master of his adopted county, both in prose and in verse. Admittedly this is a personal view and supporters of others could well argue a case of equality, but for the sheer volume and variety of his output it would be well nigh impossible to match. What we must not forget is that Kipling had many other themes outside the scope of Sussex and was a figure of influence in national and international affairs. As the laureate of the people he rose to the demands of a devoted public to voice their concerns, to support their causes and to offer prophetic warnings and to leave a legacy of the most perfect portraits of land and people.

Good fortune has continued to favour the Kipling attachment to the county, for Bateman's was bequeathed to The National Trust when Carrie died in 1939 three years after her husband. So the house in which he wrote and the garden which he loved were never subsequently owned by others who might have changed them beyond recognition. We are able to enjoy 'the good and peaceable place', to savour the spirit which still pervades the house and garden, and to feel the "feng-shui" which Kipling, always one ahead of his time, felt certain it possessed. We can drive over many of the roads on which he motored and we can absorb the legacy of events, great and small, which he wove into his stories and verses. We can still walk on Rottingdean's Green, between St. Margaret's Church and the three houses which were the focus of his initial roothold in Sussex. Although hailed as the chronicler of the Raj, and the poet of Empire, it is in Sussex where his spirit still abides most strongly.

The aim of this book is to introduce readers both to his life in the county and to consider the background to the county's history and geography as they feature in his tales. Many will already be familiar with his works and I hope that what follows will enhance that understanding. I hope also, because so much of his own written work is presented, it may draw others, previously less familiar with it, to an appreciation of what else he has bequeathed us. His own descriptions of the countryside are quoted in Italic script within the text, but the poems to which reference is made are given in full in Appendix III.

KIPLING'S SUSSEX

APPENDICES

Bibliography

Index

ACKNOWLEDGMENTS

Sir George Engle, now the President of The Kipling Society, first suggested that I could transmute a lecture I gave to the Society, *Kipling's Sussex* into a more detailed study and I am most grateful to him for that initial spur.

I am greatly indebted to Ricky Marsh who proof read every chapter and to Alastair Wilson and Michael Lacey who each commented on several chapters for me and suggested essential improvements. Also to a university colleague, Geoffrey Mead who frequently sent me snippets of very useful information unearthed in his researches into the county of Sussex. Kerr Kirkwood, an old school friend, with a lifelong enthusiasm for, and knowledge of, cattle has provided me with an enhanced understanding of Kipling's love of his herd of Sussex cattle. Former National Trust custodians of Bateman's, Jan (Wallwork-Wright) Clarke and David Fox were both exceptionally helpful and welcoming in that most magical of houses.

I'm also very grateful to many friends in The Kipling Society who have always been very supportive of the project and who have been willing to share their expertise. George Webb, a former Editor of the Society's Journal shares with Lisa Lewis an encyclopaedic knowledge and understanding of the man and his works. David Page, the current Editor has continued the exceptionally high standards of the Journal set by George, as did Sharad Keskar. Sharad's wife Jane, Meryl Macdonald Bendle, a kinswoman of Kipling and an expert on the automobilist in him, Tonie and Valmai Holt who wrote a wonderful book, My Boy Jack? were ever willing to support the project. John Radcliffe who, with genius, created the web-site which is usually regarded as being the most prestigious of any literary society. Roger Ayers and Peter Merry other former Chairmen of the Council of the Society, together with John Walker, our Librarian were also encouraging, Andrew Lycett, author of a superb biography of our man, has helped me greatly through the pages of his comprehensive work. John Morgan's painstaking work in indexing more than 300 issues of The Kipling Journal made possible much speedier access to the annals before they were translated to the web. Professor Tom Pinney, perhaps the most prolific writer on so many aspects of Rudyard's life and work was always ready with helpful advice as was fellow American, David Alan Richards who has created the definitive bibliography. John McGivering's, *A Kipling Dictionary* is ever a constant and trusty companion and John himself always ready to answer questions. I am particularly appreciative of the help of John Stachiewicz, of the National Trust, and Fiona Courage of the Kipling Archive, in giving me permission to include photographs of Bateman's and the family respectively, without which the book would have much less appeal.

The Society's web site www.kipling.org.uk is a treasure trove for admirers, and epitomises the delight with which members share their knowledge and enthusiasm. Founded in 1927 the pages of the Society's Journal bear witness to a similar joy. In the 1960s a dedicated group under the leadership of Reggie Harbord produced a monumental analysis of Kipling's work, the Readers' Guide, running to some 4,000 pages. Parallel inspiration has now translated and extended this into the New Readers' Guide electronically. The web enables both members and non-members to discover that more than seventy years after his death there is still, to paraphrase Pliny, *always something new out of Kipling.*

I am very grateful to Dorothea Berwick for allowing me to include a charming letter which Kipling wrote to her mother, Lady Elizabeth Harris.

I am very thankful to Jonathan Humphrey who masterminded the layout and printing, and to Ann Turner who was invaluable in helping me to master the vicissitudes of my computer.

I am also very fortunate in having a wife, Audrey, who has constantly supported my interest and endeavours and put up with my hours at a word processor.

 Picture Acknowledgements
All the photographs were taken by the author.
To Jill and John Dudley for permission to include one of Bob Copper's paintings of a 'hedger'.
To the late Lady Mansergh for the use of the photo of Kipling aboard a ship of the Royal Navy.

Chapter 1

BEFORE SUSSEX

For those who are not familiar with the contrasting experiences which confronted Rudyard Kipling before he and his family settled in Sussex for the second half of his life, it might be useful to give a relatively brief account of how he achieved fame as a writer and why he became so influential. His mother, Alice, was one of five surviving Macdonald girls, daughters of the Manse, four of whom married extraordinary and talented men. She herself became engaged and married in rapid succession so that her new husband could take up a position as a teacher of Architectural Sculpture at the Sir Jamsetjee Jeejebhoy School of Art and Industry in Bombay. John Lockwood Kipling, inspired by the displays at the Great Exhibition in 1851 decided to capitalize on his talent for handwork by entering the world of pottery through a Methodist friendship with the Pinder family who owned an earthenware business in Burslem, in the smoke-laden environment of 'the Potteries'. The Macdonald family has also been dedicated to the spirit of non-conformity and so the clan which was influential on the west coast of Scotland became allied with a Yorkshire branch of Methodism. Lockwood, having served his apprenticeship in the 'Black Country', with prizes awarded, moved to London to broaden his experience. After a freelance existence

he gained a position in the newly formed government Department of Science and Art, working with sculpture within the South Kensington Museum complex. Alice was the eldest daughter of the Revd. George Macdonald, having been born in 1837. Georgiana (1840), Agnes (1843), Louisa (1845) and Edith (1848) followed, interleaving with Henry and Frederick. Of her eleven children Hannah lost three in infancy. Alice's sisters, always known by their Victorian diminutives, made formidable alliances. 'Georgie' married Ned Jones, later Sir Edward Burne-Jones, the Pre-Raphaelite painter, 'Aggie' wed Edward Poynter, later knighted and President of the Royal Academy, and 'Louie', Alfred Baldwin the wealthy ironmaster industrialist. Only Edith remained

Rudyard Lake

1

United Services College

unmarried, but she outlived all her siblings and was the recipient of charming, amusing and often lengthy correspondence from her nephew. Although of somewhat humble origins, also steeped in Methodism, John Lockwood Kipling, born in the same year as his wife, was to become the foremost authority on Indian Art and was himself later honoured with the C.I.E. (Commander of the Indian Empire). He was, however, destined to be outshone by the brilliance of the son born on December 30th 1865.

The Kiplings were married in March 1865 and set sail, after making the rounds of the family, on April 12th in the paddle steamer *S.S. Ripon* for Alexandria. Crossing the desert isthmus they took ship for Bombay, which they reached in May. It was less than a decade since the Mutiny and life spans for expatriates in India could be brief, so the family back home had much to concern them. Life was not easy in Bombay at the time as the economic climate was parlous and the expected accommodation at the school was not ready. By the time Alice was prepared for the birth of a child, however, the monsoon had passed and cooler weather brought relief from the summer heat. The confinement was long and painful and by the time the servants had sacrificed a goat to propitiate the Gods, the new baby was overdue. Alice, with her usual fortitude, joked that the Creation took no longer. Joseph Rudyard Kipling was christened in the Cathedral on January 22nd, his unusual middle name, introduced at the suggestion of Alice's sister Louie, to commemorate the picnic spot at Rudyard Lake where the parents had celebrated their engagement. It was that name by which he would be recognised for the rest of his seventy years.

The earliest years were unalloyed happiness, for the new baby was cosseted by a devoted ayah, a Portuguese Roman Catholic, and protected by a Hindu bearer, Meeta. He saw far more of them, and spoke in their tongue, being reminded to speak in English to his own parents to whom he was presented before bedtime. Those years were described in his autobiography, *Something of Myself.*

My first impression is of daybreak, light and colour and golden and purple fruits at the level of my shoulder. This would be the memory of early morning walks to the Bombay fruit market with my ayah and later with my sister in her perambulator, and of our returns with our purchases piled high on the bows of it. Our ayah was a Portuguese Roman Catholic who would pray – I beside her – at a wayside cross. Meeta, my Hindu bearer, would sometimes go into Hindu temples, where being below the age of caste, I held his hand and looked at the dimly-seen, friendly Gods.

Our evening walks were by the sea in the shadow of palm-groves which, I think, were called the Mahim Woods. When the wind blew the great nuts would tumble, and we fled – my ayah, and my sister in her perambulator – to the safety of the open. I have always felt the menacing darkness of tropical eventides, as I have loved the voices of the night-winds through palm or banana leaves, and the song of the tree-frogs. There were far-going Arab dhows on the pearly waters and gaily dressed Parsees wading out to worship the sunset.

Alice returned to England for the birth of her second child, a daughter christened Alice, but always known as 'Trix' because, as her father, said she was a 'tricksy' baby. She was two and a half years her brother's junior and her welfare in later life was always of great concern to him. He returned with his mother and he was lodged with the Baldwins on the banks of the Severn at Bewdley, whilst Alice served her confinement with Georgie in Fulham. His spoilt, willful, behaviour did not endear him to his aunt's family, nor indeed to his grandparents, and so, perhaps, this was why he was placed, after a brief seaside family holiday in Littlehampton, with a foster-family in Southsea, when he had not even reached his sixth birthday, rather than with relatives. That part of his early childhood was a bitter apprenticeship to life, for he was badly treated, after her husband's death, by Mrs. Holloway and her obnoxious son, Harry, an unrepentant bully. Living at Lorne Lodge, 'Forlorn Lodge' or 'the House of Desolation' to him, was a time of torment which became crystallized in the semi-autobiographical story *Baa, Baa, Black Sheep.* The cruel realisation that he and Trix were to be, in effect, abandoned in an alien, chilly, environment is brilliantly re-created. Although Trix was more reasonably treated by "Aunty" Rosa, Rudyard was constantly picked upon and accused of misdeeds. The agony was to last for some six years, at the end of which, after a brief solace with his mother in 1877, he entered United Services College at Westward Ho!, near Bideford in Devon. Life improved because the Headmaster, Cormell Price, was a friend both of his father and of Uncle Ned. Although his very poor eyesight prevented him taking part in college games, his literary education was fostered by the Head, whose own library was put at his disposal. His schooldays provided copy for a later set of stories, *Stalky & Co.*, in which the adventures of the occupants Study 5, "Stalky" Dunsterville, "M'Turk" Beresford and "Beetle" himself are treated with a little poetic licence. "Uncle Crom", his caring mentor was thereafter regarded with respect and admiration, and treated as one of the family. In later years the fortunes of the school declined and so Rudyard produced an article for a magazine, *Youth's Companion,* in 1893, about its virtues, in an effort to restore them.

The school, an offshoot of Haileybury, produced boys who were intended to take up careers in the Indian army. Poor vision prevented Rudyard from joining that profession but as his parents, by 1882 safely translated to Lahore, had both written for newspapers in northern India, they knew those who might be of help to a lad with an aptitude for words. Accordingly he was to be given the opportunity to assist the Editor of the *Civil and Military Gazette* published in the teeming city. Making a brief second sortie into Sussex he stayed with Aunt Georgie in Rottingdean before he embarked on a career with words, a career, before the age of 17, which was to bring both honour and reward. In September he sailed from Tilbury on the P & O steamer Brindisi and ten days later was at Port Said ready for passage through the canal which had been open since 1869. From Bombay he travelled up-country 1,000 miles to Lahore in Punjab, to be re-united with his parents. So began what he called in a chapter in his autobiography "Seven Years' Hard" an allusion to a familiar prison sentence of "hard labour".

Quickly putting the earlier misery behind he established a happy family relationship in a typical Punjabi *bungalow.* Anglo-Indian residences were built to a similar design with high-ceilinged rooms and surrounded by a deep *verandah* designed to keep the fierce rays of the sun away from windows. A *punkah,* a rectangular fan, operated by a servant, the cord often being attached to his big-toe, churned the air around in an effort to make life more comfortable. The Kiplings residence differed from most others because they believed that ordinary garden plants harboured insects which could be detrimental to health and so the surrounding earth, instead of being encouraged to flower under the skill of the *mali,* was bare. So bare in fact that their friends called the house "Bikaner Lodge" after the Great Indian Desert. Kipling described the joy of reunification.

That was a joyous homecoming. For – consider! - I had returned to a Father and Mother of whom I had seen but little since my sixth year. I might have found my Mother "the sort of woman I don't care for" as in one terrible case that I know; and my Father intolerable. But the Mother proved more delightful than all my imaginings of memories. My father was not only a mine of knowledge and help, but a humorous, tolerant and expert fellow-craftsman. I had my own room in the house; my servant, handed over to me by my father's servant, whose son he was, with the solemnity of a marriage-contract; my own horse, cart, and groom; my own office hours and direct responsibilities; and – oh joy! – my own office-box, just like my Father's which he took daily to the Lahore School of Art and Museum. I do not remember the smallest friction in any detail of our lives. We delighted more in each other's society than in that of strangers; and when my sister came out, a little later, our cup was filled to the brim. Not only were we happy, but we knew it.

But the work was heavy. I represented fifty per cent of the "editorial staff" of the one daily paper of the Punjab – a small sister of the great "Pioneer" at Allahabad under the same proprietorship. And a daily paper has to come out every day even though fifty per cent of the staff have fever.

My Chief took me in hand, and for three years or so I loathed him. He had to break me in, and I knew nothing. What he suffered on my account I cannot tell; but the little that I ever acquired of accuracy, the habit of trying, at least to verify references, and some knack of sticking to desk-work I owe wholly to Stephen Wheeler.

I never worked less than ten hours and seldom more than fifteen per diem; and as our paper came out in the evening did not see the midday sun except on Sundays. I had fever too, regular and persistent, to which I added for a while chronic dysentery. Yet I discovered that a man can work with a temperature of 104, even though next day he has to ask the office who wrote the article. Our native Foreman, on the News side, Mian Rukn Din, a Mohammedan gentleman of kind heart and infinite patience, whom I never saw unequal to a situation, was my loyal friend throughout. From the modern point of view I suppose life was not fit for a dog, but my world was filled with boys, but a few years older than I, who lived utterly alone, and died from typhoid mostly at the regulation age of twenty-two.

He was able to enjoy something of a social life, as a member of the Club, and soon as an enthusiastic, but underage, Mason. His poem, *The Mother Lodge* illustrates how he valued the companionship of a wide variety of class, creed and race. Those who later accused him of 'racism' did so through wholly unwarranted prejudice. As he grew in confidence his literary horizon widened, for in addition to his editorial work he was given opportunities to file special reports from important, widely scattered, events. Even today those detailed columns of print make enjoyable reading and illustrate his extraordinary talent. They are available in the Kipling Archive, held by the Library of the University of Sussex, and a selected sample has been edited by Professor Thomas Pinney in *Kipling's India*. But perhaps, even more importantly, his insomnia enabled him to work on short stories and poems, many of which were published in the *Civil and Military Gazette* as "turnovers" and later collected into books. His association with English soldiers in the local Mian Mir garrison provided a fund of tales for *Soldiers Three* and poems in *Barrack Room Ballads*, and his knowledge of his fellow countrymen both in the grilling heat of the Punjab and relaxing in the welcome cool relief of Himalayan hill-stations provided copy for *Plain Tales from the Hills* and the verses in *Departmental Ditties*. Rudyard had one vital benefit from his early childhood in that he was able to converse in Urdu and Hindustani with Indians, and so he was able to convey the subtleties of their lives with an accuracy others couldn't match. Particularly in the soldier tales and verses he showed a mastery of English dialects and he also introduced many Urdu or Hindi expressions in a wholly authentic way. Some of these were added to the English language subsequently with the return home of time-expired soldiers who continued to use the familiar words and phrases.

He was captivated by the contrasts he experienced in India: from the palatial lives of the Rajahs to the abject misery of filthy opium-dens; from the awful heat of the Indian summer before the break of the monsoon to the stimulating air of the hill-stations; from the wealth of Hindu merchants to the grinding poverty of street beggars: by the mistreatment of native wives to the cosseting enjoyed by Anglo-Indian ladies: from the excitement of the social whirl to the loneliness impressed upon the official in his work in remote rural areas: from the prejudice experienced by those of mixed-race to the superiority of the caste conscious Brahmin or of the "heaven-born" white officials. Such knowledge, backed by a determination to explore even the meanest streets of the city and a capacity to draw from all those he met, an honest appreciation of what their life and work meant, brought immediate reality to his tales. This mental resource bank he exploited to the full in recreating the scenarios of his short stories. His capacity to describe the India he loved is perhaps at its peak with the novel *Kim* which simmered and bubbled in his mind until he eventually settled in Sussex where it was brought to fruition.

Departmental Ditties is the collection of verses, mostly generated by the intrigues, infidelities and indiscretions he found in the social whirl of life in Simla, the hill station to which the Viceroy retreated for many months of the year. In effect India was governed from there and naturally in addition to the staff, there were memsahibs refreshing themselves for several months whilst their menfolk could normally only be away from their desks on the plains for a month or less. Opportunities for liaisons were much in evidence, encouraged by the round of social events, receptions, balls, theatricals, concerts and gymkhanas. Although not of the social hierarchy enjoyed by the elite, the Kiplings were, nevertheless, invited into the Viceregal circle because Alice was a very personable lady. Indeed her daughter Trix captivated the Viceroy's son, Lord Clandeboye, which was wholly unacceptable. Because her mother was often the centre of attention to her own detriment, Trix felt something of a "wallflower". This discomfiture was highlighted in a charming and amusing poem called *My Rival* which is included in the appendix poems. Among others is *Delilah* who persuaded an elderly admirer to reveal a government secret, and *Army Headquarters* in which Ahasuerus Jenkins is commandeered by a powerful lady to transfer from his regiment by reason of his fine singing voice. When first published Kipling, to avoid the cost of binding, issued the set in the form of individual sheets enclosed in a typical Government file tied up with pink ribbon or 'red-tape'. It made an immediate impact, gaining him an early literary success. Another enterprise was his entry to the "paperback" market. In 1888, now established with the *Pioneer* in Allahabad he was approached by Emile Moreau, head of the firm concerned with railway station bookstalls throughout the sub-continent, to provide tales for six volumes of the "Indian Railway Library", bound in grey-green wrappers. Rail travel, because of the distances involved, often took many hours or even days, and so a readily disposable, light-weight, companion on the journey proved very popular, additionally spreading his tales even more widely. Not surprisingly original editions now command high prices. The covers for the series were designed at the Mayo School of Art in Lahore by his father who was the Director. This year also saw the publication of *Plain Tales from the Hills*. An unsympathetic report Kipling wrote of a meeting of the Congress Party led to recriminations, bad feeling and legal implications. As he had also annoyed the Viceroy, Lord Dufferin, with a poem about Viceregal matters, it may be that these ructions precipitated his departure. But by the time he was ready to seek new horizons back in London after two years on the staff of the *Pioneer*, his star was in the ascendancy. He was befriended during those last two years by Professor and Mrs. Hill. Edmonia Hill, usually known as "Ted", became a trusted confidante, much admired by the young journalist, who, with good humour, dedicated some of his work to her. Rudyard travelled back with the Hills to America *en route* for England in 1889 and was briefly engaged to "Ted's" sister in Pennsylvania. The return journey included brief stops in Burma, Singapore and Japan followed by fairly wide travel in the United States. His time in Japan is delightfully explored in *Kipling's Japan*, by Hugh Cortazzi and George Webb, whilst his American travels have been collected in *Kipling's America* and edited by D. H. Stewart,

AN UNLESSONED GIRL, UNSCHOOLED, UNPRAC
HAPPY IN THIS SHE IS NOT YET SO OLD
BUT SHE MAY LEARN.

Miss Kipling

The London of the last decade of the nineteenth century was lively place, full of material of use as copy. His rooms in Villiers Street overlooked Gatti's famous music hall. Another window gave on to the Thames Embankment so the city's pulse beat close to him. He was taken up by a number of leading lights in the world of publishing and his work fulsomely reviewed and re-issued. 1890 saw friendship develop with an American literary agent, Wolcott Balestier with whom he co-operated on a novel set in India and the United States. When he visited his sister at the Holloways back in 1880 he had been smitten with a young lady named Violet Garrard, and hoped that they would marry. He was rejected, but a chance meeting in London and a visit to her in Paris rekindled hope. Nothing was to come of it, but he used her as a model for Maisie in a novel *The Light that Failed*. Overwork almost caused him to have a nervous breakdown, and he was advised to take a break with a sea trip to Naples, before going to stay with Lord Dufferin at Sorrento. Towards the end of the year he met Wolcott's sister for the first time, and his parents, on home leave, realised with some dismay that Caroline intended to marry their son. She came from a distinguished New England family, but her other brother Beatty, (pronounced "Batey"), in England with them shows his "black sheep" character and is sent back home. Rudyard continued to work hard at a multitude of tasks, writing and dealing with publishers and providing some material of his father's *Beast and Man in India*. An inveterate traveller he crossed the Atlantic with his uncle Fred, hoping to see his eldest uncle Harry who was in poor health. Sadly they arrived too late and although travelling under the Macdonald name he was still hounded by American newspaper reporters. In spite of his own journalistic start he found their inquisition most irritating. He set off almost immediately on his return to take passage to South Africa on a Union Castle liner which sailed via Madeira en route to Cape Town. A fellow passenger, was Captain E. H. Bayly, sailing to take command of the naval base at Simonstown. A subsequent invitation from the Captain drew Kipling into a love of ships and the sea and a deep appreciation of the 'Senior Service'. From then on he championed the cause of the Royal Navy with just as much vigour and insight as he had already shown towards soldiers. He was drawn to the warm and colourful environment of the Cape, but could not explore it as much as he would have wished as he was to sail onward to New Zealand and Australia. His travels gave him a great deal of material to use later.

Returning from Adelaide he sailed to Colombo from where he entrained to stay for Christmas with his parents in his old home. There he learnt, in a cable from Carrie Balestier of the sudden unexpected death from typhoid of his friend Wolcott in Dresden, and so he immediately returned to England. Reaching London on January 10th he joined the sorrowing Balestier family and only a week later married Carrie at All Soul's, Langham Place, in front of a very depleted group of guests because of a serious influenza outbreak. It seemed an extraordinarily precipitate action, but Carrie a very small but determined lady protected him for the rest of his life. She was three years older then her husband although their marriage certificate gave them identical age. They stayed at Brown's Hotel just off Piccadilly and their bill for the honeymoon became the gift of the proprietor in appreciation of the enjoyment Kipling's writings had given him. It was the beginning of a long and harmonious relationship with the hotel, for the Kiplings thereafter always took a suite of rooms overlooking Albermarle Street for visits to London or *en route* on their travels. It was from there at the end of his life he was taken to hospital before he succumbed during an operation. Their honeymoon took them first to Carrie's home at Brattleboro in Vermont where they were met by Beatty for a sleigh ride from the station. Kipling's description is masterly.

Thirty below freezing!. It was inconceivable till one stepped out into it at midnight, and the first shock of that clear, still air took away the breath as does a plunge into sea-water. A walrus sitting on a woolpack was our host in his sleigh, and he wrapped us in hairy goatskin coats, caps that came down over the ears, buffalo robes and blankets and yet more buffalo-robes till we, too, looked like walruses and moved almost as gracefully. The night was as keen as the edge of a newly ground sword; breath froze on the coat-lapels in snow; the nose became without sensation and the eyes wept bitterly because the horses were in a hurry to get home; and whirling through air at zero brings tears. But for the jingle of the sleigh-bells the ride may have taken place in a dream, for there was no sound of hoofs upon snow, the runners sighed a little now and again as they glided over an inequality, and all the sheeted hills around were dumb as death. Only the Connecticut River kept up its heart and a lane of black water through the packed ice; we could hear the stream worrying round the heels of its small bergs. Elsewhere there was nothing but snow under the moon – snow drifted to the level of the stone fences or curling over their tops in a lip of frosted silver; snow banked high on either side of the road, or lying heavy on the pines and the hemlocks in the woods, where the air seemed, by comparison, as warm as a conservatory. It was beautiful beyond expression, Nature's boldest sketch in black and white, done with a Japanese disregard of perspective, and daringly altered from time to time by the restless pencils of the moon.

The Beatty who met them so hospitably was later to prove a thorn in their sides and reason for their precipitate departure from the continent. Soon Rudyard was off on a tour as far as the Rockies to write travel sketches for the *Civil and Military*, the *New York Sun* and *The Times* of London. As soon as he returned he bought some land for a house, Naulakha, named after the novel he had written in co-operation with Wolcott. The book, however, was entitled *The Naulahka: A Story of East and West*, the spelling at variance with the house name. Within a few weeks the newly-weds were off on a real honeymoon, across the Pacific to Yokohama, where just over a month later disaster struck. A day after a severe earthquake in Yokohama, the New Oriental Banking Corporation went into liquidation and they lost all their money. By cashing in the unused portion of the Cooks travel vouchers they were able to return to Vancouver and the Canadian Pacific Railway took them back to the east coast free of charge through the courtesy of William Van Horne, the Chairman of the company. Rudyard's intention of once again visiting Robert Louis Stevenson in his Samoan home was thwarted.

Back in Vermont Rudyard worked on the first of the *Jungle Book* stories, imaginatively inspired by Rider Haggard's book, *Nada the Lily*, in a rented cottage and at the turn of the year their daughter Josephine was born. Meanwhile the new house started to rise on a solid bedrock foundation, a stark long structure but with magnificent views over the river valley. The feckless Beatty was given the task of supervising the construction but his unreliability caused great concern to his sister and her husband. Once established in her new house Carrie's use of a liveried coachman and Rudyard's insistence on dressing for dinner caused amused comment among native Vermonters. On the positive side he began to establish life-long friendships with eminent New Englanders – the lively and attractive Mary Cabot, - a Harvard don, Charles Eliot Norton, and Dr. James Conland who had attended Carrie's confinement. In the spring of 1894 Rudyard and Carrie visited Bermuda where they became friends with a widow, Mrs. Julia Catlin, and her daughters and Rudyard obtained first hand knowledge of the Battle of Maiwand in the Afghan wars from a sergeant of the Royal Berkshire Regiment stationed there. Returning to the United States to collect Josephine they then crossed the Atlantic to stay with Alice and J.L.K., in their retirement home at Tisbury in Wiltshire. From there Rudyard travelled to Devon and was an honoured guest at his old school. In August they returned home and were visited by Arthur Conan Doyle. In 1895 Carrie was severely burned by flames shooting through a furnace door, and convalesced in Washington D.C. This period gave Rudyard the opportunity to meet Theodore Roosevelt with whom he began a long friendship, but his meeting with the President, Grover Cleveland, at the White House did not impress him. Constant work saw the publication of *The Second Jungle Book*. Parental devotion once again took them back to Wiltshire. The following year, following the birth of a second daughter, Elsie, Rudyard and Dr. Conland visited Gloucester, Massachusetts to learn about the techniques of the Grand Banks fishermen for a new novel, *Captains Courageous*. 1896 also saw a widening rift with Beatty whose heavy drinking gave concern and whose financial management of Naulakha's continuing development was open to question. Matters came to a head when Beatty's wild carriage driving knocked Rudyard off his bicycle, only to be followed by demands that he retracts the lies which his brother-in-law thought Kipling had made about him. Following the threat of personal violence, Rudyard unwisely persuaded the Sheriff to arrest Beatty. The hearing of the case in the assembly hall attracted enormous coverage in American newspapers but his appearance at the County Court was deferred. Unwilling to face the trauma of such publicity Rudyard fled with the family back to England, so severing what had initially seemed such a promising future in the New World.

Arriving in England in September Kipling rented Rock House at Maidencombe near to Torquay Perhaps his schooldays in the county influenced this decision, but it proved less than satisfactory for the house was gloomy and the weather abominable. The depression which pervaded Rock House is translated to 'Holmescroft' in a story called *"The House Surgeon'* collected in *Actions and Reactions*. A positive experience rekindled his interest in the Royal Navy, for he renewed his friendship with Captain Bayly at the cadet school at Dartmouth, *H.M.S. Britannia*, who invited him to sail on some naval vessels. Bad weather prevented his participation, much to his relief as he was a poor sailor. He completed a selection of verses and also *Captains Courageous*, the serial rights of which he sold to *McClure's Magazine* for $10,000. He also worked hard on *Stalky & Co.* In April 1897 he was elected, without the need for balloting, to the Athenaeum, a singular honour for one so young, where he was in the company of Cecil Rhodes, Alfred Milner and the Editor of *The Times*. He was invited to the steam trials of a 30 knot destroyer, *H.M.S. Foam*, built by Thorneycrofts at Chatham. It was an exhilarating, but nerve-wracking experience. His fame made him a sought-after guest of many of the "great and the good" and he enjoyed the opportunities presented. Closer to the family his cousin, Philip Burne-Jones, had become enamoured of the beautiful actress, Mrs. Patrick Campbell and following her rejection had painted a rather weird phantasy of a youth straddled by a witch-like creature with pointed teeth and long hair. This painting was to be exhibited in a fashionable new gallery and to promote it Kipling produced a poem called *The Vampire* which created something of a sensation. Philip's parents, Sir Edward and Georgiana Burne-Jones, had a holiday home in Rottingdean near Brighton and it was to this house that they moved from their temporary accommodation at the Royal Palace Hotel in Kensington to avoid the frenetic activity in London in preparation for the Queen's Diamond Jubilee.

Chapter 2

THE LANDSCAPE OF SUSSEX

Rudyard Kipling certainly appreciated the subtleties of the varied landscapes which compose the scenery of his adoptive county for it would have been impossible to write so brilliantly about them, either in prose of in verse, without such an understanding. His library must have made reference to the distinctive units each of which had its own well-defined physical characteristics. Only in the latter part of the nineteenth century when Kipling was at his most prolific, did the burgeoning new science of geomorphology seek to explain the relationship between the underlying geological structure and the agents of weathering and erosion which sculpted the varied strata into the scenery spread before our eyes. Only more recently had the immensity of geological time been recognized, time which allowed for a very gradual modification of mountains, hills, valleys and coastlines. Because of the clarity with which the Weald exhibited the inter-relationship between structure and relief it came to be studied as a truly classic landscape. The evolution of the area from the time in which the rocks themselves had been formed to the present attractive scenery of Down and Weald, of marsh and inlet was recognized with ever greater clarity. A glance at the map will illustrate how closely geology and scenery in the south-east of England are interrelated.

The earth has been in existence for something approaching 4,600 million years, but only the past 600 million or so can its development be interpreted with any great clarity. Geologists divide that period into four major eras, Primary or Palaeozoic (the time of ancient life), Secondary or Mesozoic (middle life), Tertiary or Cainozoic (recent life) and Quaternary. The latter division has occupied only the last two million years. The rocks of the south-east fall within the last three eras beginning about 140 million years ago. The immensity of this geological time scale is shown in the stratigraphical column and the nature of the rocks which form the basis of this landscape are shown in greater detail.

The majority of the rocks of Sussex come within the period known as the Cretaceous, the name being derived from the Latin word *creta*, meaning "chalk". Although chalk is by no means the only rock within that period it is, nevertheless, the most significant, and for that reason the founders of geology, all with a classical education, decided upon it. The Cretaceous Period lasted from about 140 million years ago to approximately 65 million years ago, and its closure coincided with extinction of the great saurians which had dominated life for so immense a length of time. The Period is divided by geologists into two, naturally the earliest being "Lower" and the later being "Upper". Most of what is now Britain was, during the Lower Cretaceous, on the edge of a large land mass, with rivers draining toward the south-east. Those rivers carried with them grains of sand and particles of silt derived from the erosion of higher ground to the north and west. Periodically the present Wealden area was an estuary and at other times either delta or swamp. The material swept down by the early rivers was deposited, accumulated and eventually compressed into the rocks which now form the central area of the Weald. Sands and harder sandstones, muds and clays, thin layers of estuarine limestone formed from the shells of the creatures living in the shallow water, and occasional ironstone are all evidence of changing depositional conditions. The accumulated grains of quartz had been brought from the decomposition of the granite masses far to the west as had the clays formed from the solution of their felspar constituents. Each type of rock reacted differently to the forces of erosion which have worked on them since they were brought to the surface. The various subdivisons of the Lower Cretaceous, together with their predominant rocks are detailed in Figure 2. Across the deltas and around the edges of the estuaries plodded some of the later dinosaurs such as Iguanadon.

About 100 million years ago the whole area subsided beneath an encroaching ocean, to create the Upper Cretaceous. This ocean was called by geologists "Tethys" – after the mythical wife of the God, Oceanus. It was deep, and because it was nearer the equator than now, it was warm. Conditions were perfect for an amazingly prolific marine fauna. Some were invertebrate, shellfish, sea urchins, sponges and the now extinct ammonites and belemnites whilst others were fish and the great marine saurians. But the creatures which had the greatest impact were infinitesimally small coccoliths, which on death fell to the sea floor in a continuous rain to form a white ooze which eventually hardened into a band of chalk, a thousand feet thick. Because of small differences in its nature, the chalk itself is sub-divided into Lower, Middle and Upper. When the Upper Chalk was being deposited, at times, conditions were favourable for an explosion in the sponge population, and the excess silica they secreted formed into nodules or bands of a silica-gel which hardened into the flint we now see in cliff faces. The distinctively visible lines of flint suggest that an over abundance of silica occurred only periodically. Once released by the solution of the upraised chalk surface or the erosion of a cliff-face they offer a seemingly unending supply of flints. Fields have to be cleared of them as they can damage ploughshares, but once collected they formed a useful building material, as did the smooth-worn ovoid flint cobbles collected from beaches. Early man mined the chalk hills to gain an important resource for the manufacture of flint tools and weapons in Neolithic times. These were touched upon in Kipling's tale *The Knife and the Naked Chalk* in *Rewards and Fairies*.

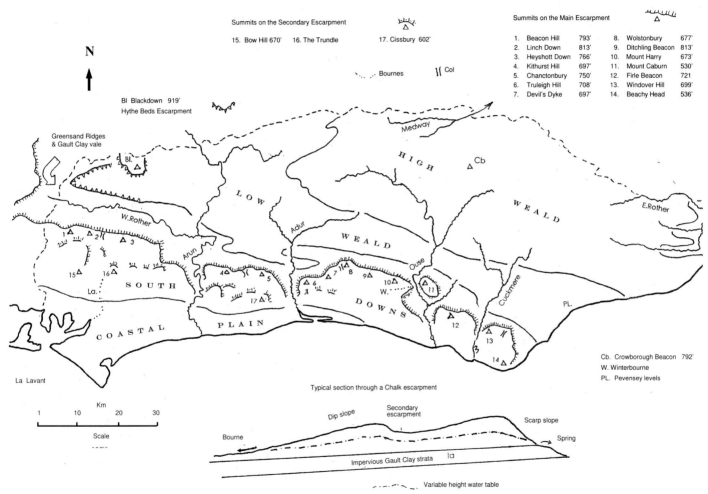

N

Summits on the Secondary Escarpment

15. Bow Hill 670' 16. The Trundle 17. Cissbury 602'

Summits on the Main Escarpment

1.	Beacon Hill	793'	8.	Wolstonbury	677'
2.	Linch Down	813'	9.	Ditchling Beacon	813'
3.	Heyshott Down	766'	10.	Mount Harry	673'
4.	Kithurst Hill	697'	11.	Mount Caburn	530'
5.	Chanctonbury	750'	12.	Firle Beacon	721
6.	Truleigh Hill	708'	13.	Windover Hill	699'
7.	Devil's Dyke	697'	14.	Beachy Head	536'

Bl Blackdown 919'
Hythe Beds Escarpment

Greensand Ridges
& Gault Clay vale

Bournes

Col

Medway

HIGH

Cb

W.Rother

LOW

WEALD

E.Rother

Adur

WEALD

Arun

Ouse

Cuckmere

PL.

4 5

1 2 3

15 16

SOUTH

La.

17

W.

6 7 8 9 10

11

DOWNS

12

13

COASTAL

PLAIN

3

14

La Lavant

Cb. Crowborough Beacon 792'
W. Winterbourne
PL. Pevensey levels

Km

1   10   20   30

Scale

Typical section through a Chalk escarpment

Dip slope

Secondary
escarpment

Scarp slope

Bourne

Spring

Impervious Gault Clay strata

Variable height water table

Figure 1

15

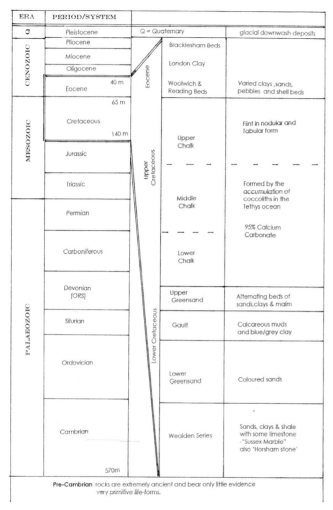

Earth began its formation about 4,800 Million years ago

Figure 2

After the chalk had been consolidated, raised above sea level and partially eroded the area was again submerged and sediments from the earliest periods of the Tertiary era were deposited on them. These are today found only in isolated patches on top of the chalk, as at Newhaven and on the low-lying coastal plain between Brighton and the Hampshire border.

About 35 million years ago the earth's crust was subjected to a slow but inexorable mountain building period, called the "Alpine orogeny". The south-east felt less severe pressures as the outer ripples of the more massive upheaval which created the Alps, so the rocks were simply folded upwards into a gentle elongated dome in which an arch of chalk covered the middle of what is now the Weald. The downfold of this structure dipped beneath what is now the Thames valley only to reappear in East Anglia. At this time there was no suggestion of an English Channel and so the anticlinal dome continued into what is now the Bas Boulonnais in northern France. Once uplifted, weathering and erosion began their destructive work, removing first, most of the Tertiary sediments before attacking the summit of the chalk itself. Weathering is the process by which rocks are broken down by rain, temperature change and the effect of plant roots, the decomposed material remaining *in situ*. Rivers flowing north and south from the central ridge began the removal of the weathered particles by erosion, which was aided by the solution of the calcium carbonate of the chalk itself. Very gradually the upper part of the dome, weakened by the stresses of the folding process, were removed, leaving the underlying varied sediments of the Lower Cretaceous exposed to the continuing erosive process. Because the nature of these rocks differed, one from another, differential erosion worked more easily on the clays than on the sands and better cemented sandstones. So, very gradually, the clays became vales, the less strong sandstones were left as ridges, and the firmer, better consolidated sandstones as the higher ground of what is now the High Weald. The process continued steadily and a number of rivers originally draining either side of the dome were reduced by "capture" into the four southward flowing rivers which maintained their courses to cut gaps through the South Downs. Only in the Pleistocene ice-age of the last two million years was the steady removal of material affected by changing conditions. Although the ice front at its maximum extent, reached only as far as the Severn-Thames line, the rocks of the south-east were under severely icy peri-glacial conditions. The result was the cutting of valleys in the chalk itself and the accumulation of a glacially cold downwash sludge in the valley bottoms. These will be considered more fully when we examine the Downs. Finally, about 10,000 years ago rising sea level created by the addition of water from the melting, world-wide, ice-sheets and glaciers broke through the former land bridge from what is now northern France and so separated the British Isles from the continent of Europe.

The South Downs

The overall effect as the crown of the dome was removed was the erosion of the chalk away from the centre, north and southward, to create a gradually retreating escarpment of the fine white limestone called chalk. An escarpment, or cuesta, is a landscape in which there is a gently inclined surface parallel to the dip of the strata and a steeply inclined scarp face. In the case of the South Downs there is a narrow stratum of a fairly similar rock called the "Upper Greensand" immediately beneath the Chalk and below that an impervious layer of "Gault Clay". Rain falling, or snow melting on the downland surface sinks through until it reaches the Gault and then builds up a reservoir of water in the porous chalk to what is called the "water-table", which tends to follow the line of the ground above. It will gush out in the form of springs where the water table intersects with the surface itself. (Fig. 1) For many millennia the water stored by nature was in much greater volume than now because it is only in the past hundred years or so that man has extracted water mechanically to serve a growing population with ever increasing needs. Thus past strong flow particularly affected the scarp face to create, mainly by solution, the scalloped edge which is now so characteristic a feature. At this stage in the erosional cycle the North and South Downs bracket the varied older rocks within, which are technically "The Weald". Some authors use that term to encompass Downs and Weald, but this is not strictly correct. The word "Down" seems strangely inappropriate for a range of fairly high and well rounded hills, but the name was bequeathed from our Saxon forebears to whom the word for "hill" was "dun". Their bold forms under a wide, ever changing, sky has attracted those who love the open air, many of whom as artists with paint or with word have left a glorious nostalgic vision.

The distinctive character of the South Downs is superbly conveyed by Kipling in his poem *Sussex*.

No tender hearted garden crowns, No bosomed woods adorn, Our blunt, bow-headed whale-backed Downs, But gnarled and writhen thorn.

This is true of the bare downs in East Sussex, but the escarpment in West Sussex beyond the Arun gap is very well covered with beech "hangers". The summits rise from a general level of about 800' and the slight eminences are individually named. Kipling used many of them in a charming poem called *The Run of the Downs*".

The Devils Dyke towards Chantonbury

The Weald is good, the Downs are best – I'll give you the run of 'em East to West.

A glance at an Ordnance Survey topographical map will reveal immediately that there are virtually no rivers or streams flowing in the area. The contour lines reveal, however, that there is a well marked series of valleys which follow a tree like (dendritic) pattern just as a river and its tributaries normally does. The valleys themselves have a "v" shaped cross section, although not always symmetrical. The long profile lessens in steepness as it reaches lower ground. Clearly they must at one time have been carved by river erosion yet they carry no water. Under normal circumstances water falling on to chalk

Ditchling Beacon – a blunt bow-headed, whale back Down

areas is absorbed, but during the many millennia of the last ice-age, the Pleistocene, the area was subject to severe permafrost conditions which froze the water in the porous sub-surface. In periods of some summer warmth, the snow cover would melt and flow downhill, and because it could not sink through, would actively erode the surface. At the end of the ice-age normal conditions were resumed and once again rainwater would be absorbed rather then flowing over the surface. The resultant landforms created in this way are known as "dry-valleys", although over many millennia brooks would flow in them occasionally in response to the accumulation of water in the chalk. Such periodically flowing streams are known as "bournes". Now only two such rills are to be seen in Sussex, one the Lavant in the west of the county behind Chichester and the other the Winterbourne, flowing through Lewes to the Ouse. Kipling recognised this distinctive feature of the chalk landscape in another stanza from Sussex.

We have no waters to delight, Our broad and brookless vales, Only the dewpond on the height, Unfed that never fails

Dewponds are a relatively modern introduction to the scenery. When enormous flocks of sheep roamed the Downs under the eye of a hardy shepherd there was always need for a drinking supply. Circular dew-ponds 20 to 30 yards in diameter were dug out and traditionally lined with puddled clay, straw and flints. Modern ones may be lined with plastic sheeting or have a concrete base. They were, and still are, dependent on rain to fill them rather than relying on the dew incorporated in their names.

Four major rivers, the survivors of the many streams which originally drained southwards from the dome, managed to maintain their courses. Throughout the ice-age sea-level rose and fell in response to the changing volumes of ice locked up in ice-caps and valley glaciers. At times sea-level was much lower than now and so these rivers cut deeply down to new base-levels. The original valley bottoms were probably some 90' lower than today. With a rise in sea-level sediments would accumulate at the seaward end of the valley, creating a flat valley floor over which the river could meander. The present rivers, Arun, Adur, Ouse and Cuckmere all exhibit this feature as they make their way through sizeable gaps in the main escarpment. Because they were less silted in medieval times and sea-going vessels were small they became arteries of trade serving Arundel, Bramber and Lewes.

The Weald

Just as the Saxons gave us the word "down" so too they left us *Andredesweald,* the Forest of Andred, the great woodland which once covered much of Sussex. The clear equivalence of the German word "wald" inspired it. In later times the 'Andred' prefix was dropped and the softer "weald" remained. At the foot of the escarpment there is, in places, a slight platform jutting northward, formed by the Upper Greensand. This has a varied lithology, siltstones, and sandy clays, called malmstones. This rather indistinct outcrop lies over the Gault Clay, which is dark blue or grey in colour but which weathers into yellowish brown clays. It is fairly easily eroded and so is seen as a shallow vale at the foot of the downs. The strata below the gault, and next in the sequence, is the Lower Greensand, a group of rocks only very rarely green in colour and having some clays and even limestones within it. In the west of the county this formation is somewhat thicker and gives rise to distinctive scenery, including a low escarpment, it is much less obvious in the area between Lewes and Eastbourne. Near Washington, inland from Worthing some spectacular colours are to be seen in the outcrops, which have been extensively quarried, - creams, yellows, pinks and reds. The vegetation of this heathland reflects the relative infertility of the soils which develop on them. Succeeding the Greensands is a much wider band of the Weald Clay, although this group of strata also contain thin sandstones and an estuarine limestone. The scenery associated with the Weald Clay is called the 'Low Weald', usually flat and undistinguished and which can easily become very muddy in wet weather. But the material of the thin sandstone and limestone layers have made an important contribution to the social history of the region. The sandstone, in thin, discontinuous beds provided the wonderfully impervious "Horsham Stone" which was used as a very valuable roofing material for centuries. It cleaves into relatively even slabs, all of which are very heavy for roofing, and were it not for the abundance of stout oak beams available locally, could not have been used. Smaller thinner slabs were used near the crown of the roof and larger thicker ones nearer the eaves. The limestone, composed of the shells of a freshwater snail

Viviparus, is erroneously called 'Sussex Marble', because the masons realised that, when sawn it could take a reasonable polish. The attractive sections of the fossil shells produce a pleasing pattern in a blue-green colour, and so it has been used as an interior decorative material for churches and homes for many centuries. In an unpolished state it was used as paving slabs, which because of the slight roughness of the rounded shells, gives a good foothold. The paths around Bateman's make appropriate use of the 'Sussex Marble' and the fossilized shells are readily discernable. Marble, itself, is a metamorphic rock in which the original limestone was transformed by great heat and pressure within the earth's crust destroying all evidence of the shells of which it was composed. The Sussex 'marble' is simply an unaltered limestone.

Wisteria on wall at Bateman's

The inner core of the Wealden anticline consists of the lowest strata of the Wealden Series, the more resistant, mainly sandstone, rocks at the base of the Lower Cretaceous system. They rise above the low-lying plain of Weald Clay to a well dissected plateau up to 900' above sea-level. These are the Hastings Beds and they curve round to the south-east to be truncated between Fairlight and Cliff End to produce quite spectacular cliff scenery. These are formed by the massive well-jointed Ashdown sandstones, and remains of an old cliff-line can be seen trending away behind the recent deposits which form Romney Marsh and the cuspate foreland of Dungeness. The Ashdown Sandstones outcrop in the side of the valley of the River Dudwell , and were quarried to provide the building blocks for Bateman's. The cream coloured sandstones contain some iron deposits and these "rust" to create the attractive streaks in the walls of the house. A series of streams drain down from the central plateau to the south and also to the north-east where they form the headwaters of the Medway. Many of these deeply incised "ghylls" were ponded back by the masters of the early iron-industry to provide water power to work ore-crushers, bellows, forges and hammers. The well-wooded landscape provided an abundant supply of charcoal with which to smelt the scattered iron deposits which had been worked since Iron Age and Roman times. Kipling was well aware of the great industry and made reference to it both in his autobiography *Something of Myself* and in the Puck tales.

The Sussex Coastal Plain

A variety of fairly soft materials deposited during the Tertiary era laid a veneer over the chalk and these form the diminishing wedge of coastal plain between the Hampshire border and where the chalk intersects with the English Channel at Black Rock, just to the east of Brighton. The picture is more complicated because there are also periglacial deposits which were sludged downward by melting snow and some wind-accumulated loess formed during the waxing and waning phases of the Ice Age. The landscape is one of a low-lying plain, fertile because of the mixture of soil types, but which for centuries were somewhat isolated and remote. The attraction of coastal settlement developed in response to changing attitudes and so from Regency times a gradual accretion of building began to spread along the plain so that by the beginning of the twenty-first century there is relatively little more which can be accommodated.

The Sussex Coastline

The English Channel was initiated only about ten thousand years ago as water released by the melting ice raised sea-level world-wide and passage was joined between the Atlantic inlet and the North Sea. The Sussex coastline was born.

Each one of the scenic units which make up the county and give it is charming and varied appeal has a counterpart on the coast, and these, too, offer many spectacular views. In the far west, near the Hampshire border, the gentle streams which drained the Downs flowed across the coastal plain in shallow valleys. A slight rise in sea level converted these into winding tidal inlets which reach inland towards Fishbourne and the lovely little mooring of ancient Bosham. So little has changed here that a crewman on a Roman galley or on a Norman longship would instantly recognise the channels. The outflow is the narrow gap between Hayling Island and West Head. Immediately east the promontory of the Manhood Pensinsula extends to its tip at Selsey Bill. Here the coastline has been changing for centuries and Selsey, originally Seal's Island, was the location which Kipling used for the arrival of St. Wilfrid, from the north, when he felt drawn to convert the pagan Saxons. Eddi, one of his companion priests, ministered to the ox and the ass in the poem *Eddi's Service* in a small chapel near the coast. Hard by is the wildlife sanctuary of Pagham Harbour, innundated by the breaking of a sea wall long ago. Large areas have been lost to the incessant ravages of the sou'west storm surges which beat up the English Channnel. "The Park" which was once a royal hunting reserve has disappeared completely and the Bill has to be protected annually by the reshaping of shingle banks to protect the low-lying ground behind. It is a continuing battle in which nature will almost certainly win.

From Selsey Bill the coastline curves gently towards the mouth of the Arun and past it to Worthing and Shoreham. The powerful effect of the waves, which constantly move material from where it has been eroded further west, is evident in a process known as "longshore drift". The prevailing south westerly winds move sand and shingle obliquely up the beach, the return rolling movement being straight back towards the waterline. That mass migration of material for long had threatened the shoreline of the coastal settlements, and so measures to slow it were attempted by the building of wooden groynes. It is not wholly effective but the curving shoreline profile between groynes and the piling up of sand and shingle against each eastern arm is a feature of the coast. This continuous drift of material was sufficient, in medieval times, to divert the mouth of the Adur eastward towards the tiny village of Hove. Only later did man cut through the shingle bar in order to improve access and to create a tide-controlled harbour.

Chalk cliff scenery stretches from Black Rock at Brighton to the great headland at Beachy Head, except where the rivers Ouse and Cuckmere flow out into the sea. The spectacular coastline has been eroded back ever since the channel was formed and it is still retreating intermittently except where sea defences protect the base. It is stabilised by the undercliff walk between Black Rock and Saltdean and again by a short stretch at Peacehaven. Elsewhere the chalk is under constant attack and since the groynes further west have slowed up the movement of shingle the speed of erosion has accelerated. A shingle deposit will, to some, extent, cushion the effect. At high tide the waves strike directly at the base of the cliff, and their force, in rough seas, compresses the air in minute cracks in the chalk. As a wave retreats there is an explosive decompression, and this continuous assault weakens the structure, which is enhanced by the waves hurling shingle at the chalk. The base can be undercut and as the upper part of the cliff is affected by alternate free-thaw conditions in severe winter weather, the upper part is also weakened. Thus, periodically, there is major slumping of broken chalk. The cliff is then protected for a period until the power of the sea removes the fallen material. The overall effect is a retreat, on average, of something approaching two to three feet in a year. Where dry valleys dissect the chalk surface a dip in the coastline is apparent, and if of sufficient depth an exploitable gap to the shore is created. One is to be found at Rottingdean, but at the Seven Sisters coastline between Cuckmere Haven and Birling Gap most of the dry-valleys are seen hanging spectacularly some height above the beach. The alignment of the beach faces south westerly and so the chalk is exposed to the full force of the traditional storm direction. Kipling recognised this in two stanzas from *Sussex*.

Clean of officious fence or hedge,
Half-wild and wholly tame,
The wise turf cloaks the white cliff edge
As when the Romans came.
What sign of those that fought and died
At shift of sword and sword?
The barrow and the camp abide,
The sunlight and the sward.

Here leaps ashore the full Sou'west
All heavy winged with brine,
Here lies above the folded crest
The Channel's leaden line;
And here the sea-fogs lap and cling,
And here, each warning each,
The sheep-bells and the ship-bells ring
Along the hidden beach

The Seven Sisters

At Beachy Head, the escarpment curls back on itself and the Upper Greensand outcrops, wave-etched on the shoreline. From there the South Downs are lost and the chalk reappears only where the North Downs reach the sea at Dover. In between the cliffs of South and North Downs Lower Cretaceous sands, sandstones and clays are responsible for the contrasting coastal scenery.

The view from Beachy takes the eye across an expansive bay towards Bexhill and Hastings. The present smooth shoreline is very different from that which greeted both Roman and Norman, for until medieval times the area was a sizeable harbour at high tide but with large areas of mud and sand exposed on the ebb, and the occasional islet. Pevensey itself was behind a low cliff, on the promontory of which the Romans established, in the late third century, one of their "forts of the Saxon Shore". At that time it would have been possible to walk across at low tide to the next firm shoreline, and it is this characteristic which produced the Roman name of Anderita or "the great ford". The Roman shore is at least a mile inland from the present strandline. Low cliffs at Bexhill are separated from more distinctive ones by a small inlet at Bulverhythe in which the Norman invasion fleet was able to anchor after departure from the brief interlude at Pevensey. They created a motte surmounted by a

Beachy Head

prefabricated wooden keep above the sandstone cliffs at Hastings. These cliffs extend past Fairlight to Cliff End, which in places are subjected to the most ferocious erosional attack by the sea, causing property to be abandoned. From Cliff End an old cliff line trends in a great curve toward Hythe. First, past Winchelsea, the trio of rivers coalesce at what was once the little island "Atter eye", which compressed as 'Rye' was one of the Cinque Ports. But since its heyday the sea has retreated some distance. Kipling, again in *Sussex* expresses the loss perfectly.

And east till doubling Rother crawls, To find the fickle tide, By dry and sea-forgotten walls, Our ports of stranded pride.

The great cuspate foreland of Dungeness was built by longshore drift carrying shingle in both directions from south-west and from north-east, so that crescent shaped ridges of pebble look pointedly, arrow-like, seaward to France. Behind that shingle is the Marsh, a land of drains and diks and sluices, with a character all of its own, whose shoreline has altered with the centuries. Once regarded as a continent in its own right by locals, it has an attraction for wildness and fantasy with an ever-changing, over-arching sky. It had a magnetic personality for Kipling who set a number of tales within its bounds. Past Camber and East Guldeford it is, of course, Kentish land. To the smuggling community mere boundaries mattered little.

Inspiration

The contrasting landscapes within the county gave him great delight and he used them for the settings of numerous stories and poems. He was a tireless walker, enjoying the company of visiting family and friends, as they strode over the Downs enfolding Rottingdean. He soon became familiar with a much wider compass as he was chauffeured, first as a pioneer motorist seeking a new home and later in the luxury of his Rolls-Royces. Although some of the scenes familiar to him have changed beyond recognition others are still almost as he described them. He found it impossible to decide which landscape claimed his greatest affection. At first, certainly, the rolling chalk downland, but once settled at Bateman's the inner weald and the nearby Romney Marsh proved equally attractive. *A Three-Part Song* underscores his indecision.

I'm just in love with all these three, The Weald and the Marsh and the Down countree, Nor I don't know which I love the most, The Weald or the Marsh or the white Chalk coast.

Later he recognised that the Sussex Downs because of their great power to attract an ever increasing number of visitors might hold the seeds of their own desecration. In 1926 he wrote *Very Many People*.

On the Downs, in the Weald, on the Marshes, I heard the Old Gods say:
"Here come very many people: We must go away".

"They take our land to delight in, But their delight destroys,
They flay the turf from the sheepwalk. They load the Denes with noise".

One of the greatest benefits his words bring to us is his capacity to bring into focus a landscape of a less frenetic time, parts of which have disappeared for ever. Through his meticulous eye for detail we meet shepherds and their faithful dogs caring for their flocks, craftsmen hedgers practicing their ancient arts, the local builder with an accumulated knowledge of wood and stone, smugglers who plied their nefarious trade in the dark of the crescent moon and a host of characters who moulded the history not only of the county but of England itself.

Philology

The term "Downs", normally associated with the strong rounded contours of the chalk uplands seems paradoxically "topsy-turvey" until one realises that it is derived from the Saxon word 'dun', meaning a hill. The word 'dene' or its later version, 'dean' means a valley. The curved parentheses of the North and South Downs enfold an area which is technically the "Weald". That name is derived from the Saxon name "Andredesweald" – ' the forest of Andred' – a softening of the harsher Germanic 'wald'.

The majority of Sussex place names were derived from the Saxon language, and they can be interpreted to demonstrate the gradual advance of pioneering settlement of the coast fringe to the well wooded centre, used for pannage of pigs before the clearings or 'hursts' were taken into cultivation. Just a few words take us back even before Roman occupation. An example is, possibly, the very old word for water – 'us' which is transmuted to Ouse. Some relate to the Romano-British settlement and others from the time of the Norman conquest. Kipling introduced place names and old Sussex words vigorously into his texts. Appendix I is a glossary of Sussex dialect words and Appendix II is concerned with some place names of special significance.

A dew pond

Cliff end

Camp Hill

Seaward view of Rye from the church tower

Chapter 3

DOWNLAND IDYLL

For more than a century Rottingdean has taken a justifiable pride in its connection with so notable a resident as Rudyard Kipling, for it was his family home between 1897 and 1902. Rudyard and Carrie were, however, inveterate travellers and much of each winter was spent avoiding the worst of the English weather so that their residence was not continuous. Even so the period was of great moment, not only because Rudyard completed a number of important works but also because so many notable figures came to visit him. The years brought for the family both great joy and awful sadness and peace as well as conflict.

A postcard of Rottingdean in 1900

It might have been thought that, on returning to England, settling in the village would have been a foregone conclusion because it held a comfortable holiday home for Kipling's "beloved aunt" Georgiana, and her Pre-Raphaelite painter husband, Sir Edward Burne-Jones. Another positive attraction was the fact that his cousin, Stanley Baldwin, had married "Cissie" the daughter of the Ridsdales of The Dene, and was, thus, a frequent visitor to the home of his "in-laws" close by. So there was thus a ready-made family circle which he valued. The picturesque location in a dry-valley running to The Gap in the chalk cliffs gave the benefit of healthy sea-air advocated by the medical profession. In addition the village was within easy reach of Brighton's railway station and the magnetic attraction of London. It was not, however, their first choice. Devon's "English Riviera" was particularly attractive to Carrie because it was the home of the mother of a close friend and also some considerable distance from her mother-in law. It was, in addition, the county where Ruddy's schooldays stability compensated for the bitter apprenticeship of Southsea. Love of nearby sea and ships was a comforting bonus. But even there, at Maidencombe, near Torquay, the drear Rock House granted no favours in an uncomfortably dismal winter, so the Kiplings soon set out to find an alternative. Perhaps persistent toothache made life seem even more uncomfortable for Rudyard and discomfiture is exemplified by visits to his parents at Tisbury and to London's clubs. The dark oppression felt at Rock House is pictured in a later story *The House Surgeon* published more than a decade later.   The expected panacea of taking up tandem bicycling, wearing specially designed CTC suits, pedalling through the steep, and often muddy, lanes or around the town's velodrome didn't relieve the oppression of the damp weather. Neither did fishing and long walks with "the Pater" solve the problem, although work carried on steadily. One contact did, however, give great and lasting pleasure. As a guest at the Training School of the Royal Navy aboard H.M.S. Britannia at Dartmouth he renewed the acquaintance of Captain E. H. Bayly and was given sea-time aboard a cruiser which triggered great admiration for both mess deck and wardroom and thus just as active a support for naval affairs as he had already developed for the British soldier.

Leaving Torquay they went to London where on April 2nd Rudyard was elected to the Athenaeum, under Rule 2 which admitted distinguished people without the normal need for balloting. A busy social diary included an Academy dinner and a reception at the Royal Society as well as house-hunting in Kent. He sat for a portrait by William Strang in early May and a fortnight later was invited to Thorneycroft's yard at Chatham for the trial of a torpedo-boat destroyer. He was fêted at Oxford's Balliol College and then travelled to Brighton to discuss an offer of housing from Georgiana Burne-Jones. That invitation was fulfilled in Rottingdean on Derby Day 1897, but even then taking up full residence just across the Green was not a foregone conclusion. Until, eventually, they signed a tenancy for The Elms in September, their eyes and attentions were drawn to possibilities around the county town of Lewes and in the Hastings area. The arrival was documented in *Something of Myself*, but as the words were written in the last year of Rudyard's life a few errors of recollection have crept in.

Our flight from Torquay ended almost by instinct at Rottingdean where the beloved Aunt and Uncle had their holiday house, and where I had spent my very last days before sailing for India fourteen years back. In 1882 there had been but one daily bus from Brighton, which took forty minutes; and when a stranger appeared on the village green the native young would stick out their tongues at him. The Downs poured almost direct into the one village street and lay out eastward unbroken to Russia Hill above Newhaven. It was little altered in 96. My cousin, Stanley Baldwin, had married the eldest daughter of the Ridsdales out of the Dene the big house that flanked the green. My Uncle's North End House commanded the other, and a third house opposite the church was waiting to be taken according to the decrees of Fate. The Baldwin marriage, then, made us free of the joyous young brotherhood and sisterhood of the Dene, and its friends.

As their arrival was in June 1897 rather than '96 it was actually fifteen years after leaving for India. He had also mistaken the local pronunciation of 'Rushey Hill' which he has transposed to 'Russia Hill'. The map of the time shows distinctly the nature of the village, set just four miles to the east of Brighton, as a single street occupying the floor of a dry-valley which intersected the cliffed coastline at a slight angle at the 'Gap'. The seaward end consisted of an extension to the High Street before the track dropped steeply to beach level, above which was the pier built to receive the Daddy-Long-Legs railway. The modest 'White Horse', formerly 'The King of Prussia' overlooked its forecourt and a badminton green, at the side of which was a latticed shelter. It was here

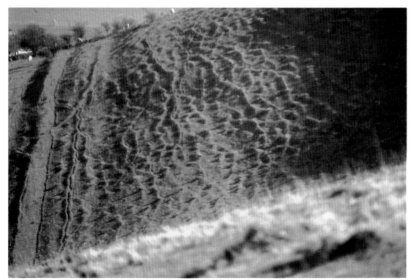

Tangled Sheep Tracks

that the local photographer would take typical 'seaside photos'. Across the main Brighton to Eastbourne road, in the area now a triangular car park, was a block of housing which supported another public house, 'The Royal Oak'. The single High Street, with two more pubs, in addition to butchers, bakers, sweet shop and Post Office led to the picturesque hub, of the village, Pump Green. Two rough tracks formed a saltire above the pond across the green itself and continued northward, following the old trackway over a downland rise to Falmer. At the heart of the green was the pond, which had for centuries provided water for the community founded around it probably in the seventh or eighth century. The name of the village was, naturally, of Saxon derivation – the elements being 'ingas' (the people of), Rota, the name of the first family elder and the word 'dean' for valley. The 'valley of Rota's people'. It had been primarily a farming community, with the sea playing only a minor role in its economy, the rock-pools in the chalk platform below the Gap, supplying prawns and shrimps, and with pots sown offshore, lobsters. It was never a fishing village as such. An idea of its pleasant northern focus at the time, around the Green, is seen in the postcard showing St. Margaret's and the properties enfolding Pump Green. Open downland, now partially built over, enfolded the settlement, with Beacon Hill to the west opposite East Hill. Water for human consumption was obtained from a well, the pond water being used for animals. Only recently had a piped supply been installed through the initiative and generosity of Mr. Edward Ridsdale, before which it was either carried home in a couple of pails slung from a yoke or bought from a wheeled water-cart toted around the village. It was a difficult farming environment for the thin chalk soils, never abundantly productive, needed intensive labour and substantial "muck-spreading" to keep it in good heart. Of some three thousand acres locally only a third was under arable and the process of ploughing was powered either with draught horses or with teams of eight bullocks. Large flocks of seagulls would certainly have followed the ploughshare. Seed sowing was traditionally broadcast by hand. The harvest was reaped with scythes and sickles, and the grain threshed in the barns with flails, the "threshold" across the double doors preventing the heavier seed from being blown away. Traditional haystacks dotted the fields. Golden-red mangel-wurzels were pulled and clamped for use as cattle fodder in the winter, so that a milk supply could be maintained. The remaining two thousand acres were grazed by enormous flocks of sheep, each under the care of a shepherd and a dog. The Downland shepherds were incredibly tough characters, out in all weathers, and especially at lambing time working from small wheeled cabins for weeks on end. Each group of sheep had a leader, - a bell-wether – the distinctive tone of its iron bell telling the shepherd where each cluster was grazing. Kipling described the scene with great clarity in *The Knife and the Naked Chalk* in which the children, returning from Bateman's to stay with Aunt Georgie, accompany their father's friend, the shepherd Ben Dudeney and his dogs, Old and Young Jim. John and Elsie are transposed for the stories into Dan and Una, fictional names which sprang from the little menagerie, which included a lion cub, which so enhanced their time in Cape Town. Kipling captured the essence of the downland character in a few succinct paragraphs. It was, for him, the beginning of a long and expert training in the ways of farming which he developed later in his estate in the Weald. Kipling often plucked names from those of the local community for use in his stories and his normal practice was to cloak the name with a fictional character. Here, however, name, character and occupation coalesced.

They made friends with an old shepherd, called Mr. Dudeney, who had known their father when their father was little. ..... He had a tiny cottage about half a mile from the village, where his wife made mead from thyme honey, and nursed sick lambs in front of a coal fire, while Old Jim, who was Mr. Dudeney's sheep-dog's father lay at the door.

One afternoon when the village water-cart had made the street smell specially townified, they went to look for the shepherd, as usual, and, as usual, Old Jim crawled over the door-step and took them in charge. The sun was hot, the dry grass was very slippery, and the distances were very distant. ..... 'Show, boy! Show!' said Dan, for the Downs seemed as bare as the palm of your hand. Old Jim sighed, and trotted forward. Soon they spied the blob of Mr. Dudeney's hat against the sky a long way off. .... Two kestrels hung bivvering and squealing above them. A gull flapped lazily along the white edge of the cliffs. The curves of the Downs shook a little in the heat, and so did Mr. Dudeney's distant head. They walked toward it very slowly and found themselves staring into a horse-shoe-shaped hollow a hundred feet deep, whose steep sides were laced with tangled sheep -tracks. The flock grazed on the flat at the bottom, under charge of Young Jim. Mr. Dudeney sat comfortably knitting on the edge of the slope, his crook between his knees. ..... The air trembled a little as though it could not make up its mind whether to slide into the Pit or move across the open. But it seemed easiest to go down-hill, and the children felt one soft puff after another slip and sidle down the slope in fragrant breaths that baffed on their eyelids. The little whisper of the sea by the cliffs joined with the whisper of the wind over the grass, the hum of the insects in the thyme, the ruffle and rustle of the flock below, and a thickish mutter deep in the very chalk beneath them.

After a day's adventuring when they meet a man of the Neolithic age and learn of the sacrifice he had made, the homeward trek is exquisitely described.

The Downs which looked so bare and hot when they came were full of delicious shadow-dimples; the smell of the thyme and the salt mixed together from the south-west drift from the still sea; their eyes dazzled with the low sun, and the long grass under it looked golden. The sheep knew where their fold was, so Young Jim came back to his master, and they all four strolled home, the scabious-heads swishing about their ankles, and their shadows streaking behind them like the shadows of giants.

The cottage, at the top of the track leading to the downs was later to become Bazehill Road, and the Dudeney home was "Shepherd's Cottage". He was known to

Ben Dudeney and young Jim

his friends as 'Bung' as he enjoyed his ale.   Rudyard was adept at inventing words which seemed to illustrate their meaning. "Bivvering" seems perfectly to evoke the fluttered hovering flight of kestrels, and he modified a golfing term in the wind which "baffed" on their eyelids. Shepherds were essential figures in downland villages and Rottingdean had a delightfully eccentric one in 'Steve' Barrow. He wore a distinctive moleskin cap and delighted in his picturesque image, being noted for interminable songs accompanied on his concertina. He was also a renowned story-teller and had been immortalized as 'Old Bramble' in Alfred Noyes poem *The Silver Crook*. He was wary of Rudyard as he felt that his own rich vein would find its way into the Kipling canon. Steadfastedly refusing to let the author hear his stories, he avowed "that Rudyard Kipling would be sendin' 'em to Lunnon and makin' a mort of money out of 'em".

On the opposite hill the stark outline of the Mill on Beacon Hill was one of the features which so impressed Georgie Burne-Jones. In the two-volume work in memory of her husband, *Memorials of Edward Burne-Jones*, she described her first view in 1880.

It was a perfect autumn afternoon when I walked across the downs and entered the village from the north; no new houses then straggled out to meet one, but the little place lay peacefully within its grey garden walls, the sails of the windmill were turning slowly in the sun, and the miller s black timber cottage was still there. The road I followed led me straight to the door of a house that stood empty on the village green, and we bought it at once.

This was Prospect Cottage and a few years afterwards she and Ned bought the adjoining property, Aubrey House, employing an architect friend, W. A. S. Benson to create a more spacious home, called North End House. It was so named because their London house, The Grange, was in North End Road, and perhaps also because their new holiday retreat was near to the north end of the village. Their grand-daughter, later Angela Thirkell, wrote a loving memoir of the house she remembered as a child, the third of *Three Houses*. Benson created a studio for Ned on the first floor of what was Aubrey Cottage, with a long window to let in the strong light from the east, and with a small, but elongated bow by it. As the two winding staircases were impossible of access for large canvases, a thin trap door was engineered alongside the bow so that canvases could be lifted up and through. The frame of the infilled hatchway can still be seen. The redesign provided much more space, including a bower curtained and draped with Morris chintz for their daughter Margaret, with a pear tree just outside one of the windows. Ned turned a small downstairs kitchen into a smoking room – normally a strictly male preserve. It was called the "Mermaid" where members of the Pre-Raphaelite set, including William Morris of "The Firm" together with

Rudyard's father, Lockwood, and his old Headmaster, Cormell Price, enjoyed a glass of stout or ginger-beer, and played draughts, backgammon and dominoes. Conversation flowed congenially with such relaxed and intellectual company. The name of the snug was derived from a painted bas-relief of a mermaid with flowing hair disporting with fishes in a turbulent sea, over the mantle. The fireplace itself was of ruddled brick and only wood was burnt in it. The floor, too, was of brick and the furniture reminiscent of a Dickensian inn. German steins hung on the dresser and the oak furniture burnished with the polish of ages gleamed in the candlelight. Its austere hard upright settle and massive chairs gave very little comfort, for which

North End House

Ned and his friends seemed to have scant need. The garden, framed by the 'L' shape of the joined houses must have been a delight, for a painting of it at the turn of the century by Thomas Matthews Rooke shows shaped bushes, twining creepers on the walls and colourful flowers along the flint-edged garden paths. This, then, was the Kipling's first base in the village, which he introduced thus:-

The Aunt and Uncle had said to us: Let the child that is coming to you be born in our house, and had effaced themselves till my son John arrived on a warm August night of 97, under what seemed every good omen.

The interim was, however, both full and memorable. Less than three weeks after their arrival came the solemnity of thanksgiving for Queen Victoria's Diamond Jubilee on June 22nd. The event was more than a mere date on a calendar; it was the culmination of an age of achievement and a glow of devoted enthusiasm enveloped the 'Great White Queen', who, as Empress reigned supreme over the largest empire in the history of the world. It had been suggested to Kipling that he might pen something suitable, and he toyed with the idea, though lacking urgent motivation. The arrival of a new tandem bicycle, a gift from S. S. McClure, offered slight distraction from more momentous activity the following day.   On the overcast day of celebration the Kiplings enjoyed the sound of bells ringing from the ancient tower of St. Margaret's Church just across the green.   With skies clearing they walked up to Beacon Hill in order see the bonfire responding to the signal chain which flamed along the south coast, as it had done in time of trial or jubilation ever since the Armada. A poem began to take shape in his mind but he was dissatisfied.   Having received an invitation to witness, with his father, the great Fleet Review off Spithead he escaped the immediacy of the task.   One hundred and sixty-five ships drawn up in five ranks with parade-ground precision was, he admitted, almost beyond his powers of description. Back in Rottingdean he was invited, almost immediately, to return to board H.M.S. Pelorus for fleet manoeuvres by his old friend, Captain Bayly, now in command. Whilst a guest in Pelorus he dined aboard the flagship with Prince Louis of Battenberg. Ever active he worked on a poem about Torpedo Boat Destroyers, published the following year in *McClure's Magazine* entitled *"The Destroyers"*.   The company of seamen, whom he revered, revitalized him and so, on returning home, he set to work on a poem, then called *After*. Frustrated with an inability to compose the verses as he wanted, he discarded several sheets of paper. Sallie Norton, the daughter of his old friend, the Harvard academic Charles Eliot Norton, had joined the family on July 12th and she retrieved, with Rudyard's permission, the stanzas from the waste-paper basket. Her delight with what she read, and with Aunt Georgie's encourage-ment, persuaded him to emend the work. The result was a reduction in the number of verses and a new title – *Recessional*. The following day Georgie, a guest in her own home, together with Sallie, carried the manuscript off to Printing House Square to show it to Moberly Bell, the Editor of *The Times*.   He published it on July 17th, with a laudatory leader.

The deep sense of religious feeling and moral obligation which has coloured the whole of the Queen's life will bring her heartily into unison with the spirit of the fine poem by Mr. Rudyard Kipling which we print this morning.   There is a tendency, in these days, to rush into dithy-rambic rapture of every great exhibition of national power. It is well that we should be reminded by a poet, who perhaps more than any other living man, has been identified with the pride of Empire and with confidence in the destinies of our race, that there is a spiritual as well as material side to national greatness.

Two personal experiences are encapsulated in one of the stanzas. With the ending of the fleet review at which he was a guest, Her Majesty's ships dispersed to the stations at the ends of the oceans to resume their duties, and joining the villagers at the celebratory beacon on the hill above, he and Carrie witnessed the fiery rejoicing.

Far-called our navies melt away; On dune and headland sinks the fire:
Lo, all our pomp of yesterday, Is one with Nineveh and Tyre!

The poem met with national approval and reinforced Rudyard's place as the unofficial Laureate of Empire. It attracted considerable misinterpretation and even opprobrium. The phrase "lesser breeds without the law" was construed as an attack on subject races, whereas Kipling was aiming at the Germans, who had turned away from international law in their aggressive rearmament. The poem was to be seen as a counter to the excessive euphoria of imperial achievement. He was suggesting that once the exuberance of celebration had faded the nation should think reverently of the responsibilities imperial power had brought; that humility should replace vanity; and that above all, thanks should be offered to the Almighty, the words "Lest we forget", borrowed from Deuteronomy, being, then, an exhortation to remember our duty to God. The phrase was, of course, used later, in a different context, on the memorials to those killed in the Great War through his work for the Imperial War Graves Commission.

St Margaret's

There is a note in the family diary that on July 19th, only two days after publication in *The Times,* that Sir Arthur Sullivan wrote to suggest that he wished to set it to music. Much as he tried he was unable to come up with a matching tune. Mrs. Bambridge, Kipling's daughter, noted, later on, that the only tune which ought to be used for the poem was Melita, that for "Eternal Father, strong to save" and she said that when he wrote the poem he had the cadence of the hymn in his mind. The title suggests that the most appropriate time for its use would be when clergy and choir recess from the chancel through the nave at the end of service. In spite of the poem's plea for reflection it drew some amazingly adverse comments, one from the Rector of a Birmingham church, Canon Rogers, that there are "lines in that hymn which are distinctly 'sub-Christian' " presumably suggesting that they opposed the precepts of Christianity. Kipling was immensely gratified by a letter of congratulation from Jack Mackail, an Oxford classics don and ardent pacifist who was the husband of cousin Margaret. In his appreciative response, after describing his recent naval experiences, predicted that "the big smash is coming one of these days sure enough".

There is an engaging footnote to the poem *Recessional*. On a visit to England in 1937, the owner of Forest Lawns Memorial Parks in Glendale, California, Dr. Hubert Eaton, sought inspiration for the design of another chapel to be built in his ground. He wished to locate a church which had historic interest and was associated with a well known personality. He looked in vain for some time and then, by chance, was dining in London with two friends, Oliver St. John Gogarty, a former Irish senator, and Frank Owen, the newspaper editor. In the course of conversation he recounted how he had disciplined his son by making him learn, by heart, famous pieces of literature. He recalled that the only one his son still knew perfectly was *Recessional* and wondered if he could find where it had been written. Both his friends knew that it was in Rottingdean. The following day Dr. Eaton and his architect reached the village and discovered St. Margaret's Church. Entranced by its beauty and its history Dr. Eaton saw it transported, in his mind's eye, to a Forest Lawn hilltop. Its name, chosen immediately, was to be "The Church of the Recessional". An exact replica was created, including the pulpit and the font. His dream, translated to reality was dedicated only four years later. Just inside the entrance is a room devoted to memorabilia associated with the author, including the "Sussex" Edition of his works, a page from *The Times* of July 17th, the story of the poem by Sir Roderick Jones, a later resident of North End House, a bronze bust done by P. Synge-Hutchinson , a copy of Philip Burne-Jones portrait, and a watercolour of St. Margaret's. The vestry walk has a wall inscribed with Kipling's poem *When Earth's Last Picture is Painted* commanding a panorama of green valleys, blue hills and distant mountains.

Elsie, John and Josephine in 1898

Simultaneously Rudyard began work on another poem which was to be the centre of much debate. *The White Man's Burden* was influential comment on American relations with the Philippines and more controversial than *Recessional*. He was also bringing together the *Just-So Stories* begun in Vermont and added to in Rottingdean. It was an exacting time.

Exactly a month after the publication of *Recessional*, Carrie, after a very difficult pregnancy, was safely delivered of a son, named John in the time-honoured sequence of the Kipling family. Their first and only son arrived in the small hours of August 17th. Full of promise, and with the hindsight of autobiography, "under what seemed every good omen" John's short life was destined for sorrow. But with the recent stimulus of sea trials in a torpedo-boat destroyer, Kipling joyfully described the arrival in suitably nautical terms to a friend W. J. Harding.

Ref: t.b.d. trials. My attention is at present taken up by one small craft launched from my own works - weight (approx) 8.957 lbs: h.p. (indicated) 2.0464, consumption of fuel unrecorded but fresh supplies needed every 2½ hours. The vessel at present needs at least 15 years for full completion but at the end of that time may be an efficient addition to the Navy, for which service it is intended. Date of launch Aug 17th 1.50 a.m. No casualties. Christened John. You will understand that the new craft requires a certain amount of attention- but I trust ere long to attend a t.b.d. trial.

On an unusually domestic note, many years later, Kipling avowed his pleasure in being with the infant. In a letter to Dora Clarke, the wife of his old naval friend, congratulating her on the birth of her daughter, Hilary, for whom he stood as Godfather, he said *When my boy was born I wheeled the pram up and down across Rottingdene* (sic) *Green – and was rather proud of it.*

Rudyard, with a fervent enthusiasm for the Senior Service, intended that John should become a cadet at H.M.S. Britannia, not at that time knowing that he would inherit the poor eyesight from which his father suffered. Stanley Baldwin came to Rottingdean at this time and he and Rud enjoyed each other's company. But the inherent restlessness, so apparent in Torquay, continued. Rudyard continued to look for a suitable home, and he thought one possible in Hastings. In another amusing search he was taken by Thomas Hardy to view a house near Dorchester; each independently mentioned the name of the other to the lady who wished to sell. They were somewhat taken aback later to discover that she recognized neither's name as anyone of note. On September 25th Rudyard signed the lease of The Elms at three guineas a week. *Something of Myself* details what The Elms meant to them.

Meantime we had rented by direct interposition of fate that third house opposite the church on the green. It stood in a sort of little island behind flint walls which we then thought were high enough, and almost beneath some big ilex trees. It was small, none too well built, but cheap, and so suited us who remembered a little affair at Yokohama. Then there grew up great happiness between 'The Dene', 'North End House' and 'The Elms'. One could throw a cricket ball from any one house to the other, but beyond turning out at 2 A.M.. to help a silly foxhound puppy who had stuck in a drain I do not remember any violent alarms and excursions other than packing farm-carts, filled with mixed babies – Stanley Baldwin's and ours – and despatching them to the safe clean heart of the motherly Downs for jam-smeared picnics. Those Downs moved me to write some verses call "Sussex".

The poem *Sussex* is a remarkable evocation of the county which shows how deeply he loved the varied landscapes and coastal scenery and how fully he understood the outlines of the history fashioned by its peoples. Its universal appeal is the line *Ordained for each one spot should prove Beloved over all.* He continues with the observation that for some it is Baltic pines, or Surrey glade or the sound of the tropic wind through the palms of Levuka in the Fijian islands. For him, however, it was the short springy, thyme scented, turf of the roundly contoured *blunt, bow-headed whale-back downs.* He continues with an understanding of the nature of the dry valleys and the inexorable recession of the cliff-line, and then extends the scope to the deep ghylls of the inner weald. He recognised that it took a long time to convince the Saxon peasant of the benefit of conversion to Christianity and that a port like Rye had been stranded by the build up of the foreshore in the Romney marsh area. He describes the rounded tower of Piddinghoe Church as capped mistakenly, by a *beguilded dolphin* when it is, in fact a sea-trout. This was so dilapidated in the 1970s that it neither veered nor was still golden. A request from the Parochial Church Council elicited a small monetary contribution towards restoration from The Kipling Society. His *fair ground* was *Sussex by the sea.* The phrase was to be used as the title of a stirring song adopted as a county anthem. The composer was William Ward-Higgs (1866 – 1936) and there is a memorial tablet to him in South Bersted Church Hall, Bognor Regis.

The first record of The Elms, the home which they now rented, appears in 1750 which stated that a grant had been made to William and Elizabeth Ridge to erect a new house. There had, however, been a cottage on the north-east corner of what was to become the enclosed land. By 1785 a James Ingram bought the land with that cottage, which was inherited by his daughter, Elizabeth. In 1824 another James Ingram was able to buy 5½ rods of the land in front of the house before which the residents of the house would have stepped straight out on to the village green on which the villagers had common rights. This, presumably, was when the enclosing wall was built, allowing some privacy. By 1853 the house was leased to a George Morpeth and six years later the Ingrams sold it to Josiah Olding who also took ownership of the seven cottages contained within the enclosing wall opposite 'Hillside'. Soon after it was sold to the Rev. Jacob Stanley, a cleric not connected with the parish church, and he passed it on in 1869 to Baron de Bliss, who had a Portuguese courtesy title. During Kipling's time it was his son, Mr. A. H. A. Bliss who let 'The Elms' to the writer. There was, at that time, a small dairy farm within the enclosure owned by 'Trunky' Thomas, and the cattle were looked after by his nephew, Bill Noakes. When, soon after taking up residence, Kipling offered to buy the property but the price was so exorbitant that it led him to suggest that "you must think that there is a goldmine under the Green." In 1908 Bliss sold to a Major Sidney Goldman who added a spinney which he purchased from Colonel Moens, the owner of Down House, opposite the northern part of the enclosure. In 1929 Sir Roderick Jones, Chairman of Reuters, who had joined North End House and Gothic House bought the whole of The Elms enclosure. In 1951, during the Festival of Britain, the house hosted an exhibition of Kiplingiana, the first and only time it had been open to the public. Books and pamphlets, portraits and pictures, letters and memorabilia were displayed along with sections on 'Rottingdean through the Ages', with an input from Arthur Negus, and 'Rural Rottingdean' arranged by Bob Copper. At that time the tenants were Mr.

Village postcard of The Elms with the small dormer windows

and Mrs. Ernest Beard. In 1960 it was leased as a Boarding and Day School for Girls with Miss K. Birney as Headmistress. It passed to Sir Roderick's daughter Laurian, the Comtesse d'Harcourt, who, in 1980, sold the house and immediate garden to the present owner. She had hoped to sell the remaining area for building development, but after strenuous protest action by the Rottingdean Preservation Society, planning permission was refused. This effort was followed with close interest and concern by The Kipling Society. As a result of the refusal the Preservation Society bought the unkempt and overgrown garden for £55,000 in 1983 and by co-operative effort restored it to its present most attractive state in order that local residents and visitors alike could enjoy the beauty, peace and quiet which it offers. The Society presented the 'Kipling Gardens' to the then Brighton Borough Council under covenants, on trust. It was handed over, officially, on April 23rd 1986 when the Mayor declared it open to the public. Rudyard's gardener's cottage, once occupied by old Bill Whale, (now 'Kipling Cottage') was restored by Sir Roderick and has remained separate from The Elms and the Kipling Gardens.

Having taken up residence in The Elms he worked as energetically as ever, although repeated visits to the dentist may have had a temporary debilitating effect. Verses for *An Almanac of Twelve Sports* to accompany William Nicholson's block prints must have been a light-hearted diversion. Nicholson first came to the village to prepare a woodblock of Kipling in his first series of "twelve portraits" to be published by Heinemann in 1899, and the convergence of interest led to the collaboration in the *Almanac*. Nicholson was so taken with the village that when, a few years later, the Vicarage came on the market he bought it and renamed it The Grange. The *Almanac* carried the Heinemann 'logo, a woodcut of a rather straggly windmill. It became an easily recognised colophon in the years to come. Two decades later Enid Bagnold, wife of Reuter's chairman, Sir Roderick Jones, promoted, vigorously, the idea that Sir William Nicholson had used Rottingdean's mill as his model. As the local mill was a smock mill and the colophon was of a post mill such a claim was far fetched. Indeed the son of a friend of Nicholson's stated quite specifically that his father had seen Nicholson trace the logo from a seventeenth century panoramic Dutch battle map. Such was the force of her argument however, that her own publishers, Heinemann, contributed annually to the Preservation Society's funds for its upkeep. The incumbents who had lived in the spacious and elegant Vicarage before Nicholson, included some remarkable men. One of these was Dr. Thomas Redman Hooker who had been appointed in 1792 as the result, somewhat quixotically, by the Patron of the living, of the fall of the dice between two of the candidates. His talents were extraordinarily wide for in addition to being a much loved shepherd to his flock, he was a brilliant rider to hounds, and excellent cricketer, an accomplished cellist and a reasonable artist. He enlarged the vicarage in order to board pupils in his school, among whom were Henry Edward Manning, the celebrated theologian who converted to the Catholic Church and became Cardinal Archbishop of Westminster, and Bulwer Lytton a formidable novelist. He was also, because of his fine horsemanship, the "look-out man" for the local smugglers, the Rottingdean Gang. Kipling must have learnt of this side of his character and probably knew that Hooker's study had a trapdoor concealed beneath his desk which led to the cellars and so into the smuggling tunnel which ran under the buildings in the High Street from the cliffs. It would be nice to think that *Brandy for the parson,* from his poem, *A Smuggler's Song,* had been inspired by the Vicar's illicit nocturnal adventures, although it first appeared in print in *Puck of Pook's Hill.* Hooker served his flock for 46 years and was greatly loved by them. He still keeps an unwavering eye from his white marble bust above the pulpit, much to the discomfiture of some preachers. A decade after his death another much loved parson, Arthur Thomas, was to dedicate almost another half century to the welfare of his parishioners. He died only a year before the Kiplings arrived, when Francis Champeneys began a short ministry. The next vicar was an Australian, Frederick Tower for whom Kipling had a great deal of respect, for he took an active part in the Rifle Club and supported the Boy's Club, both of which were close to Rudyard's heart. On his return from the Cape in May 1901 Kipling was saddened to learn that Tower was to move on and as a result wrote to Sir Edward Carson, who lived nearby in Northgate House, to seek support for preferment as a reward for his outstanding services. In the letter Kipling admitted that *I am not, as you, know, a Churchman, but I have been watching him from the outside…. He is the kind of padre badly needed these days… and has done much for the village in a sane and straightforward fashion.* Tower's successor was not as highly regarded, as he seemed to Rudyard to lack the patriotism England deserved at a time of conflict.

Stanzas on the insane posturing of the Kaiser and continuing efforts on "Stalky" stories also occupied his time. This work was set within a background of socializing with William Black, a very popular Victorian novelist who lived locally, and discussing with Cope Cornford how to set up a pension for W. E. Henley. His parents and sister came for Christmas and their presence could not have made things easy because of the mutual antipathy between Carrie and Alice. Trix, too, was in one of her periodically unstable mental states. The diary reveals, however, that they thought 1897 to be the richest of their married life. Enthused by meeting Sir Alfred Milner and Cecil Rhodes at the Athenaeum and Rider Haggard at the Savile, the Kiplings, with father in tow, plus nurserymaid and governess, set off for Cape Town, in early January 1898, aboard Union Castle's *S.S. Dunvegan Castle.* Whilst in the Cape he established a firm and friendly relationship with those in power, Rhodes understanding that Kipling's greatest attribute was his ability to communicate saw in him an effective ally. He was also entertained at the Simonstown naval base by his old friend, Captain Bayly. A journey which had a significant effect on one of the *Just So* stories he was composing, was one that Rhodes suggested to visit his up-country province. He left for Kimberley by special train on March 5th to Khama's country towards Bulawayo. By the Limpopo, at Mmabalel Pool he conceived the idea for *The Elephant's Child,* which was to become the most popular of all the collection. The repetitive "great, grey-green, greasy Limpopo River, all set about with fever trees" became part of childish vocabulary. Not long before Dr. Jameson was asked by Rhodes to nurse Rutherford Harris who had been badly bitten by a crocodile at that very spot. Perhaps Kipling heard of the incident which triggered the idea of stretching the baby elephant's nose. There are no fever trees there now, possibly because they are sensitive to frost and could so easily be wiped out, although there are some further inland.   The present owner of the farm, which has a "Kipling Pool" is hoping to re-establish a grove. After returning via the Matapo Hills and Johannesburg the family encounterd a rough passage home aboard *Norham Castle*.

Back in London by April 30th Rudyard discussed the Spanish-American war with an old friend, John Hay, now U.S. Ambassador to Britain. Returning to Rottingdean by May 5th he was immediately back at work, putting together *The Day's Work* and writing a dog story, *Garm*. For relaxation he returned to the horsemanship last practiced in India. Initially he enjoyed it until a few days later he was badly shaken when thrown. The following month saw a dramatised version of his story *The Light that Failed* gaining some approval, but all was overshadowed by the sudden death of Uncle Ned at The Grange in Fulham. Ned, having been cremated, Philip, the new holder of the Baronetcy, brought his ashes back to Rottingdean. Most of the family gathered in the village, and the casket were placed in the church for an overnight vigil, attended for a two hour period by Rudyard.   He was very distressed by the loss and sought solace by riding the tandem with Carrie to Newhaven. A stone in the outside west wall of St. Margaret's is Ned's memorial, where, more than twenty years later, it was joined by that for Georgie. Edward Burne-Jones left a wonderful legacy in the church. To celebrate the marriage of his daughter, Margaret, to an Oxford don, Jack Mackail, in 1892, he gave the magnificent three-light East window the following year. At the base of the window is the inscription "Pro unica filia Margareta in hac S. Margaretae aede feliciter nupta Edwardus Burne-Jones pictor dedicavit". In addition to his painting he also designed stained glass for the Morris Arts and Crafts "firm". These three, depicting three archangels, St. Gabriel, the Messenger of God, St. Michael, the symbol of the Church Militant and St. Raphael, guardian of pilgims and children, each with a small inset below, are spectacular.   This trio with another four installed later by the firm in St. Margaret's, are most highly regarded because of their quality and the real personal connection. Almost a hundred other churches are beautified with his work.

The early part of the family's life in the village was idyllic. Josephine, Elsie and other close young relatives were able to enjoy the beach and swimming from one of Trunky Thomas's bathing machines. Angela Mackail, Josephine's best friend, described the thrill of a swim from one of them in *Three Houses* changing into heavy serge, all-enveloping, bathing costumes and emerging into the paralysing coldness of the tossing sea.   Finally the excitement of the machine being drawn up by the capstan with attendant scrunching noise as the wheels turned over the shingle moving slowly up the beach. Once dressed, with their costumes being wrung-out by Trunky's horny hands, the children enjoyed warm buns from the bakery of an exceptionally rotund Mr. Stenning. A charming vignette of life at this time was given in an article published in The Kipling Journal (KJ 169) by Lucy Hilton. She recalled how the children had a number of friends in the village, one being Molly Stanford, daughter of the Headmaster of the Prep School. Kipling amused them by inscribing their initials with a pin on to the gourds growing in the garden so that they could watch the letters increase in size. It was at this time that Miss Anderson was engaged as Kipling's secretary and she lived above Dr. Ridsdale's surgery opposite the Black Horse. On one occasion Lucy was asked to light the fire. As she was having difficulty

Daddy-Long-legs at Rottingdean Pier

Rudyard walked in and gave her a demonstration of how it ought to be done. She also saw, on one occasion, a visitor asked him where Kipling lived, and he was courteously shown The Elms without recognizing the author.

An additional attraction at the Gap was the new pier installed to accommodate the carriage of the "Daddy-Long-Legs" railway. One of the most bizarre contraption ever invented this was, officially, "The Brighton and Rottingdean Seashore Electric Railway". Designed and built by Magnus Volk it extended the already operating, more conventional, "Volk's Railway" from the Aquarium to Paston Place to reach Rottingdean through the waves. "Pioneer" was supported by a bogey of wheels below each 24' stilt, which ran on rails attached to concrete blocks fixed to the solid chalk abrasion platform. The carriage was comfortably appointed with padded benches and potted palms in the typical Victorian fashion. On top was a promenade deck to whose rails were attached lifebuoys and at one end, hanging from davits, a small lifeboat placed at the insistence of the Board of Trade, the only "railway carriage" ever to have to carry one. It had a chequered history, its rails being battered by storm waves, but it ran, with the occasional break from 1896 to 1901 – almost coincident with the period of the Kiplings residence. It was, naturally, an attraction on arrival and often a small crowd would welcome the passengers transported from Brighton for sixpence. As it was powered by electricity, through catenary wires above, it had a generator to which Lady Burne-Jones, a forthright member of the Parish Council, objected vociferously because of its polluting smoke. It was, however, a small haven for Rudyard and the children because they were able to fish from the pier. Normally subjected to requests for an autograph, Rudyard maintained a privacy protected by a coastguard friend at the pier entrance gates who, armed with a sheaf of pre-autographed strips, was able to sell them in aid of a good cause. Angela Mackail, also described the wonder of the arrival of "Pioneer" in *Three Houses*. It was she wrote "more like a vision of the Martians than anything you ought to see at a peaceful seaside village." Much as the children would have liked to have been passengers they were not allowed to be so because 'Pioneer' had a habit of getting stuck opposite the ventilating shaft of Brighton's main sewer and being marooned there till nightfall.

Kipling used the view from the Gap in a story called *Brother Square-Toes* which starts with a tale of smugglers in Sussex but ends up in Philadelphia.

It was almost the end of their visit to the seaside. They had turned themselves out of doors while their trunks were being packed, and strolled over the Downs towards the dull evening sea. The tide was dead low under the chalk cliffs and the little wrinkled waves grieved along the sands up the coast to Newhaven and down the coast to long, gray Brighton, whose smoke trailed out across the Channel. They walked to The Gap where the cliff is only a few feet high. A windlass for hoisting shingle from the beach below stands at the edge of it. The coastguard cottages are a little farther on, and an old ships's figure-head of a Turk in a turban stared at them over the wall.

Cordery, the coastguard, came out of the cottage, levelled his telescope at some fishing-boats, shut it with a click and walked away. He grew smaller and smaller along the edge of the cliff, where neat piles of white chalk every few yards show the path even on the darkest night. 'Where's Cordery going ?' said Una. 'Half-way to Newhaven,' said Dan. 'Then he'll meet the Newhaven coastguard and turn back. He says if coastguards were done away with, smuggling would start up at once.'

The children are then introduced, by Puck, to an old-time smuggler who they heard singing the first stanza of an old folk song about *Telscombe Tye* –

The moon she shined on Telscombe Tye – On Telscombe Tye at night it was – She saw the smugglers riding by, A very pretty sight it was!

Contemporary accounts mention the old-figure-head, and smuggling, in its heyday a century before gave lucrative returns to the members of the Rottingdean Gang. The white piles of chalk defining the cliff-edge track had been in use even before that to allow Riding Officers to gallop close to the edge in search of a 'drop'. Sadly the smugglers, wise to the stratagem, would replace the line to lead the official over the edge to his death. Many of the clergy sympathized with those engaged in running cargoes, and churches were often used as stores for illicit tobacco, tea and brandy. *A Smuggler's Song* with "*Hal o' the Draft*" in *Puck of Pook's Hill* has as its refrain.

Five and twenty ponies, Trotting through the dark –Brandy for the Parson, 'Baccy for the Clerk; Laces for a lady, letters for a spy, And watch the wall, my darling, while the Gentlemen go by!

Most coastal communities were happy to take advantage of the cheaper price of goods available, although the cosy image of Kipling's poem bore little relationship to the often vicious and brutal trade which was regarded by the government as a national evil. The guile and ingenuity of the Brotherhood was, without question, of a very high order and for the most part the Preventive Men were outwitted and outnumbered by the smugglers. In Rottingdean there was an easily portable hoist, ostensibly to rescue shipwrecked mariners from the beach below the cliff, but which could equally well lift contraband to the cliff top from which tubmen would remove it, speedily, to a convenient, first night's hiding place, en route to the London market. Vital intelligence could be passed by the position of the sweeps of the mill on Beacon Hill to a lugger offshore approaching with cargo, and the mill itself could be, and was, used in concealing the contraband.

Not only the children enjoyed the freedom of the beach as a relaxation from the task of writing, for in *Something of Myself* he shows how.

(Uncle Ned's) golden laugh, his delight in small things, and the perpetual war of practical jokes that waged between us was refreshment after working hours. And when we cousins Phil, his son, Stanley Baldwin and I, went to the beach and came back with descriptions of fat bathers, he would draw them, indescribably swag-bellied, wallowing in the surf. Those were exceedingly good days, and one's work came easily and fully.

The garden of The Elms was enclosed by a long flint wall, and within it there were a number of smaller walled sections, part pasture, part kitchen garden and part ornamental. It offered a delectable haven for play and was equipped with a sandpit for the very young. On one occasion Josephine and one of her friends, Christabel

Macnaghten, were playing when Rudyard came out to say that Carrie wanted Josephine indoors for something. The young visitor had walked over Long Hill from Ovingdean, where she was staying with her grandfather, to be with her 'best friend' Jo. Rudyard was thus left with Christabel and with his usual flair for being at ease with the young, asked her how she had enjoyed her recent holiday. Christabel replied that the New Forest had frightened her because of its strange sounds and because whereas some branches were twisting and shaking, others close by were perfectly still. She then asked Rudyard if he believed in ghosts because she was sure that they existed in woods. A few days later Rudyard said to her "I've written a poem about ghosts in a wood; it's a very lonely wood and no one sees the ghosts: you only hear the sound of a horse galloping and the sound of a lady's skirt swishing as she rides; I shall give you the poem." As she recounted in her autobiography as Lady Aberconway, *A Book of Memories*, sadly the manuscript never arrived, but she read *The Way through the Woods* in *Rewards and Fairies*. It is certainly a short, but very nerve-tingling, poem which some authorities claim as his finest work.

With the Royal Navy

The diary shows a number of welcome visitors were entertained, including Henry James, who had "given Carrie away" at her wedding, over from Rye, and Lockwood de Forest, a wealthy American artist and collector of Indian art. Work on *Kim* was absorbing and for afternoon exercise Rud would often cycle into Brighton to talk with another naval friend, Surgeon Captain Gilbert. The marine connection was enhanced in September, when he joined his friend Captain Bayly on H.M.S. Pelorus for manoeuvres in Bantry Bay. He was to dine with Prince Louis of Battenburg and was asked to recite some of his verses at a ship's concert. He was thrilled to be carried shoulder high by the seamen, but as always was eager to learn all he could about the ways of the different aspects of a warship's life – particularly engines and armaments. There is a charming photograph of him sitting cross-legged on deck, beaming with happiness at his experience. He was to use the naval details in the later Pyecroft stories, but the more immediate result was *A Fleet in Being*. The material, an account of the life of a ship's company and including some concerns which they felt, was published first as six articles, in the *Times* and in the *Morning Post* in November 1898 and then 'collected' a few weeks later. It was reissued in 1913 to raise awareness of the importance of the Royal Navy in the defence of the realm.

Throughout that summer the children listened with rapt attention to the tales written especially for them. They became *Just So Stories for Little Children* and since they were published, generations of children have found these extraordinary fables to be full of delight, particularly if they were read to them by a grown-up who spoke with understanding and with emphasis. In the Preface to the first story – *How the Whale Got His Throat* – Kipling explained his raison d'être. In his introduction to the book Kipling refers to "Effie", the disguise he used for his adored daughter Josephine.

Some stories are meant to be read quietly, and some meant to be read aloud. Some stories are only proper for rainy mornings, and some for long hot afternoons when one is lying in the open, and some are bedtime stories. In the evening there were stories meant to put Effie to sleep, and you were not allowed to alter those by a single word. They had to be told JUST SO, or Effie would wake up and put back the missing sentence.

Many of the repeated phrases became well-loved catch phrases, such as "best beloved" and "the great grey-green greasy Limpopo river" with some even having child-like mispronunciations such as "satiable curtiosity" instead of "insatiable curiosity". Angela, who was usually one of the avid listeners, recorded that the printed version was poor compared with the fun of hearing them told in Cousin Ruddy's deep unhesitating voice. There was a ritual about them, each phrase having a special intonation, an inimitable cadence and an exaggeration of certain phrases which made his telling unforgettable. Another charming feature of *Just So Stories* was that he illustrated them, in black and white, himself. Within each illustration is his own rebus, consisting of a simple Noah's Ark enfolded in a capital "A", so that "Ark A" became the equivalent of his initials, "R.K". In 2002, on the centenary of the publication of the collected stories, Royal Mail issued a charming set of 10 stamps, by an Israeli artist, Izhar Cohen, each representing one of the animals featured in the original set. Rottingdean celebrated the occasion with an exhibition of art work on a "Just So theme" by children from local primary schools and the production of an attractive special "First Day Cover" for the stamps. This included mention of both the Kipling Society's 75th anniversary and the Preservation Society's museum which houses a "Kipling Room".

Entertaining "Uncle Crom" he read some of the stories from *Stalky and Co* which his old, and much respected, Headmaster thought were more fancied than factual. As with *The Jungle Books* and *Just So Stories*, the Stalky tales published collectively in 1899, had been read first in magazine form the previous year. They recorded the adventures of Kipling himself, "Beetle" or "Gigs" and his study mates, Lionel Dunsterville and George Beresford in outwitting masters and local inhabitants. Dunsterville – "Stalky" – was to become a distinguished soldier, and having served in some remote parts of the Empire was to retire as a major-general. Beresford – "M'Turk" – was a civil engineer in India and later a well-known photographer. Both published reminiscences and both were involved in the founding of The Kipling Society in 1927, Stalky becoming its first President. Even so, heavily occupied in work on *Kim* and a number of poems, Rudyard still devoted a great deal of time organizing a club for the boys in the village. They, however, were less impressed when he tried to introduce them to a "reading room." The year ended somewhat gloomily with the funeral of Willam Black and with the news that Trix's mental condition was in one of its downward spirals.

At about this time, and involved with the writing of *Kim*, that the family were disturbed - *the sou'wester raged day and night till the silly windows jiggled their wedges loose (which is why the Committee vowed never to have a house of their own with up-and-down windows)*. As a result Rudyard employed his cousin Ambrose Poynter ("Ambo") to replace the small top-floor dormer windows. The structural shortcomings of his work prompted a poem, intended solely for family amusement, called *The Architect's Alphabet* – one line of which read - *T, the tornadoes he told us were draughts*.

The children were given a 'governess cart' – a light two wheeled trap with inward facing seats, which must have been an enjoyable means of transport. Their father published a collection of tales mainly set in India called *'The Day's Work* and he was writing up some naval stories as well as some major verses. In early January of 1899 Rud went to his parents at Tisbury to discuss the Pater's comments on *Kim* and back in the village they entertained the Bensons and Beerbohm Tree.

On the 25th the family left from Euston and embarked on S.S. *Majestic* at Liverpool bound for New York. The weather on the crossing was cold and very stormy and during the voyage they all succumbed to illness. By the time their liner docked a week later the children were taken to the Grenoble Hotel and treated for possible bronchitis. Their Nanny, Lucy, had been ill right from the start of the voyage. By February 20th Carrie and

Rudyard also developed symptoms, and whilst his wife rallied quickly, Rudyard soon became feverish with just a brief respite. Carrie's sister Josephine had married a doctor, Theodore Dunham, and he soon called in a specialist. For some inexplicable reason Josephine, whose condition gave cause for concern, was taken to stay with Lockwood de Forest's sister some distance away. Sadly she never recovered and died on March 6th. By this time Rudyard's infection had spread to both lungs, and he became delirious. He was now critically ill and world-wide concern was focused on him, with goodwill messages arriving hourly. There was one from 'the working people of Rottingdean', as well as from Mark Twain, Henry James and, incongruously, the Kaiser. His strength began to return but he could not be told of his beloved daughter's fate until the middle of the month. Their intended objectives, for Carrie's return visit to Brattleboro, and Kipling's need to establish his copyright came to nought.

The Idyll shattered.

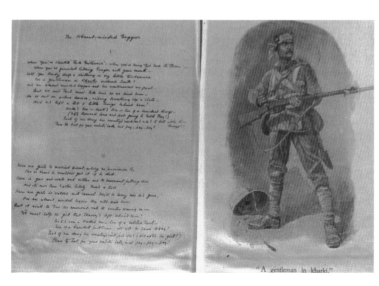

Silk Souvenir of The Absent-Minded Beggar

Needless to say the return to Rottingdean was dispiriting. Carrie's diary entries show the agonies endured in those frightful weeks, and her stricken conscience at putting Josephine with friends. Her diary entry "Josephine left us at 6.30 this morning" is heartrendingly simple. Rudyard's gradual convalescence in New Jersey was enveloped in the kindness of F. N. Doubleday, 'effendi', the Caitlins, the de Forests, McClure and the 'pater'. Even amidst such sorrow proof reading and business transactions are still noted. Carrie, at last, had a chance to revisit Naulakha with her mother, although they did not stay in the house. In London on June 23rd with the Doubledays who had sailed with them, they were given a muted welcome by the family and Mr. Watt, his agent. The following day they returned to The Elms 'quietly' and to take up the threads of life. Forays to Brown's Hotel, with the Doubledays, friends who had been constant support for six bitter months, after which some work is resumed with the help of a new secretary, Miss Anderson. Cousin Phil worked on the portrait of Rud in his study. It proved to be the most popular and enduring of his likenesses and Kipling delighted in it, writing a few months later to C. E. Norton.

They say (I'm the poor devil that had to sit for it so I don't know) that Phil's portrait of me is a Regular Stunner and shows specially well in reproduction. I resent the sleek baldness of my head, but the intellectual air and the tummy are beyond dispute. It's just me at my writing table, and as like one pea to another down to the flap of my pocket and the pipe at my side.

It shows him sitting at his writing-table in the study at The Elms, pensive, with a favourite pen in hand and a comforting pipe lying in an ashtray weighing down some manuscript pages. The well-loved pewter inkwell and a small globe are close, and below a wicker waste-paper basket which his habit was to fill regularly with work with which he was dissatisfied. Above a well filled bookcase is a picture of H.M.S. Pelorus, alongside some cigar-boxes.

In early August recuperation continued as guests of the Carnegies at Kingussie, walking and fishing with family and friends, whilst Phil began the matching portrait of Carrie. The return south in September witnessed a resumption of writing and involvement with political discussion. Oddly enough the diary does not mention the visit of Alfred Harmsworth, which Rudyard describes at some length in *Something of Myself* both for the request to write some verses for the South Africa Fund and as the trigger for his motoring passion. By Trafalgar Day he had completed the task entrusted to him by Harmsworth. *The Absent-Minded Beggar* verses reverberated throughout the land. Set to music by Sullivan, it was recited and sung in every village hall and music hall theatre in the country, as well as being committed to silk, paper, porcelain, leather and metal. The theme of the rousing chorus 'Pay, pay, pay!' saw an enthusiastic shower of coins to add to the sales of souvenirs, and well over a quarter of a million pounds was raised for the benefit of our troops fighting the Boer War and for those they left behind. Kipling himself gave a public recital of the appeal in the village. The autographed copy of the words were accompanied on the souvenirs by a suitably defiant picture of a British Soldier, head bandaged, and with rifle and bayonet fixed. His pith-helmet is on the ground and seems to enclose a skull. The art-work was contributed by a popular military artist Richard Caton Woodville, entitled 'A gentleman in kharki'. A note on the nature of the war, which caused Rudyard so much deep anguish, is to be found at the end of Appendix VII about the Rifle Club he set up in the village.

The setting up of the Rifle Club was a very practical expression of his belief that a major war was looming. He had been alarmed at the Kaiser's expansion of the "Grand Fleet", a German Navy expected to outgun the Royal Navy, and he believed that in order to prepare for a possible invasion every able bodied Englishman should be trained to offer some resistance. He raised a tin Drill Hall in the grounds of what is now the Our Lady of Lourdes Convent. It contained a 25 yard rifle range and the weapons used were .303s modified by the insertion of a Morris tube, which took .22 ammunition. The men belonged to what was in effect a local volunteer detachment, the forerunner of the Territorial Army. In addition he designed a full 900 yard range across the adjoining Lustrell's vale towards the steep slopes bordering Telscombe Tye. His assistants in this venture were an ex-service man, Mr. J. S. Johnson, who was employed as a Sergeant Instructor at one of the prep-schools in the village and Petty Officers of the coastguard. He took a very active role in the running of the club and for competitive shooting contests, making meticulous arrangements for his occasional absences. We have a facsimile of his signature on a score sheet when he acted as "Range Officer". As something more powerful Kipling obtained a Maxim Nordenfeldt machine gun which was anchored on the cliff edge and fired seaward for practice. The villagers welcomed this added protection. He used this venture later on when asked to write about Army and Naval training schedules. The ideas crystallised in his *Army of a Dream* published in 1904 the object of which was to arouse interest in the defence of Britain.

He continued his naval interests with a visit to H.M.S. Nile as a guest of Commander H. J. L. Clarke. On his return he sent a gift to the Wardroom accompanied by a an amusing letter.

To the President WR Nile

Dear Sir,
I have the honour to forward herewith for information and reference one (1) compete set of the works of Mr. Rudyard Kipling an author for whom (though I never yet had the pleasure of meeting him) I entertain a sincere regard. You will find his works elevating, innocuous and strictly moral. Some of his sentences are beautiful while others are even more so & the refinement of his language is only equalled by the aristocratic interests of his characters.
If the perusal of his pure and lofty style should in any way tend to the amelioration of the manners and customs the King's Navy, a service which I undertand is composed exclusively of large hairy men without boots I shall feel that Mr. Kipling's labours have not been in vain.

Vy sincerely yours

Rud K

PS   The bulk of the works have gone down direct from London. The volume that accompanies this is a little tract upon Life in the Army & is distinguished by a clarity of diction & a pungent lucidity of intellect which has seldom been equalled.

The recipient, his friend Commander Clarke was later to become a resident of the village when he bought Hillside from Ernest Beard in 1911.

The wartime years absorbed his energy, and the early months of 1900 were spent in South Africa where he was engaged in hospital visiting and general assistance, and by offering comfort on the ambulance trains bringing back the wounded. There was even time to support Cecil Rhodes who initiated the remodelling, with the aid of Herbert Baker, of 'The Woolsack' which was to be his winter retreat within the grounds of the Premier's residence, Groote Schuur. General Roberts asked him to edit a paper for the troops and so he, with a group of trusted correspondents, established *The Friend* published in Bloemfontein. A sally almost to the front line was memorable enough to suggest that he had seen action. Back in Rottingdean on May 1st, after a diversion to the parents at Tisbury he is immersed in volunteer and rifle club activities as well as arranging a rousing welcome for the Relief of Mafeking. It was at this time that the second John Collier portrait is posed and completed, and there was time for leisurely motoring to Seaford and Alfriston. Visitors abound, some of who stayed as house guests, with relief occasionally in his London clubs and talk with Austen Chamberlain. All the while being driven around the county he absorbed a wealth of material for later use in the setting of *They*. The beauty and heritage of the Sussex countryside is described in the story which is, in part, a heartfelt cry for Josephine. The text reinforces the depth of understanding about the physical and human landscape so succinctly painted in his poem *Sussex*. The opening of the story tells of how the narrator's car reaches a charming house and garden in which children live; children who are not seen by everybody. The route followed is clearly from Bateman's to Rottingdean and along the coast as far as Worthing and then inland through the Findon valley up to and beyond Washington. Although the area has developed enormously in the century since the tale was crafted, many of the features described are easily identifiable today.

One view called me to another; one hilltop to its fellow, half across the county, and since I could answer at no more trouble than the snapping forward of a lever, I let the county flow under my wheels. The orchid studded flats of the East gave way to the thyme, ilex and grey grass of the Downs; these again to rich cornland and fig trees of the lower coast, where you carry the beat of tide on your left hand for fifteen level miles; and when, at last, I turned inland through a huddle of rounded hills and woods I had run myself clean out of my known marks. Beyond that precise hamlet which stands godmother to the capital of the United States, I found hidden villages where bees, the only things awake, boomed in eighty-foot lindens that overhung grey Norman churches; miraculous brooks diving under stone bridges built for heavier traffic than would ever vex them again; tithe- barns larger than their churches, and an old smithy that cried out aloud how it had once been a hall of the Knights of the Temple. Gipsies I met on a common where the gorse, brackens, and heath fought it out together up a mile of Roman road; and a little farther on I disturbed a red fox rolling dog- fashion in the naked sunlight.

As the wooded hills closed about me I stood up in the car to take the bearings of that great Down whose ringed head is a landmark for fifty miles across the low countries. I judged that the lie of the country would bring me across some westward-running road that went to his feet, but I did not allow for the confusing veils of the woods. A quick turn plunged me first into a green cutting brimful of liquid sunshine; next into a gloomy tunnel where last year's dead leaves whispered and scuffled about my tyres. The strong hazel stuff meeting overhead had not been cut for a couple of generations at least, nor had any axe helped the moss-cankered oak and beech to spring above them. Here the road changed frankly into a carpeted ride on whose brown velvet spent primrose-clumps showed like jade, and a few sickly, white-stalked blue-bells nodded together. As the slope favoured I shut off the power and slid over the whirled leaves, expecting every moment to meet a keeper; but I only heard a jay, far off, arguing against the silence under the twilight of the trees.

Still the track descended. I was on the point of reversing and working my way back as best I could ere I ended in some swamp, when I saw sunshine through the tangle ahead and lifted the brake. It was down again at once. As the light beat across my face my fore-wheels took the turf of a smooth still lawn from which sprang horsemen ten feet high with levelled lances, monstrous peacocks and sleek round-headed maids of honour – blue, black, and glistening – all of clipped yew. Across the lawn – the marshalled woods besieged it on three sides – stood an ancient house of lichened and weather-worn stone, with mullioned windows and roofs of rose-red tile.

The story in *They* has for long been the focus of question as much as comment, and regarded by many as 'obscure'. It is certainly intriguing and seems to have a semi-autobiographical input. Two specific elements tease the reader, the topography and the nature of the paranormal experience of the narrator. As far as the motoring element it is fairly easy to trace the route, but the location within the Weald of the 'house beautiful' is much more problematic. Indeed it seems likely that no actual house was intended, for it seems to be a 'composite' of the real and the imagined. The description of the entrance hall is clearly based on that at Bateman's and the ornate topiary of the garden part fanciful and part factual. There is an attractive and elegant half-timbered property called Ravello at Rusthall on the western outskirts of Tunbridge Wells.   It was painted by Ernest Rowe, who specialized in detailed studies of old world gardens, and in one of Ravello completed about 1909 there is displayed a magificent topiary peacock. Kipling knew the area intimately and it seems likely that this garden art caught his imagination. The fictional location of the house must be somewhere in the region to the north east of Washington probably in the direction of Ashurst. Bob Thurston Hopkins who wrote extensively about Sussex in general and Kipling in particular attempts to identify the location in *Kipling's Sussex Revisited,* but without much success. The drive along the coast from Rottingdean was straightforward, crossing the River Adur by the old Norfolk Bridge and thence to Worthing *keeping the beat of tide on your left hand for fifteen level miles.* West Tarring, now a suburb of Worthing was famous for a garden of an old Archbishop's Palace full of fig trees. The turn northward would take the gentle gap through Findon, beneath the Iron-Age fort at Cissbury, directly to Washington. There is evidence for all the descriptive elements within close range of the village which *stands godmother to the capital of the United States.* A Roman road, the 'Greensand Route' follows the foot of the chalk escarpment from their fort of the Saxon Shore at Anderita as far as Washington, and there are short identifiable offshoots further westward. Nearby, too, is a village called Sompting Abbots which has a ruined chapel built by the Knights Hospitallers, perhaps the *Knights of the Temple* of the text. It has, also, a Norman nave and chancel built around a very distinctive Saxon church tower with its 'Rhenish helm'. Thurston Hopkins favours the impressive Early Norman church at Shipley also built by the Knights Templar who laid a massive causeway of Horsham stone to keep them dry-shod. Bridges abound in the Adur valley.   Wiston Lane at the foot of the *great Down whose ringed head is a landmark,* Chanctonbury, was a favourite haunt of the true Gipsy. Chanctonbury itself was crowned by a circular clump of beech, saplings planted and nurtured devotedly by the young Charles Goring of Wiston in 1759. It was his greatest wish that he should live to see the ring develop to almost maturity, and so it proved. Sadly, however, saddened by all save the archaeologists, the great storm of 1987 erased those proud trees of the Ring.

The story itself, with Kipling himself as narrator, is more difficult to comprehend because we are taken beyond the bounds of normal belief into the preternatural. This is almost certainly in order to come to terms with the devastating loss of Josephine, whose presence he felt with him The Elms and its garden. We are given a clue to the narrative in the poem *The Return of the Children* which precedes it. Children in heaven, taken before their time, feel bored by an adult paradise and are released to slip back to earth by the compassion of Mary the Mother. So after the first encounter with the blind lady at the ancient house he makes a second visit and only then realises that the children so happily playing and so familiar to their hostess can only be seen by parents who have suffered so grievous a loss. Miss Florence, who knew not the joy of motherhood, but was blind was thus able to offer them sanctuary. On a second visit the narrator is able to find nursing care for a desperately ill village boy. Sadly by the final visit little Arthur has relapsed and died. The villagers are aware that children who have met untimely deaths may be seen in the woods which almost encircle the house. Miss Florence shows him over the house in which the rooms are laden with toys which would amuse the children. When she is called to discuss problems with a tenant farmer, Rudyard, sitting, half hidden, feels a childish brushing kiss on the palm of his hand which he knows can only be from his adored daughter. He now understands that it was she he had seen waving from the window during his first visit. He then accepts that he can never again visit the house as such desire could become obsessional. Rudyard's own sister, Trix, was much absorbed during her life with the supernatural, and he recognised what harm it could do and so disassociated from all metaphysical contacts.

One other descriptive piece in *They* would be certain to be wholly familiar with those who daily look seaward from the chalk cliffs.

As I reached the crest of the Downs I felt the soft air change, saw it glaze under the sun; and looking down at the sea, in that instant beheld the blue of the Channel turn through polished silver and dulled steel to dingy pewter.

Arriving in Cape Town on Christmas Day 1900 they found that The Woolsack, the gift of Cecil Rhodes, was fully equipped and staffed. It its described by Carrie as " dream of beauty". Naturally being so close to the Premier's residence they see much of him, not only with concern for the conflict, but looking into the future the possibility of the establishment of "Rhodes Scholarships" at Oxford. The gift of a lion cub,

Rottingdean Mill overlooking the polished silver sea.

mistreated by its dam, was recorded in a story *My Personal Experience with a Lion* published in the Philadelphian *Ladies Home Journal.* John and Elsie, who were allowed to help with the rearing of the cub, and are called, in the story, Daniel and Una. Dan's name must have alluded to "Daniel in the Lion's Den". The lion cub was called "Sullivan"- the nearest they could get to the Matabele word for lion *'umslibaan*, but the children's names were translated later into their 'alter egos', Dan and Una in the Puck stories.

Arriving home in May 1901 Rudyard quickly took up the reins of village life, in which his rifle club featured prominently, recording a win in a local competition.. Life had its ups and downs, for Carrie was unwell, but there was considerable picnic exploration of the Sussex and Surrey countryside in a new car. In between work, and a trip to Paris, notable callers at The Elms included Sir Edward Carson, who had a few months earlier moved into Northgate House, Cecil Rhodes himself and the Australian poet 'Banjo' Paterson. It was he who described an amusing motoring incident in which the chauffeur, with enormous 'sang-froid' allowed the car to slide backwards towards a cliff edge in order to demonstrate how efficient were its brakes. The Just So stories were nearing completion and Lord Roberts and Rudyard conspired to raise the importance of conscription for the security of the state. In December he produced a major plea for the nation to take the defence of the realm more seriously than many of its gentry took their field sports, and the majority who were absorbed by cricket and football. The oft-quoted lines *With the flannelled fools at the wicket or the muddied oafs at the goals* caused resentment across the social spectrum. He was commenting on the absurdity, as he saw it, of the perceived importance of a test match 'down under' whilst our troops were fighting a bitter war. *The Times* also recognised the disproportionate column inches devoted to a game of cricket, although it stopped short of full agreement with conscription. Later Kipling was to confide to Rider Haggard that he ought to have used the word 'hired' rather than 'flannelled' in order to suggest that payment to professional cricketers, at such a time, was anathema.

The 1902 winter-spring visit to the Cape was overshadowed by the illness of Cecil Rhodes in early February which resulted in his untimely death the following month. Rudyard, having visited his friend almost daily during the decline was closely involved with the arrangements, with Jameson, for the funeral which took place in the Anglican Cathedral after a Lying-in-State at Groote Schuur. Kipling, so devastated by the loss, could not be persuaded to travel with the body to the summit in the Matapo Hills called by Rhodes "View of the World". His moving tribute, *The Burial,* was, however, read by the author at the private ceremony in Cape Town and as the coffin was lowered into the grave after its solemn journey by train and by a gun-carriage drawn by twelve oxen. It was during this period of sadness that Kipling composed his paean to his home county, *Sussex*. Clearly Rhodes' 'ordained' place would have been the view from the kopje summit overlooking his beloved Rhodesia.

Back at The Elms at the beginning of May *Just So Stories* are ready for publication, and Rudyard plucks a local name for use in *The Comprehension of Private Copper*. The Copper family had been engaged as farm-workers and farm bailiffs for more than 300 years, and well regarded, but this time it was simply the name which had been appropriated for a story with a South African location. Bateman's was again on the market and this time the deal was clinched, almost at the same time as the Peace of Vereeniging brought to a close the bitter conflict. Aunt Georgie's anti-war banner, "We have killed and taken possession" caused something of a commotion until the protesters were pacified by her nephew. A week after the Peace Treaty, Rudyard was heartened to learn that *Recessional* was to be sung at the services of Thankgiving. Dr Jameson came to the village, as the country was being prepared for the Coronation of King Edward VII on June 26th, a ritual which had to be postponed at very short notice by emergency surgery. The Kiplings had accepted seats in Westminster Abbey, but remained quietly at home for the delayed ceremony held in August. A drive to the sheltered park belonging to Sir Edmund Loder at Leonardslee, with its own collection of exotic animals, provided copy before long for *Steam Tactics*

The move to Bateman's had been dictated by the haunting memories of an adored daughter and the fact that Rudyard's privacy was increasingly jeopardised by the wiles of fans wishing to glimpse one they admired so much. Mr. Thomas, landlord of The Royal Oak at the cross roads, had introduced a tourist double-decker horse bus which brought trippers the four miles out to the village for sixpence. The conductor was often Charlie Tuppen, a famous post-horn player who would entertain the travellers. The driver used to bring his vehicle so close to the flint wall of The Elms that his upper-deck passengers had an unobstructed view into the garden and over the study which stood alongside the front door. On one occasion the bus broke off an overhanging bough of

The double-decker Rottindean horse bus.

one of the Quercus oaks. Oral tradition has it that such vandalism infuriated the owner, who had commented on the flint walls in his autobiography which *we then thought high enough* was proved wrong. He wrote a letter of complaint to the landlord, who showed it to his cronies in the 'snug' that evening and sought their counsel. They suggested that he ignore it, but one among the company, realising that an autographed letter was valuable offered the landlord half a guinea, an offer which was accepted. Not having received a reply Kipling wrote again and this time it changed hands for a pound. With still no response Kipling decided to beard the villain in his den and stormed to the inn in person. The landlord with devastating Sussexian logic answered the charge by saying "why, zurr, I was 'opin' as how you'd send a fresh letter every day. They pays a deal better than bus-drivin'." The astute Kipling recognised that he had been outgunned. Stories abound about trippers who wanted to know where he lived. Mrs. Ridsdale, the mother of Stanley Baldwin's wife, was a wonderfully eccentric character, who enjoyed striding up and down the High Street dressed in an assortment of garish clothes and accessories she found in the attic. When asked where the poet lived she would counter by demanding to learn what of his works the enquirer had read. If unable to do so she would say "Then I won't tell you!" The gates of the Elms often saw a number of visitors gathered around and a small spy-hole

The Elms more recently, seen from across the Pond.
Note the two large dormers designed by 'Ambo' Poynter.

had to be cut into one of the pair so that a welcome visitor could be admitted. Carrie Kipling had, frequently, to ask to be let through the throng in order to enter her own home.

The record of those who were entertained at The Elms during the Rottingdean years is really very remarkable. Few places of comparable size could match it. In addition to the family clans and their devoted friends from the United States there were those from the literary world, J. M. Barrie, Henry James, William Black and the Australian poet 'Banjo' Paterson. William Nicholson, who later was to take up residence at the old vicarage and John Collier both produced portraits. The world of the theatre was represented by Beerbohm Tree and the house was awash with the gentlemen of the press, including Alfred Harmsworth, Perceval Landon, John St. Loe Strachey and Leslie Cope Cornford. Sir Edward and Lady Carson had become near neighbours, but it was the South African connection which possibly overshadowed all. Cecil Rhodes and Dr. Jameson, Herbert Baker (Rhodes' architect) and Sir Percy Fitzpatrick the Chairman of Witwatersrand Chamber of Mines. The village continued its attraction to people of note for decades to come.

The months leading up to the move to Burwash were fully occupied by the thoughts of what needed to be done and action to accompany them. Literary output continued amidst concern for the health of Edward VII. Frequent visits to Bateman's after the purchase had been completed with the help of Rudyard's uncle George Mcdonald ensured a fairly smooth transition to the welcome peace of the Dudwell valley. A "farewell reception", on September 1st, at The Dene was given by the Ridsdales which might have fortified Carrie for the "chaos and black night" of moving the following day. The first half of life was complete and the second was about to begin, with the pithy comment from Carrie "the foreman of the removers was drunk".

First day cover

The Seven Sisters

Trunky Thomas

Chapter 4

PIONEER MOTORIST

The poison worked from that very hour. Kipling's words in his autobiography define the catalyst which gave him a wholly new outlook on life, and provided the means by which he was able to explore his adopted county and so come to respect and understand it even better. The incident was the arrival in Rottingdean of Alfred Harmsworth, proprietor of the *Daily Mail* to ask Kipling's help in a project very dear to his heart. His paper espoused the cause of the British troops sent to South Africa to fight the Boers. Initially only some 25,000 were sent but Harmsworth realised that combat with hard, determined, fighters, born to the saddle, would call for a much larger force. There would thus be a need for a public appeal to fund support for our men and their dependents. Early in October 1899 Harmsworth drove down in his Panhard to The Elms to enlist Kipling's talent. The result as far as the Boer War was concerned has already been discussed, but the enthusiastic motorist invited Rudyard for a short spin. His car must have been one of the first horse-less carriages to disturb the peace of the village. *A friend cried out at our door: Mr. Harmsworth has just brought round one of those motor car things. Come and try it! It was a twenty minute trip. We returned white with dust and dizzy with noise. But the poison worked from that very hour.* Harmsworth, later Lord Northcliffe, was devoted to each new development in what he called "the coming street revolution" and soon had a 75 h.p racing Mercedes, the first in England. He said that driving was "like being massaged in a high wind". Clearly his enthusiastic demonstration converted Rudyard immediately for before long:-

Somehow an enterprising Brighton agency hired us a Victoria-hooded, carriage-sprung, carriage-braked, single-cylinder, belt-driven, fixed-ignition Embryo which, at times could cover eight miles an hour. Its hire, including 'driver' was three and a half guineas a week. The beloved Aunt, who feared nothing created, said 'Me too!' So we three house-hunted together taking risks of ignorance that made me shudder through after-years. But we went to Arundel and back, which was sixty miles, and returned in the same ten-hour day! We and a few other desperate pioneers, took the first shock of outraged public opinion. Earls stood up in their belted-barouches and cursed us. Gipsies, governess-carts, brewery-waggons – all the world except the poor patient horses who would have been quite quiet if left alone joined in the commination service, and The Times leaders on 'motor-cars were eolithic in outlook'.

The hired 'Embryo' cost more per week than the rent of The Elms and clearly it was in use for some time. He took delivery on December 6th 1899, from London, presumably arranged by the Brighton agency, and was immediately driven to the town. A leading motoring correspondent could find no such make as an "Embryo" and concluded that it was an embryonic development of one of the main car-makers. Kipling worked energetically on a number of projects, although the depressing news from the war weighed heavily on their minds. In mid-December he organized a 'volunteer corps' and rejected the offer of a K.C.B., but by the 22nd the diary records that the car has broken down. As a man with financial acumen he would surely have cancelled the hire contract for the period the family was away in South Africa, from mid-January until late April. The diaries show that thereafter they used the car quite frequently. To Seaford and Alfriston, and then on June 15th 1900, 50 miles to Guildford to stay with the family of John St Loe Strachey, Editor of *The Spectator*. The following day was occupied by a drive through a number of picturesque villages. The return via Tisbury to see 'the Pater' seems to have put a strain on the car for in a letter to Strachey dated June 21st he notes that *We came home to find our motor suffering acute gastritis.* The following few weeks saw outings to Cuckfield, to Arundel, to Uckfield and to Haywards Heath to inspect a house. It did not suit, so on August 14th when they had an appointment to consider Bateman's, the car was again out of commission, and they had to take a train to Etchingham and a 'fly' to the house with which they fell in love. Sadly for them it had just been let and so they were forced to bide their time. The car tempted them on to the coast road, which crossed the glorious valley of the River Cuckmere at Exceat Bridge into the superb Downland behind the Seven Sisters cliffline. They went as far as the village of Friston, where, by the pond, the tapsell gate leads to an ancient church. The following month they motored to Hawkhurst to view another Jacobean house which delighted them but it was in a very poor state of repair. In October an American automobile was tried out and finding it 'rather good', arrangements were put in hand to purchase one. Sailing in early December from Southampton for Cape Town, they arrived on Christmas Day to find The Woolsack, 'a dream of beauty' equipped and staffed for them by Cecil Rhodes. By early May they came back to Rottingdean and on June 18th 1901 the diary heralds the arrival of the new motor, described as 'most beautiful'.

Initial adventures of the new motor are amusingly recounted in a letter to John S. Phillips on July 4th. Phillips who had acted as an agent on Rudyard's behalf, was general manager of *McClure's Magazine*, for which Kipling often provided material for publication. The letter, written at The Elms says:-

Dear Phillips,

I enclose herewith a cheque for £100 which I understand is what you advanced on the Locomobile. We are tremendously indebted to you for all the trouble you have so kindly taken over the business and it proves once more the busiest men are always readiest to help other folk.

As to the Locomobile herself, she is at present a Holy Terror. If ever you meet Amzi Lorenzo Barber who, I gather, is President of the Company [Locomobile Company founded at Bridgeport, Connecticut in 1899, having begun as a firm run by the Stanley brothers, and later sold back to them] *you may tell him that I yearn for his presence on the driving seat with me.*

I suppose she will settle down some day to her conception of duty but just now her record is one of eternal and continuous breakdown. She disgraced us on the June 26th when I took two friends over 13 miles of flat road. The pumps failed to lift and we had to pump dolefully every few miles home. Also she took to blowing through her pistons. We overhauled her on June 27th (all of the day). She did some run-about trips on June 28th. On June 29th we laid out a trip of 19 miles out and back. I took the wife. She (the Loco) betrayed us foully 12 miles out – blew through her cylinders, leaked, and laid down. It was a devil of a day. It ended in coming home by train. The wife nearly dead with exhaustion.

On June 30th I telephoned up to town and got the London agents to send a man down to overhaul. She needed repacking throughout, and the main steam valve leaked. (Another day off.) I left her alone on the 31st (being Monday) went up to town on the 1st. Came down on the second of July. She covered the five miles from the station to my home in fine form. Yesterday, July 3, I went for an evening trip – a few miles only along the road. Her steam was beautiful, but she shut down her fire automatically, and amid the jeers of Brighton we crawled to the Brighton repair shop, where we left her. The explanation was that her petrol pipe was choked. She apparently must be taken to pieces every time anything goes wrong with her. She is today in the shop being cleaned, and I shall be lucky if I get her tomorrow night.

I tell you these things that you may think once or twice ere you get a Locomobile. It is quite true that she is noiseless, but so is a corpse, and one does not get much fun out of a corpse. Is McClure's open to a story of her performance – say 5000 words under the caption "Locoed"? If the worst comes to the worst I may reimburse myself that way for the cost of her repairs during the past ten days. It isn't as if we wanted her for long tours – it isn't as if we ever tried to get more than 10 miles an hour out of her. We got her for a carriage – a refined and lady-like carriage – and we treat her on that basis. Her lines are lovely; her form is elegant; the curves of her buggy-top are alone worth the price of admission, but – as a means of propulsion she is today a nickel-plated fraud. I guess Amzi Lorenzo goes about the world in a B'way surface car.

Yours locomobiliously, but always sincerely,
Rudyard Kipling

This account was augmented by a letter written on the following day to his mother-in-law Anna Smith Balestier. Carrie was fully occupied dealing with domestic affairs and so had asked her husband to send news. It was, as ever, a very full letter and he explained their plans and writes of their recent stay with the Baldwins at a rather unprepossessing flat opposite the Kensington Palace Hotel.

Dear Mother:
*   The news is Motor, nothing but Motor and now I believe in a personal devil. You won't know Brighton or Brighton seafront so you will never understand the joy of breaking down for lack of fuel under the eyes of 5000 Brighton Hackmen and about 2,000,000 trippers. We were taking Aunt Georgie for a little run and – but its no use talking. We had to run her, or crawl her (the Locomobile) to the Repair Shops. This happened on Wednesday. She has just come out with all her innards rejuvenated and for the time being is going like a dream. C and I are going out this evening to test her as we have an appointment with the Stracheys (of the Spectator) tomorrow on the north edge of Sussex. They run down from Merrow Down in Surrey to Handcross where we meet and I pray that Coughing Jane won't disgrace herself.*
I don't know whether C gave you any details of our trip to Crowborough – about 25 miles N of here. Coughing Jane lay down on a hill and dissolved into clouds of steam and oil and water. She did everything vile that a motor could do and we wearily tramped the roads till we found a cottage and a kind Irishman who fed us on chicken and ham sandwiches and beer and was an angel unto us. We came back by train from Crowborough. …….. If the motor stands up we propose going down to Salisbury to see a house that has taken our fancy. (Norrington is its name and I daresay C has told you all about it). We shall leave on Tuesday and shall make two days of the ninety mile run, halting at Petersburg (really Petersfield) and Winchester.

The ninety mile route to Salisbury took them through Pulborough where they stopped for lunch. Kipling signed the visitors book at The Swan, adding the comment "thirty miles from Rottingdean in three hours". Most certainly the joy of motoring at this period was well and truly offset by the anger and frustration that frequent breakdowns had on the intrepid motorist. It was probably even worse for the chauffeur, an appropriate name for the driver of a steam car because the boiler in which the steam had to be created was situated beneath the seat. Kipling, however, always referred to his "engineer", who drove him. Heat was provided by petrol burners which were unreliable in the extreme. The vertical boiler beneath the seat contained a myriad of tubes heated by the burners. The drive was by means of a chain to the rear axle. Steering was either by means of a tiller or, in the case of Kipling's locomobile, by a lever. Lucy Hilton, a Rottingdean resident, recorded that warning of approach was made by a bell rather than a horn and that on one occasion the "steamer" went only 50 yards from home when it stopped. Kipling jumped down and said "Carrie, my dear, American girls are the best in the world, but American cars – damn 'em". This at a time when the force of the expletive was much more shocking than today! So meticulous a planner as Kipling would undoubtedly have used "Batholemew's Touring Atlas and Gazetteer of the British Isles" which was published yearly between 1897 and 1903. T. W. Wilkinson's Introduction to the 1900 edition, taken from his *The Highways and Byways of England,* gives a well-considered judgement of the development of the country's road system. The growth of the railways in the nineteenth century caused the development of much-needed road improvements to be delayed, and so the state of the roads was appalling. Although the popularity of cycling had been a small spur to making the roads better, it wasn't until the advent of the motor that the needs of the "automobilist", and of the motor vans of The Post Office, that action began to be taken. Even so the state of the surface, varied according to the availability of local material, was by our standards often abysmal. Ruts and pot-holes would have caused havoc within the delicate engineering of the power source, and punctures were a constant annoyance. Drought created an all-enveloping dust to swirl about and rain could turn the surface into a quagmire. It is hardly surprising that frequent delays were inevitable. The Emancipation Act of 1896 relieved the driver of the necessity of being preceded by a man bearing a red flag, but even so much police effort was devoted to curbing speed. It is likely that Kipling's troubles with his "steamer" inspired a story, and the one offered to McClure's to offset the cost of repairs may well have been translated into *Steam Tactics*. In *Something of Myself* he wrote *"Then I bought me a steam-car called a 'Locomobile' whose nature and attributes I faithfully drew in a tale called "Steam Tactics". She reduced us to the limits of fatigue and hysteria, all up and down Sussex".* Some 400 Locomobiles were sold in England in 1900 and 1901. The most persistent problem with them was that it steamed-off so much water that the boiler had to be refilled every 20 miles. A very distinctive mode of transport, it carried a single Cyclopian headlamp on the front of the dashboard and a further two more traditional lanterns on either side of the front seat.

Steam Tactics, first published in December 1902 in *Windsor Magazine* and the *Saturday Evening Post,* following Kipling's usual practice, was collected in a volume of short stories *Traffics and Discoveries* in 1904. The essence of the story, which involved the abduction of a plain clothes police officer, was based on an actual happening when Dr. F. W. Lanchester "kidnapped" a policeman in Warwickshire. (see Chapter 6) The Lanchesters became friends of Rudyard when, later, they supplied him with their marque to replace the temperamental Locomobile. Kipling is the narrator of the story, and when out for a drive, meets his naval friends, Emmanuel Pyecroft, a Petty Officer, and Henry Salt Hinchcliffe, an Engine Room Artificer. Invited to board the car, they are naturally intrigued by this *"land-crabbing steam pinnace"*. Hinchcliffe soon learns to drive the monster, coming to terms with all its foibles, but is stopped for apparently breaking the speed limit. The policeman is tricked into becoming a passenger, a fifth person in what was really only a four-seater. The car then breaks downs, as usual, and a motoring friend, Kysh, in his 24 h.p. Octopod, one of the Lanchester stable, stops to offer assistance. Kysh was modelled on Max Lawrence, Works Manager of the Lanchester Company, and incidentally the brother of the two Misses Lawrence who founded Roedean School. The two chauffeurs are left to deal with the temperamental "steamer" and the roundabout journey continues until, eventually, the policeman is decanted in the wildlife park belonging to Sir Willam Gardner. That park was based on a real one near to Lower Beeding, called Leonardslee, owned at the turn of the century by Sir Edmund Loder, who kept a collection of exotic animals. Kipling enthusiasts have for long been keen to follow the track of the adventure and to identify the fictional place names with their real-life equivalents. The description of the various instruments on the two cars are very carefully drawn and some of the manoeuvres described had been experienced by the author. The possible route and the location of the places are shown on the map "Kiplings Sussex" and the story is more fully explored in the chapter on Sussex Stories.

An old friend of Kipling's, W. E. Henley, an editor for whom he had great regard, had retired to Worthing, a few miles along the coast. Clearly he wished to experience the joys of motoring, but as Rudyard says in a letter of September 1901 his car was undergoing extensive repairs in London and so he wasn't able to oblige. His caustic comments reveal his growing impatience with the "Holy Terror" and when he returned from wintering again in South Africa he wrote to Strachey to enquire about joining the Automobile Club, founded in 1897, from which he felt that he would be able to get sound advice about a replacement. Max Lawrence brought round a Lanchester and as it happened a well-known Australian poet, 'Banjo' Paterson, the librettist of "Waltzing Matilda" was a guest at The Elms and he joyfully shared the ride which "scattered tourists right and left". It was during this escapade that Max demonstrated the power of the brakes as he let the car run backwards towards a sheer cliff-edge, an event which scared his passengers but was included, in disguise, in *Steam Tactics*. Max, who worked for the Lanchesters, was the brother of the wife of a good friend and associate of Kipling, Leslie Cope Cornford, a Brighton resident.

The inventor of the car was F. W. Lanchester, a son of an architect who had designed the most prestigious parts of neighbouring Hove. Leaving university without taking a degree he set up as a mechanical engineer near Birmingham with his brother George. He created his first experimental car, a two-cylinder air cooled model developing 5 h.p., in 1896. A mutual interest in poetry and cars drew F.W. and Kipling together and they soon became firm friends, by which time his design for a 10 h.p. vibration-free engine and cantilevered sprung body was a technical masterpiece. Kipling found that even this new car was fallible for on an occasion when F.W. drove him to Worthing, to visit W. E. Henley, it ground to a halt. He recorded in *Something of Myself* " *Once the proud designer – she was his newest baby – took me as far as Worthing where she fainted opposite a vacant building-plot. This we paved completely with every other fitting she possessed ere we got at her trouble. We then re-assembled her, a two hours job, After which she spat boiling water over our laps, but we stuffed a rug into the geyser and so spouted home.*

Kipling continued his practice of dubbing each car with a nickname. Occasionally the Lanchesters lent him experimental models to try out, one of them being that which collapsed in Worthing. It continued to misbehave, a characteristic which attracted the name "Jane Cakebread", after a well-known Soho character who amassed 93 convictions for being "drunk and disorderly" in a year. Once she spluttered to a defiant halt just north of the Downland scarp. The inevitable telegram to the works in Birmingham read "Jane disembowelled on village green, Ditchling. Pray remove your disorderly experiment".

He took delivery of the first Lanchester he purchased, on June 5th 1902. Graced with the name "Amelia", she proved only slightly less reliable than Jane. It is probable that Rudyard took cousin 'Ambo' over to Bateman's twice in a week in order to discuss what needed to be done to the house, the purchase of which was settled only the day before the first visit. During a stay with the Stracheys in Guildford, by train on the outward journey because Rudyard didn't feel up to the drive, Carrie was exhilarated by a drive in Harmsworth's 45 h.p. racing Mercedes. The difference in style was not lost on Rudyard who wrote of the return to Rottingdean in their own car.

We came down from Guildford in our own humble little motor which, after the giants among whom we had moved, felt very like a perambulator. However it carried us quietly and noiselessly from Guildford to Rottingdean (50 miles) without a single accident or delay. We were enormously pleased as the day was fine and warm and a modest 10 miles an hour came as a relief after the rattling charging motors that had called at the Stracheys all through the Sunday.

The demands of Bateman's saw constant journeys in early July, an attractive run through the Downs at Lewes, over the Wealden countryside to the crusaderly Cross in Hand and along the ridge to Burwash. In the middle of the month they spent two days with the Loders at Fern Chase, where Sir Edmund owned the private zoo immortalized in *Steam Tactics* on which Kipling was then working. The move to Bateman's at the beginning of September occupied all their energies and their car, in the charge of Mr. Colgate, joined them on the 26th. Clearly something seemed to have been awry as a week later a visit from F. W. Lanchester convinced them that all was well. It was a short lived relief, for a much vaunted drive to Henry James in Lamb House at Rye ended embarrassingly. In a letter to C. E. Norton, Kipling wrote:-

Because we swaggered and boasted about Amelia (she being a virgin) and told him we would drive him all over Sussex, in two hours Amelia was took with a cataleptic trance then and there – opposite a hotel- and she abode in Rye stark and motionless till we wired the place where she was born (it happened to be Birmingham) – for an expert mechanician or obstetrician or whatever the name is, and after two days Amelia came back to us. But Henry James's monologue over her immobile carcase … would have been cheap at the price of several wrecked cars.

R K being driven in his Lanchester

Henry James, who had an acerbic wit, was rather pleased by Kipling's discomfiture for his younger friend in the same profession had made immensely more money than he had. He recounted the incident, in his usual, rather long-winded way, to Ford Madox Ford, one of a group of literary folk then living on or by Romney Marsh, and Ford described his thoughts on the matter.

.... Mr. Kipling ...has just been to see me. And- - such are the rewards of an enviable popularity! – a popularity such as I – or indeed you my young friend if you have any ambitions which I sometimes doubt – could not dream of far less imagine to ourselves – such are the rewards of an enviable popularity that Mr. Kipling is in the possession of a magnificent one thousand two hundred guinea motor car. And, in the course of conversation as to characteristics of motor cars in general and those of the particular one thousand two hundred guinea motor car in the possession of our friend .... But what do I say? .... Of our cynosure! Mr. Kipling uttered words which have for himself no doubt a particular significance but which to me at least convey almost literally nothing beyond their immediate sound .... Mr. Kipling said that the motor car was calculated to make the Englishman ... '- and again came the humorous gasp and the roll of the eyes' –' was calculated to make the Englishman ... think.' And Mr James abandoned himself for part of a second to low chuckling. 'And' he continued, 'the conversation dissolved itself, after digressions on the advantages attendant on the possession of such a vehicle, into what I believe are styled golden dreams – such as how the magnificent one thousand two hundred guinea motor car after having conveyed its master and mistress to Bateman's, Burwash of which the proper pronunciation is Burridge would tomorrow devotedly return her and reaching here at twelve would convey me and my nephew Billiam to Burridge in time to lunch and having partaken of that repast to return here in time to give tea to my friend Lady Maud Warrender who is honouring that humble meal with her presence tomorrow under my roof ... And we were all indulging in – what is it? – delightful anticipations and dilating on the agreeableness of rapid – but not for fear of the police and consideration for one's personal safety, too rapid - speed over country roads and all, if I may use the expression, was gas and gingerbread when ....there is a loud knocking on the door and – avec des yeux éffarés .... ' and here Mr. James really did make his prominent and noticeable eyes almost stick out of his head...' in rushes the chauffeur .... And in short the chauffeur has omitted to lubricate the wheels of the magnificent one thousand two hundred guinea motor car with the result that its axles have become one piece of molten metal ... The consequence is that its master and mistress will return to Burwash, which should be pronounced Burridge, by train, and the magnificent one thousand two hundred guinea motor car will not devotedly return here at noon and will not in time for lunch convey me and my nephew Billiam to Burwash and will not return here in time to give tea to my friend Lady Maud Warrender who is honouring that humble meal with her presence tomorrow beneath my roof or if the weather is fine in the garden....'

Which concluded the Master after subdued ho,ho,ho s of merriment is calculated to make Mr.Kipling think.

Rudyard was mortified and so sent a letter of apologetic explanation to his amused host on October 17th, from his new home.

Dear Mr. James,
Touching motors and Amelia specially it s not as easy as it looks a sick motor. The wretched engineer laboured with her all that night and next day wired that he could do nothing but would return and explain all. Late on Wednesday evening he came home and I wired to Birmingham where Amelia was born and bred, that she lay comatose at Rye, and please would they do something.

They sent a man from Birmingham to Rye (two towns that are fairly remote) and he had a smack at her and on Thursday evening wired that our engineer should come over and help him. But our engineer, who had been helping saw wood on our circular saw, was at that moment in bed with two fingers rather cut (this comes of saying nothing and sawing wood) and so we had to tell the Birmingham man to wrestle on alone.

He (the Birmingham specialist) brought Amelia back yesterday morn and vowed that the accident which had befallen her was unique in all mechanics and motoring. (I know about fifty similar accidents – all unique).
So there you are, and now you can keep a motor or not as you please. But won't you and your nephew come over on Monday next by train (which tho' slow is safe) and we'll send you back by Amelia. If you leave Rye by the 11.22. you can reach Etchingham 12.32 and we'll meet you.

Ever sincerely,

Rudyard.

Clearly Henry James thought discretion the better part of valour and so failed to reach Bateman's for lunch. Kipling wrote subsequently:-

Don't say I told you but Amelia is a bitch – the petrol-piddling descendant of untold she-dogs. Today was divine. We waited for your chariot wheels till we felt you weren't coming and then we went to see Aunt Georgie at

Rottingdean – 28 miles in an hour and 25 minutes. Amelia with a scientific frontier, I mean reconstructed interior – did it like a kestrel, and one way and another we put in 61 miles ere we came back for tea through woods lovelier than a partridge's breast. Amelia is very female. If she thinks she isn't giving pleasure but helping to improve the world she'll toil like a yankee school ma'am.

Their friendship didn't suffer, for in 1903 after their return from South Africa the diary records them motoring back to Rye to lunch at Lamb House. Hospitality was reciprocated in September when Henry James brought an American cousin with him and was entranced by Bateman's. In 1904 an 18 h.p. Mark II Amelia is delivered but she too, soon misbehaved, although there are no further reports of serious motoring frustration. A Siddeley car came and was considered but not adopted, and then in May 1906 earlier tribulations were put aside and more luxurious and genteel motoring age was inaugurated by a Daimler. Later motoring tours through Britain and France from Bateman's will be reviewed later.

The fury which police speed curbs aroused was common amongst the early pioneers. Kipling himself featured in a Punch cartoon, produced by L. Raven Hill in 1903. A sporting type of foreign car driven by a well-swaddled enthusiast approaches close to Kipling's chauffeur-driven Lanchester. In the rear seat of the Lanchester the passenger says to the owner "Going about thirty are we? But don't you run some risk of being pulled up for exceeding the legal pace?" Kipling responds "Not in a sober, respectable car like this. Of course if you go about in a brass-bound, scarlet-padded, snorting, foreign affair, like **that**, you are bound to be dropped on, no matter how slow you go!" The artist had been a recent guest at Bateman's and Kipling supplied the caption.
F. W. Lanchester wrote a letter of thanks to the Editor of Punch for such excellent publicity, and later, to appease the Editor's anger he bought the original of the cartoon for £25.

When traveling to the Cape aboard *Kinfauns Castle* in 1900, Rudyard had enjoyed the company of a young writer, A. B. Filson Young whom he had amused with details of his motoring escapades. Clearly in response to a request from him Rudyard wrote a "Letter" for publication in a book Filson Young was preparing with W. G. Aston, *The Complete Motorist.* It was a wonderful account, part hilarious and part serious, but for Sussex and adjacent counties it has a very special significance.

But the chief end of my car, so far as I am concerned, is the discovery of England. To me it is a land of stupefying marvels and mysteries; and a day in the car in an English county is a day in some fairy museum where all the exhibits are alive and real and yet none the less delightfully mixed up with books. For instance, in six hours, I can go from the land of the Ingoldsby Legends by way of the Norman Conquest and the Baron's War into Richard Jefferies country, and so through the Regency, one of Arthur Young's less known tours, and Celia's Arbour, into Gilbert White's territory. Horses, after all, are only horses; but the car is a time machine on which one can slide from one century to another at no more trouble than the pushing forward of a lever. On a morning I have seen the Assizes, javelin-men and all, come into a cathedral town; by noon I was skirting a new built convent for expelled French nuns; before sundown I was watching the Channel Fleet off Selsea Bill, and after dark I nearly broke a fox's back on a Roman road. You who were born and bred in the land naturally take such trifles for granted, but to me it is still miraculous that if I want petrol in a hurry I must either pass the place where Sir John Lade lived or the garden where Jack Cade was killed. In Africa one has only to put the miles under and go on; but in England the dead, twelve coffin deep, clutch hold of my wheels at every turn, till I sometimes wonder that the very road does not bleed. That is the real joy of motoring – the exploration of this amazing England.

In this account there are resonances of phrases he uses in the story *They* which he was preparing only a few weeks earlier. The *Ingoldsby Legends* were written by Richard Barham, a minor Canon of St. Pauls who had been born in Canterbury. The whole of the southern Weald is steeped in the history of the Conquest, and the decisive battle of the Baron's War was fought on the Downs above Lewes in 1264, when Henry III was defeated by Simon de Montfort. The naturalist Richard Jefferies wrote of Wiltshire and Sussex, the latter in *Nature near London* is quite magical. Brighton is famed for its Regency associations of the Prince and his exotic Royal Pavilion, and nearby Rottingdean gave succour to expelled French nuns, in the "Star of the Sea" Convent. *Celia's Arbour* by Sir Walter Besant is set in Portsmouth and Gilbert White was the Curate at Selborne which featured in his outstanding *Natural History*. Jack Cade, a rebel had been killed at what is now Cade Street, near Heathfield, and a series of Lades lived at Warbleton. Kipling may have been referring to 'Jack' Lade, coaching tutor to the Prince Regent, the most wildly notorious of them all.

The Muse among the Motors

The success of the Daily Mail's support for the troops in South Africa, for which *The Absent -Minded Beggar* was the catalyst, encouraged Alfred Harmsworth to think that Rudyard might well provide publicity material for the "Thousand Mile Trial" which he sponsored. Although he didn't rise to that particular bait, Carrie's diary entry for 15th May, 1900 showed that "Rud declines a further publicity scheme for the *Daily Mail*". He, nevertheless, worked on a scheme of a series of poems which would have a motoring theme, eventually published in the paper in series in February 1904. He employed a favourite trick of parodying the style of poets of either side of the Atlantic. The initial fourteen were, "The Advertisement" (Early English); "The Engineer" (Geoffrey Chaucer); 'To a Lady Persuading Her To A Car' (Ben Jonson); 'The Progress of the Spark' (John Donne); 'The Braggart' (Mat Prior); 'To Motorists' (Robert Herrick); 'Lord Byron' (Byron); 'The Idiot Boy' (Wordsworth); 'The Landau' (W. H. Praed); 'The Dying Chauffeur' (Adam Lindsay Gordon); 'The Inventor' (R. W. Emerson); 'Contradictions' (H. W. Longfellow); 'Fastness' (Lord Tennyson); and 'The Beginner' (Robert Browning). A further twenty-two were added over the years, to complete *The Muse Among the Motors*.

Many have very humorous themes – especially on driving faster than legally allowed.

Chapter 5

THE VERY OWN HOUSE

The search for a home which would provide relief from the pressures of his celebrity, and as a refuge from the haunted visions of an idolized daughter came, at last, with the discovery of Bateman's, a house snuggled in the valley of the Dudwell below the ridge on which Burwash stands. The first view came, not as recorded in *Something of Myself*, by the 'heartbreaking locomobile' but by train to Etchingham and a 'fly' to the house on a hot August day in 1900.

We had seen an advertisement of her, and we reached her down an enlarged rabbit-hole of a lane. At very first sight the Committee of Ways and Means said: 'That's her! The Only She! Make an honest woman of her – Quick!' We entered and felt her Spirit – her Feng Shui – to be good. We went through every room and found no shadow of ancient regrets, stifled miseries, nor any menace, though the 'new' end of her was three hundred years old. To our woe the Owner said: 'I've just let it for twelve months.' We withdrew, each repeatedly telling the other that no sensible person would be found dead in the stuffy little valley where she stood. We lied thus while we pretended to look at other houses till, a year later, we saw her advertised again, and got her.

Bateman's

Bateman's is a supremely beautiful house, reputedly belonging to a local Ironmaster. Its cream Ardingly sandstone is flecked with stained swags of rust which emphasize that the area was at the heart of the great iron-industry which had been so important from even before Roman times. The visit, the following year, which clinched the deal was also without the 'steamer' which, yet again, was in a trance. Perhaps it was a fortunate omen because the owner, who had his horses broken by the steepness of the lane, said that had he realised Kipling was a motoring man, he would have asked twice the price. As it was the property, which included the mill and 33 acres, changed hands for £9,300, with George Macdonald acting for them. A 'reception of farewell' was given for them at the Ridsdales on September 1st. Carrie, ever the practical partner, left The Elms on September 2nd 1902 and was equal to the task of dealing with foreman of removers, somewhat taken in drink, and met 'chaos and black night'. Rudyard, wisely, joined them the next day, having stayed overnight at 'The Bear', where he met Colonel Henry Feilden for the first time. The thrill of taking up residence in so attractive a house had not waned when he wrote Christmas greetings to Charles Eliot Norton during the first week of December.

We left Rottingdean because Rottingdean was getting too populated; though we didn't want to part from Aunt Georgie. Then we discovered England which we had never done before (Rottingdean isn't England: it's the Downs) and went to live in it.

England is a wonderful land. It is the most marvelous of all foreign countries that I have ever been in. It is made up of trees and green fields and mud and the Gentry: and at last I'm one of the Gentry! – I'll take a new pen and explain.

Behold us the lawful owners of a grey stone lichened house – A.D.1634 over the door – beamed, panelled, with oak staircase all untouched and unfaked. ...... It is a good and peaceable place standing in terraced lawns nigh to a walled garden of old red brick and two fat-headed old oast houses with red brick stomachs and an aged silver grey dovecot on top. There is what they call a river at the bottom of the lawn. It appears on all the maps and that, except after heavy rain, is the only place where it puts in any appearance.

The oast houses were evidence that the area was once dedicated to the growth of hops for the making of beer, but Rudyard quickly abandoned hop production and expanded his ownership in the farms around so that no neighbours could disrupt their new-found peace. In the same letter he reports on a very cold snap which had gripped the south of England.

A cold wave has hit us and driven us indoors – a venemous snowing blowing frost. All the country looks like a Christmas card. .... We are fighting the cold with logs – five foot long – in the hall; with stoves that close not day or night with two foot baulks; with hot water pipes. We have vanquished it indoors but outside it is untempered, and all the birds of the wood have come to beg rations. Figure to yourself a blackguard jay – a beautiful ruffian in blue – coming into our garden cowed and penitent – and being received with howls of indignation from the blackbirds and robins who stand in with the landed and householding classes. Tits, wagtails and finches are all in the crowd and, unless they migrate, I don't despair of getting sight of kingfishers. The moorhens daily feed nearer the house. If the cold lasts they'll come in among the fowls. A great deal of England is explained by its winter climate.

The hall must have presented a delightfully welcoming sight with the roaring logs casting streaks of golden glow on the dark panelled walls. Later the doorway offered an even more especial reception, for as he noted in *Something of Myself:*

But, for a month each year I possessed a paradise which I verily believed saved me. Each December I stayed with my Aunt Georgy, my mother's sister, wife of Sir Edward Burne-Jones, at The Grange, North End Road. At first I must have been escorted there, but later I went alone, and arriving at the house would reach up to the open-work iron bell-pull on the wonderful gate that let me into all felicity. When I had a house of my own, and The Grange was emptied of meaning, I begged for and was given that bell-pull for my entrance, in the hope that other children might also feel happy when they rang it.

Such thoughtfulness epitomised his ability to relate to the young, and certainly many children were welcomed through that doorway over the ensuing decades. The hallway inside was, clearly, of great joy, for as with so many other of his visual experiences he transposed it as the hall of the house beyond Washington, the location in *They* of his imaginary visits to the blind lady and the wraithe-like children.

I waited in a still, nut-brown hall, pleasant with late flowers and warmed with a delicious wood fire – a place of good influence and great peace. …. A child's cart and a doll lay on the black-and-white floor, where a rug had been kicked back ….. I looked on either side of the deep fireplace, and found but a half-charred hedge-stake with which I punched a black log into flame. …… The red light poured itself along the age-polished dusky panels till the Tudor roses and lions of the gallery took colour and motion. An old eagle-topped convex mirror gathered the picture into its mysterious heart, distorting afresh the distorted shadows.

As with the descriptive introductions to the locations of his short-stories, whether in India, South Africa, New England or Sussex, he drew on real places. The garden of the house in *They* nurtured a collection of clipped-yew topiary figures, among which were 'monstrous peacocks'. These he probably saw in a famous house, but a few miles to the north near Tunbridge Wells - Ravello at Rusthall.

The Bell pull inside the porch at Bateman s

Bateman's is a glorious home which provided for a firm base for all their needs for the remaining decades. It became the spiritual heart of the Sussex he loved. After Kipling's death in 1936, Carrie remained there just into the conflict he had predicted until she joined him. Happily she bequeathed the estate to The National Trust and so it remains almost exactly as it was during their residence, except for one of the bedrooms which found a new role as the Exhibition Room. On the ground floor the parlour has a Knole style sofa and a Tiffany studio lamp, reputedly brought back from Brattleboro although this is now a doubtful assumption. Opposite the parlour is what originally was a schoolroom for Elsie and John and was later converted to a sitting room. The dining room, lined with a most exotic 18th century English 'Cordoba' leather lies off the other side of the hall. Overlooking the hall, just up a few stairs, is a room used by Carrie as an office and from which she could see, though small windows, anyone seeking entry. Up the main staircase, above which hangs a Brussels tapestry, lie bedrooms and the hub of his working life, a fabulous, book-lined study, his desk and day-bed, together with a host of souvenirs of eventful travels. Soon after arrival he decided that the mill, which had once ground corn, should be converted to supply electricity to light the house, and enlisted the help of Sir William Willcocks to do so. Sir William's pedigree was impeccable as he had installed the first Aswan Dam, humorously recalled by Kipling as 'a trifling affair on the Nile'. A water turbine drove a generator which supplied power through a buried deep-sea cable to storage batteries in an outhouse. It was thus able to light only ten bulbs for a few hours each evening, but Kipling's enthusiasm for new-fangled ideas was satisfied.

He found in the landscape, which contrasted so markedly from the Downs around Rottingdean, a wealth of new inspiration right on his own doorstep. Its historical resonances spoke to him strongly of almost every period of English history which had shaped the destiny of an emerging nation, just as surely as the agents of erosion had created the scenery. *Puck's Song* is a precis of that destiny delving back in time. He explained exactly what triggered his enthusiasm

Just beyond the west fringe of our land, in a little valley running from Nowhere to Nothing-at-all, stood the long overgrown slag-heap of a most ancient forge, supposed to have been worked by the Phoenicians, Romans, and since then, uninterruptedly till the middle of the eighteenth century. The bracken and rust-patches still hid stray pigs of iron, and if one scratched a few inches through the rabbit-shaven turf, one came on the narrow mule-tracks of peacock-hued furnace-slag laid down in Elizabeth's day. The ghost of a road climbed out of this dead arena, and crossed our fields, where it was known as 'The Gunway,' and popularly connected with Armada times. Every foot of that little corner was alive with ghosts and shadows. .... You see how patiently the cards were stacked and dealt into my hands ? The Old Things of our Valley glided into every aspect of our outdoor works. Earth, Air, Water and People had been – I saw it at last – in full conspiracy to give me ten times as much as I could compass, even if I wrote a complete history of England, as that might have touched or reached our Valley.

The children were given a shallow draught canoe in which they ventured onto the bubbling little River Dudwell. The valley was the focus of their existence and the usually placid slightly meandering waters their intimate playground. On the stream they felt that they could be travelling imaginatively in far distant lands and seas. The little craft, sometimes *The Golden Hind* sometimes the *Long Serpent*, but actually *Daisy* could transport them to up the Nile or down the Amazon or even to the North Cape. The river was so narrow that it wasn't possible to row, so the children manoeuvred it by poling or pulling on branches of the overhanging trees. It was so particularly their own private domain that their father, with his usual imaginative genius, drafted a mock medieval document, elaborately scrolled in red and black ink, which 'granted and confirmed' to John and Elsie 'the liberties, freedoms and benefits, all and singular, of that portion of the Dudwell River lying and situate between Turbine Point and the Great Ash, commonly called Cape Turnagain'. It was The Charter of the River signed and sealed on June 19th 1906.

Their father enjoyed the rather limited fishing offered by the Dudwell. He was first attracted to the sport when living in Rottingdean where from the Daddy-Long-Legs pier he and the children would use the hand line, so popular at that period, to catch inshore fish, partially for sport and perhaps also to add very fresh fish to the table. At Bateman's he was accustomed to take Irish Guards officer friends of John out to cast for trout. He was amused by the fact that most of them, hardened veterans of the horrors of warfare, were quite squeamish about baiting a hook or removing one from the fish they had caught.

Thus was born some of the most enduring and much loved stories, ostensibly for children in general but Elsie and John in particular, the Puck stories, published as *Puck of Pook's Hill* and *Rewards and Fairies*. The children had been encouraged, with their father's keen participation, to act scenes from Shakespeare's *A Midsummer Night's Dream*. He had arranged for a modelled Ass's Head and Fairy wings to be sent from a London costumier and they performed in the Quarry Garden. With poetic license he transposed the setting of the performance to 'the long-slip meadow' on Midsummer's Eve, when Puck appears suddenly. From the first story, 'Weland's Sword', Puck becomes the instrument by which the children, now Dan and Una, are introduced to characters, real and fictional, who welded the nation or contributed to its well being. He acknowledged that he was not the first to bring history alive from a mere recitation of dates, for a neighbour from Romney Marsh, Edith Nesbit, had just earlier, written immensely popular tales for children.

His new environment entranced his imagination and he was torn between love for the Downs, over which he had spent so many happy hours tramping, and the eastward directed Wealden valleys below the High Weald converging at Rye. Beyond its medieval walls and gates lay out the contrasting flatness of Romney Marsh with its tortuous dykes and its wide skies above the shingle cuspate foreland of Dungeness. The dilemma was posed in *A Three-Part Song*. With the companion volume to Puck, he explained that 'grown-ups' could also respond to the three or four overlaid tints and textures. Certainly the intricacies of the stories, conceived a century ago, are so great that a look at The Kipling Society's 'New Reader's Guide' to them will prove most valuable. At the same time

As Rudyard looked in 1902

we have an indication of his writing process. He 'hatched' stories, during which he was 'a brother to dragons and a companion to owls', and unavailable even to his children. Then he let the tales 'drain' before re-drafting. Indeed when he was 'hatching' he was in a trance-like state which made normal courtesies irrelevant. The process could take place just as easily when he was trudging the local lanes as in his study. Sometimes he would ignore friendly pleasantries from folk he passed because his mind was focused exclusively on the story or verse with which he was engaged. He admitted that the physical process of writing was one he enjoyed, but that depended upon the tools of his trade being exactly where he needed them on his desk. His way of finding perfection in his writing was the shortening of his original draft by considering it line by line and excising anything superfluous, using a simple expedient of using a camel-hair brush and Indian Ink. The process could last over considerable periods of time whilst letting the text 'drain'.

Only a year after the publication of *Puck of Pook's Hill* he was honoured with the presentation of the Nobel Prize for Literature valued at seven thousand guineas. The ceremony in Stockholm was naturally subdued because Sweden was in mourning for King Oscar II who died only three days before. The prize was put to excellent use in the addition of the shallow, concrete lined, rectangular pond, which was to be the base for his 'navy' – a small hand-cranked paddle-boat – and a source of much merriment when visitors occasionally fell in. With any young and enthusiastic sailor he would seat them at the handle and say "I'm the passenger list, you are the Engine Room". A young Arthur Gordon was invited to "come and inspect my navy". The pond also occasioned much merriment when a visitor slipped accidentally into the water. Each time it elicited the letters FIP inscribed into the book which contained the names of guests. It, of course, meant "fell in pond". The rose-garden, the crisply trimmed hedge of yew and the semi-circular

Bateman's Garden and pond

wooden seat within it as well as a sundial with a cryptic message 'it is later than you think' to spur the departure of overstaying guests, all benefited from the proceeds. The extraordinary avenue of pleached limes were already in place when they bought the house, but with their love of gardening they were able to potter contentedly, perhaps playing at weeding and planting. A small band of gardeners was employed and Carrie was particularly critical of anything less than perfect horticulture, particularly where weeds were concerned. Rudyard was really interested in the minutiae of the plant world, and was grateful for occasional gifts of exotic species from friends in various parts of the world. With the coterie of distinguished family and friends the Kiplings must have been very familiar with the sights and scents of magnificent gardens with manicured lawns, borders, shrubberies and hedges, but it would be nice to think that it was his and Carrie's own creation which inspired *The Glory of the Garden*. This was published, only four years later, as the final poem in *A School History of England* for which C. R. L. Fletcher wrote the text and Kipling the accompanying poems. The pathways between house and garden are of the distinctive Sussex limestone enclosing fossil snail shells, whose rough surface have ensured a non-slip texture. By the south door this paved area is known as the 'Quarter-deck', and the interstices between the slabs are alive with sweet smelling herbs.

In the cold heart of each winter, until 1908, the family returned to the Woolsack for the reviving warmth of summer in the Cape, and to socialize with the great and the good of the land for which Rhodes, before his death in 1902, has such high hopes. Whilst they were away Kipling's firm friend Colonel Henry Feilden, who lived in the beautiful 'William and Mary' house, Rampyndene, in the High Street, oversaw Bateman's affairs when they were abroad. The major part of the year was concerned with farming enterprises, with entertaining, with discussions with those in power in London's clubland, and of course with writing. There is a revealing note in the diary that just about a year after their arrival they borrowed the Church records in order to trace details of previous owners. This perhaps triggered a fanciful interest in those who had been masters of those woods and fields before records began which culminated in a wonderful poem called *The Land*. He had already recognized the wisdom of men whose roots had been planted in the soil for generations. He epitomized that unerring instinct in one of his own men, a hedger and ditcher called William Isted, transmuted to a character called 'Hobden'. To each succeeding line of owners one of the 'old, unaltered, line' is called on for advice. Through Julius Fabricius, a Roman, and Ogier the Dane, to William of Warenne, made Lord of Lewes by William of Normandy, he arrives at his own stewardship in the time of George V. The Hobdens all followed extra-curricular traditions of poaching game-birds and rabbits to add to 'trout-tickling'. Even so Kipling accepts this as a *quid pro quo* for folk-wisdom on tap. Some archaeological treasures had been unearthed during the normal course of estate development and the significance of such finds is incorporated in Roman drainage schemes. *And in droughty middle August when the bones of meadow show, we can trace the lines they followed sixteen hundred years ago.* Isted's 'flagrant' poaching is accepted with - *Shall I dog his morning progress o'er the track betraying dew? Demand his dinner basket into which my pheasant flew? Confiscate his evening faggot under which my conies ran, And summons him to judgement ? I would sooner summons Pan.*

Kipling took a great interest in the ways of the countryman and was able, at first hand to admire their rural skilled craftsmanship. He had long been absorbed by the mysteries of agriculture and had observed Rhodes's enthusiasm for experimental farms to assess best practice for Cape farmers. Back in England his great friend Rider Haggard was considered an authority and he took heed of his wisdom alongside that of a sixteenth century author, Thomas Tusser, whose book *Five Hundred Good Points of Husbandry* he treasured. Such was his command of farm lore that *A. G. Street in Moonraking* comments of him:-

But nowhere have I read anything which stresses the one phase of his work which appeals to me the most. I mean his stories and verses which deal with rural England and its inhabitants. To me, a farmer, his insight into the minds of countryfolk was uncanny. He never made a mistake. When he was writing about a farmer, he was himself a farmer; when the need arose he became himself a farm labourer.

This assessment parallels those judgments made by engineers, law-makers, soldiers, sailors, bridge builders, medical men and many other professions whose daily routines were grist to his mill. Maintenance of field boundaries is ever of prime importance to the farmer, and where stone is in abundance dry-stone walling with limestone, or variations with flints embedded in mortar give a very characteristic appearance to the landscape. Elsewhere the layering of hedges provides an animal-proof enclosure which, most importantly, also acts as a haven for birds and small mammals. Nowhere is this technique better observed than in the opening of *Friendly Brook*, which precedes *The Land*.

The valley was so choked with fog that one could scarcely see a cow's length across a field. Every blade, twig, bracken-frond, and hoof-print carried water, and the air was filled with the noise of rushing ditches and field drains, all delivering to the brook below. A week's November rain on water-logged land had gorged her to full flood, and she proclaimed it aloud.

Two men, in sackcloth aprons were considering an untrimmed hedge that ran down the hillside and disappeared into mist beside those roarings. They stood back and took stock of the neglected growth, tapped an elbow of hedge-oak here, a mossed beech-stub there, swayed a stooled ash back and forth, and looked at each other. 'I reckon she's about two rod thick,' said Jabez the younger, an' she hasn't felt iron since – when has she Jesse?' Call it twenty-five year, Jabez, an' you won't be far out. 'Umm !' Jabez rubbed his wet handbill on his wetter sleeve. 'She ain't a hedge. She's all manner o'trees. We'll just about have to –' He paused, as professional etiquette required. 'Just about have to side her up an' see what she'll bear. But hadn't we best -- ?' Jesse paused in his turn, both men being artists and equals. 'Get some kind o' line to go by.' Jabez ranged up and down till he found a thinner place, and with clean snicks of the handbill revealed the original face of the fence. Jesse took over the dripping stuff as it fell forward, and, with a grasp and a kick, made it to lie orderly on the bank till it should be faggoted.

By noon a length of unclean jungle had turned itself into a cattle-proof barrier, tufted here and there with little plumes of the sacred holly which no woodman touches without orders.

In the early years at Bateman's John returned to his Prep School, St Aubyns in Rottingdean, where he had the additional comfort, on 'exeat', of the welcome warmth of great-aunt Georgie, and occasionally both children would stay with her. These visits provided the trigger for both *The Knife and the Naked Chalk* and *Brother Square-Toes*. Farming occupied both the Kiplings, although Carrie seems to have had the daily round of management very much under her control. She could be a hard taskmistress and a summons to the little office over the hall could be daunting. A village garden-boy, Albie Waterhouse, cheekily tried to counter her remonstrances for his lateness at work without much luck and later declared her to be 'a devil'. As leases expired they were not renewed and Rudyard extended his farming activities, particularly in the war years. Increased pasture allowed him to develop a herd of Guernsey cattle for dairy produce. Each new calf was lovingly registered and named, appropriately with 'Bateman's' as a prefix, whilst the second name always began with a "B". Farm accounts showed that they didn't really earn their keep but they did accumulate rosettes from agricultural shows. Kipling was particularly proud of his "Sussex" Shorthorn breeding stock which provided animals for fattening. He understood their capacity for growth and fine quality and his eulogy for them is found in *Alnaschar and the Oxen*. His joy is therein compared to Lobengula's pride in seeing his vast herds moving across the veldt, although his herd numbered only 26. Alnaschar was a character in *The Arabian Nights* who invested in glassware in the hope of making sufficient fortune to claim the hand of the daughter of the Grand Vizier. His dream was shattered when his stock was broken, so perhaps, with his customary humour, Kipling thought it unlikely that his herd would make him another fortune. There is an amusing account of the pedigree stud bull, normally docile, taking exception to Mrs Sands as she went to feed the poultry. She was alarmed at his unaccustomed aggression and so took shelter in a wheeled hen house. The bull trundled the whole contraption along with all its frenzied occupants wailing, before battering it in earnest. The inmates were eventually rescued by farm hands and the bull sentenced to solitary confinement. Many cattlemen believe that the breed is supreme, with its deep rich dark red skin and sleek seal-like coat. The quality of the meat was unrivalled, but because their care was so labour intensive and that they took so long to mature, they never made the farmer a reasonable profit. Before the turmoil of the Great War farming was a way of life rather than a business. The cattle were fed hay, sliced mangolds and turnips, treacled bran, ground nut cake and flaked maize. In the early years the cattle were dual purpose, draught animals before beef. It was normal to have eight to ten Sussex oxen to draw the iron plough, painfully slowly, across the cloying Wealden clay. Kipling knew and loved his little herd and he, like so many farming folk, believed in the theraputic quality of simply watching them. All their qualities are cleverly introduced within the beautifully balanced stanzas. There was a considerable export trade of the breed to Natal, the Orange Free State and Rhodesia, because their red-pigmented skin was less susceptible to sunburn. Agricultural fairs would have figured strongly in the life of the farmer and his farmhands, with coveted rosettes being sought eagerly for the perfection of the stock chosen for each event. One of the nearest fairs was held at Heathfield, a few miles along the ridge to the west. One of the annual events there was held in early spring, traditionally on April 14th, when an Old Woman released a cuckoo from her basket as its official opening. It has always been known as Heffle (or Hefful) Cuckoo fair, which Kipling celebrated with *Cuckoo Song*.

The farm was 'mixed', having some arable as well as hens, geese, pigs and orchard produce, with sheep introduced at times to take advantage of the 'bite'. From his experience at Rottingdean he knew a great deal about the ways of sheep and their shepherds. New fangled mechanization had been introduced for harvesting but two dray-horses, 'Captain' and 'Blackbird' were employed to move the crop. 'Captain' was quite a character with a mind of his own and a liking for escaping from normal drudgery. On one occasion he rolled in a pond in an effort to remove his loose harness. He stood up blackened in mud and remained beyond the reach of his driver's lash till the working day was over. 'Blackbird' was normally more amenable. Rudyard maintained a keen interest in farming throughout his life and was instrumental in encouraging schemes which provided opportunities for British children to undertake rather more extensive agricultural experience in the Dominions. Being close to the country scene, he had a great enthusiasm for trees, shrubs and flowers. His poem *A Tree Song* is a heartwarming evocation of that delight. Oak, Ash and Thorn, the charm which Puck lays upon Dan and Una after their encounters with characters from history, was wonderfully recalled when a spray of the three was sent by the estate workers to his interment.

The first decade at Bateman's saw many gatherings of the clan and their friends enjoying all the delights that a well-staffed estate could provide. Lady Lorna Howard, a favourite cousin, and Elsie's special friend, daughter of Stanley and Louie Baldwin was a frequent guest and she recalled in a series of ten articles entitled *'Uncle Ruddy', Remembered* (The Kipling Journal Nos 232 – 243) the simple joys of family life undistracted by the pressures of life today. Charming vignettes such as "Uncle Ruddy" struggling, suitably gauzed, with his beehives which were dotted in the Quarry Garden, or Aunt Carrie getting happily into the weeding of the rose garden. Lorna Baldwin, as she then was, was particularly favoured because her build and colouring reminded the Kiplings of their adored lost daughter. His fervent wish that the iron bell pull should bring happiness to young visitors was amply fulfilled. The domestic scene she described was typical of the delights open to the gentry. There is an account of much anticipated 'teenage-ball' in August 1913, with the hall beflowered, and dancing in the drawing-room. Autumn afternoons were taken up with woodland walks. A large basket was filled by Elsie and Lorna with fir cones from the pines on the hillside above the mill. The cones were added to the fire in order to produce a fragrance which today is supplied only from bottles. Much later, in 1923, the same delicious scent was remarked upon by a welcome visitor, Coudurier de Chassaigne, the London correspondent of *Le Figaro*. There was also a good grass tennis court which the girls could enjoy. In letters to John in 1912 Rudyard described the building of a squash court and later revealed that Elsie, a keen tennis player, could not really master the game in which the ball comes back so frighteningly quickly. Uncle Ruddy's constant companionship with his dogs is noted as was his habit of spending the time after breakfast at a hall table awash with all the morning papers. Some of the short articles relate to their frequent trips abroad and of the enjoyment of their own particular brand of 'Franglais', for they spent a great deal of time travelling to allow Carrie to 'take the waters' in their beloved France or to enjoy the crispness of Swiss snow, ice and air.

An estate the size of Bateman's needed considerable staffing, both indoor and out. Entertaining family friends, some of whom were world statesmen, and even occasional unexpected visitors demanded a sizeable domestic staff, managed by Carrie with her usual brusque efficiency. The most important was the cook who would in most households be addressed as "Mrs", whether married or not. Carrie, as a determined chatelaine, used the more succinct "Cook". Next in the hejrarchy was the mistress's Lady's Maid, responsible for the personal comfort of her employer. A Parlour-maid would serve food and wine at table, assisted, when there were guests, by the Head Housemaid, whose main task was to ensure that the Master's clothes were set out and to bring her employers their early morning tea. The under-maid would do the sweeping and tidying and would also have to collect the waste paper from Rudyard's study and make absolutely sure that it was incinerated, at least three times a day. This was considered as vitally important to ensure that nothing discarded could eventually find its way on to the literary market.   In many households a Housekeeper would head the domestic staff but Carrie herself fulfilled that role. The keys at her waist in Philip Burne-Jones portrait of her emphasized her role as chatelaine. Neither did the Kiplings employ a Butler. The Head Housemaid would be helped by an Under-Housemaid, and the Kitchen Maid would scurry unseen in kitchen and scullery. The "living-in" staff were accommodated in the old oast houses where there was also the Servants' Hall.   As in all major houses the day started early.   At 6.30 the kettles would be put on to prepare for morning tea for family, guests and staff. Although there was a bathroom for each, Carrie usually preferred to use a washstand in a recess in their bedroom, and Rudyard certainly washed and shaved in what was originally the 'Powder Room' where seventeenth century wigs would be prepared.   In later years Rudyard used to stay in bed until 11 o'clock if he felt unwell, but normally breakfast was served at 8.30. The Servants Hall breakfast was half an hour earlier and was of the traditional kind. The maids were dressed in blue or pale grey cotton, with white apron and cap, but changed into black alpaca with white collar and cuffs for afternoon and evening.

When the children were young a Governess supervised their lives. Between 1904 and 1909 the post was filled by Miss Mary Blaikie who developed a memorable rapport, both with her charges and with their parents over and above the normal employer/employee relationship. The genuine friendship lasted over many years, maintained by much detailed correspondence from Rudyard about John, whom she called 'Juno', as to his progress and his departure to war. She lived in Park Mill Cottage adjacent to the mill, as did Dorothy Ponton who came, as an inspiring tutor, with a real ability to motivate a reluctant John, from 1911 to 1913. She added to her flock during the school holidays when Oliver Baldwin and his sister Margot joined their cousins. When John was at Wellington College an unsatisfactory report prompted Mary to coach him in Maths and English in Engleberg where the family were staying for the winter sports. In 1913 Carrie recommended Miss Ponton as Governess to Lord Cecil's daughter Helen at Great Wigsell, their home near Hawkhurst. Active suffragettes objected strongly when Kipling published *The Female of the Species* in 1911. Threats that they would burn down Bateman's perturbed Carrie more than Rudyard, and she ensured that lights were left on in the house, even when no one was there.

She reasoned that even suffragettes would not start a fire if they thought the house was occupied. After the Great War the Kiplings asked Dorothy to return to Bateman's as a secretary and helper to both of them. In a memoir published in the Kipling Journal and later extended into a monograph entitled *Rudyard Kipling at Home and at Work*. Miss Ponton shed much light on the duties the Secretary was expected to undertake. During her period as his secretary he was at what he called his "great work", the masterpiece history of the Irish Guards in the Great War. This was truly a labour of love for which the proceeds went entirely for the widows of those killed. She gradually learnt to decipher his handwriting, although occasionally had to take what she called 'pot shots' at it. It was during this work that Carrie's domination was exemplified. A typescript ready for dispatch had been modified by a few emendations in Rudyard's hand. Carrie spotted this, and in spite of her husband's assertion that a typed revision was unnecessary she insisted upon it to the frustration of the two most closely involved. It was at this time that her employer bought a small portable Imperial "Good Companion" typewriter. He was not particularly adept at its use and complained bitterly that "the beastly thing won't spell". Dorothy's term of office must have been exceptionally busy, for in addition there were the arrangements needed to be made in respect of work for the Imperial War Graves Commission as well as the visit he inspired His Majesty to make across the channel. In addition to handling a variety of requests from the reading public, Dorothy was expected to collect rents from some cottages in the village which he had bought out of kindness to a widow of a Hobdenesque poacher to prevent her from being turned out of her long cherished home. Rather surprisingly, for one so much attuned to technical developments, the telephone was never installed at Bateman's, the desire for privacy being paramount and his objection to talking to someone he could not see. Bateman's headed notepaper printed symbols of a telegraph pole, aligned with Burwash, and a railway engine to indicate the nearest station at Etchingham. The normal means of communication was the telegram, agreeable for receipt but inconvenient for outward transmission as a trek to the village Post Office had to be made. Only after Rudyard's death was a telephone installed in Carrie's bedroom.

In June 1922, a few weeks before the completion of *The Irish Guards*, Clare Sheridan and her brother Oscar, children of an old friend, Moreton Frewen, who lived at Brickwall, came as guests. The reason was, ostensibly, that she, as an artist, could make a sketch of Rudyard for the *New York World*. A piece appeared in a New York paper, which seemed to suggest anti-American views, much to the consternation of the Kiplings. He had said, in private conversation, that American entry to the war was too late and that their negotiations at Versailles had been unhelpful. Rudyard also made disparaging remarks about Charlie Chaplin having mislaid his patriotism by staying in America throughout the war. Perhaps Kipling hadn't realized that the comic genius had recently been linked amorously with Clare, and the spiteful piece published in September was most regrettable.

Kipling's last secretary was Cecily Nicholson, who came of a distinguished military family. Her engaging reminiscences appeared in six short instalments in The Kipling Journal, *Something of Himself*, shortly before she died in 1982. (K.J. Nos 215 – 221) She worked for Rudyard from 1932 until his death and remained with Carrie until she died. Cecily then transferred to assist Elsie with the mass of her father's papers at Wimpole Hall between 1949 and 1954. She gave a valuable insight into life at Bateman's and enjoyed her long hours of work greatly, although she suffered from the somewhat Spartan life style she was expected to lead. She admired Rudyard immensely but found Carrie a more difficult person to get on with. Cecily had to cope with a vast incoming correspondence, and many of the letters requested his autograph. These were prepared in advance but would only be sent if return postage had been included, perhaps a reflection of his mother's Scottish ancestry. He enjoyed receiving letters from children and responded most kindly to them. Cecily described his way of working, reinforcing Kipling's own account in his autobiography. She commented on the love both had for their Aberdeen terrier Michael, who was allowed into the study but not on their bed. She exercised the dog daily on her walk to lunch at Dudwell Farm where she lived, some distance down the valley, where the pet was fed by the staff. Rud and Carrie played with Michael in the garden, but were away so frequently that their contact was relatively sparse. His undoubted love of dogs was immortalized in a series of quite remarkable 'dog' stories and poems, the most heart-rending of all must be *The Power of the Dog*. When Kipling died Cecily was called to Brown's Hotel to help Carrie with the very detailed arrangements for the Service in Westminster Abbey and with responding to condolences. She reported that the only time Carrie's reserve broke was on receiving a carefully wrought wreath of Ash, Oak and Thorn from the staff at home.

Secretaries had been an important adjunct ever since the much respected and admired help of Sarah Anderson in Rottingdean. A succession of others followed. Elsie Parker replaced Sarah in Rottingdean as she had worked as an assistant nanny there. But she had a number of disputes with Carrie, ever suspiciously ready to take umbrage that she was being treated with prejudice and being underpaid.   Laid off for a time in 1902, Carrie surprisingly begged her to return and actually increased her wages, but she eventually resigned in 1904. She retaliated by removing some draft letters and typescripts of stories when she left and these came to light when auctioned in 1996. They were bought for the Sussex University collection with the aid of a fund and a generous contribution of an anonymous donor.

The Head Gardener would have four or five assistants and an 'odd-job' man who would also ensure that there were sufficient logs for the hall fire to be kept alight day and night in the cold of the winter. He would clear the resultant ash which would then be spread in the garden.

The peace and comfort of the valley was destroyed with the mental agony of his long-predicted arrival of the 'Armageddon' which, in September 1915, claimed John's life at Loos. The theme has been brilliantly recorded in *My Boy Jack?* by Tonie and Valmai Holt, the title springing from the poem Kipling wrote as a response to their loss. His other memorials were the dedication he used to serve as a very active Commissioner of the Imperial War Graves Commission, and in the writing of the history of The Irish Guards into which John had been gazetted. With the Great War at its height the sound of heavy guns booming in Flanders could occasionally be heard in their quiet valley. Many of John's friends had met a similar fate, but surviving ones would be welcomed in the house as a tangible link with their son. In St. Bartholemew's Church in Burwash a plaque was commissioned to record John's sacrifice. Rudyard's old friend Herbert Baker recommended a young sculptor, Charles Wheeler, to produce it, but on seeing the loose strap surrounding the laurel wreath in the clay design, Rudyard asked him to tighten it. The first bronze casting had a flaw, immediately spotted by Kipling, to the anguish of the sculptor, and needed to be recast. The epitaph read *Qui Ante Diem Periit*, "who perished before his day". Clearly the Kipling's liked the new casting and actually commissioned Wheeler to make a bust of their son from photographs. When it was completed the sculptor invited Rud and Carrie to come and see it, but in spite of several reminders he found they simply couldn't bring themselves to do so, and so it was destroyed. Charles Wheeler became a most distinguished contributor to the work of the War Graves Commission. There is a striking War Memorial at Burwash in the road junction in front of the Parish Church. Lt. John Kipling's inscription is a couple of names below that of Lance Corporal Alfred Isted, one of the 'Hobden' clan. There is a most moving tradition that on the anniversary of the death of each of those on the Roll of Honour the lamp at the top of the cenotaph is lit. For many years, the former garden boy, Albie Waterhouse, faithfully filled the role as guardian of the lamp.

Aftermath

Life could never be the same again and the latter years, although occasionally ameliorated by travel, were depressed, lonely and beset with medical problems. There were some highlights, particularly when Rudyard was able to serve his monarch. He and Carrie accompanied King George V to the cemeteries across the Channel, and having produced the inscriptions he was also asked to compose the speeches for the King to make. This gladly accepted task was to be extended, long unacknowledged, when His Majesty was about to make the first Christmas broadcast in 1932 and subsequent ones. Their partnership ended when they died within two days of each other, and it was said that "the King is dead, and he was preceded by his trumpeter." He and Carrie were *en-route* for Cannes, and whilst at Brown's Hotel, he was taken ill. An operation was unable to save his life and so on January 18th 1936 he died, only recently having passed his 70th birthday. He was cremated, secretly, at Golders Green and his ashes were taken to the Burial Service at 12 noon on the 23rd January in Westminster Abbey. The pall-bearers included his cousin Stanley Baldwin, the Prime Minister, an Admiral of the Fleet, a Field Marshal and other very distinguished men. It seems that the same ceremonial as when he was a pall-bearer at Thomas Hardy's interment was carried out for him. The Ashes Casket was placed inside a coffin carried by the Pall-bearers. The Service began with the Opening Sentences of the Burial Office and was followed by Psalm CXXI. The lesson was taken from 1 Corinthians xv, after which H.F. Lyte's Devonian hymn *Abide with Me* was sung, during which the mourners moved into Poet's Corner. Following prayers by the Dean and the Precentor, the clergy and mourners returned to their places whilst *Recessional* was sung. The introit had been Parry's *Elegy* and Harwood's *Requiem Aeternam* and the service ended with *Solemn Melody* by Walford Davies and the *Sonata in G* by Edward Elgar. Carrie's reserve almost broke when the bouquet of oak ash and thorn sent by the staff at Bateman's was placed on the coffin. A telegram came to Carrie from Queen Mary saying "The King and I are grieved to hear of the death this morning of Mr. Kipling. We shall mourn him not only as a great national poet, but as a personal friend of many years".

Carrie battled on for almost four years and when she passed away on December 19th 1939, her ashes could not join those of her husband but were placed beneath a tree in the walled garden. At her death, as they had agreed, Bateman's was handed over to The National Trust, and thus remains virtually as it was during their life there, which is, of course why a visit to the house is so very special, for no other family has occupied the main part of the property. Carrie, ever the astute negotiator, drew up a list of wishes, which were partially accepted by the

Trust, in return for which an endowment of £5,000 was forthcoming. This was, however, quickly absorbed by inflation. After her death the estate was declared inalienable land so that it could never be sold. The first tenant, the Trust's custodian, moved in during 1940.

Carrie had a very quiet private existence after her husband's death, with two nurses living in the attic in attendance. One, Nurse Mander spoke of her duties which included preparing her diabetic injections and reporting to the doctor in Burwash who made a regular weekly visit to his patient. She dined with Carrie and tried to see that she kept to an appropriate diet, often in vain. She was surprised to learn that Carrie wore a wig during the day. The maid was responsible for ensuring that one of a pair was always ready. When nurse saw her at night she wore a night-cap tied beneath her chin.

Bateman's today.

The greatest joys of Bateman's are threefold. The house still exudes the aura of the family and the extraordinary authorship to which it gave birth, and secondly, the exquisitely beautiful formal garden and the wilder garden beyond, and thirdly the setting within so charming a valley. Few could fail to be moved by Bateman's ambience in a golden age before the world was beset by the garishness which now assails our eyes and ears.

The heart of all must be the study at the top of the stairs. Set with oak bookcases filled with a library which Kipling considered essential reference and inspiration, the focus has to be his sixteenth century French work table raised on a base

Kipling's Study at Bateman's

shaped as the Cross of Lorraine. This was his craftsman's bench set in what he called his 'mould-loft', now neat and tidy bearing the tools essential to his physical enjoyment of writing, but often, then, a chaotic amalgam of sheaves of paper. With his writing blocks there is a large blotter with silver angle corners and an iron paper weight with a clenched brass hand as its handle. This is supposed to have belonged to Warren Hastings, the first Governor-General of India, who transformed the East India Company into a major civil administration. His incorruptibility must have stirred Kipling's own ideal of Imperial 'service'. On the blotter lies a photostat of the original manuscript of *'Recessional'* which, it ought to be made clear, was not written here as the tribute to the Queen's Diamond Jubilee but was conceived at North End House. Nearby is a large pewter Post Office ink pot on which the author scratched the names of each of his works as they were published, and few other typical desk items. There was always a monumental pen-wiper stitched each year by a faithful maid. A pair of terrestrial globes flanked the desk which emphasized the great deal of travel which he and Carrie had experienced. On one a famous airman, Sir Geoffrey Salmond, had painted the pioneer air routes to the East and Australia he had been instrumental in setting out. Close to his chair, raised on blocks, is a large Algerian woven waste-paper basket, which had accepted a great deal of unsatisfactory script. One particularly important item of furniture was an oak day-bed, uncomfortably hard for all but Rudyard, who used to lie there waiting for his 'daemon' to strike. Occasionally an especially favoured guest would be invited to use it whilst he read to them a newly composed verse or text. When writing he was invariably alone and incommunicado, except when Rider Haggard was a guest. As the great friends were both writers. Rudyard was never disturbed by his presence. The room is full of mementoes of an exciting past. Above the north wall bookcase is a terracotta bas-relief, a self portrait profile of Lockwood, inscribed 'Fumus Gloria Mundi' which clearly extolled their shared delights of a smoked leaf. Portraits abound, chief of which, above the fireplace, is the oil of Carrie painted at Andrew Carnegie's Skibo Castle by Sir Philip Burne-Jones for which she sat in August 1899 when she was 37. Sir Edward Poynter, Philip's uncle admired the one he had done of Rud, but was less appreciative of Carrie's likeness. Other photographs or prints represented

Burwash War Memorial

are the adored Josephine, Dr. Jameson, Lord Roberts, and an Aberdeen terrier. Kipling's own water-colour design for the rose garden hangs on the south wall. A *Punch* cartoon depicting RK in armour kneeling to receive the Nobel Prize from a Queen, bearing the caption, "A Verray Parfait Nobel Knight" is on the same wall. A number of what are described as 'miscellaneous objects' are dotted around, including a large ornamental silvered replica of a Canadian Dollar presented by 'The Stroller' Club in Toronto. One very nostalgic item is a hardwood box, the lid decorated with oak and ash leaves in white gesso, reflecting the last couplet of *A Tree Song* which followed *Weland's Sword*. There are also a couple of fossil sea-urchins, *Echinocorys*, which he must have brought from Rottingdean where the genera form part of the fossil fauna of the strata known as the Upper Chalk. Among other souvenirs of India is an antique red lacquer bridal chest from Punjab, which is decorated with flower sprays, and a curved Indian sword with a hilt overlaid in silver, set in a leather scabbard. Another sword is much more poignant for it almost certainly belonged to John. Two leather cases, each inscribed, held the motoring maps used for tours in Britain and France.

Next door to the Study is the only room with a different function to that which it had when Rudyard and Carrie were in residence. Originally almost certainly their bedroom, its walls panelled with oak from the estate, it was, when taken on by the National Trust, used to display memorabilia about his life and work. The contents are self-explanatory and they include Lockwood's bas-reliefs illustrating characters in *Soldiers Three, Kim* and other early works. The pages of the visitors book are turned regularly and the Citation for the Nobel Prize for Literature is elegantly framed. Just off to the side is a small room, which would have been used in the seventeenth century for the messy business of powdering wigs. Rudyard used it for washing and shaving. It now houses one of the watercolours used for the set of illustrations by the Detmold brothers to illustrate first *The Jungle Book* which shows *Kaa, the Python*. The Detmold set is usually accepted as the finest of those produced by three different artists for the various editions. The brothers story is extraordinary and tragic. The twins, Maurice and Edward, were born in 1883 and early on displayed a talent for drawing the animals they viewed in Regent's Park. Their tastes in everything were identical and both could work on the same theme, and none could tell which brother contributed which part. A few years after this collaboration, very tragically, Maurice took his own life at the age of 24. He had at one time lived at Horsebridge Common in Sussex. Naturally his death was very distressing for Edward, but the latter continued a career as a successful illustrator for Hodder and Stoughton. In later years he became reclusive and almost 50 years after his brother's death he killed himself. On the window ledge in the Powder Room is a charming brass model of Zam-Zammah, the giant cannon set outside the museum at Lahore, astride which Kim is introduced at the beginning of the novel. It is one of two presented to the author.

Beyond the Exhibition Room is the room later used by Carrie as her bedroom, a jealously guarded private retreat. It is almost certainly a myth that they occupied it for the whole of their life there. The bed is an oak four-poster, and it has a replica of the original bedspread which had their initials upon it. This was made and presented by the East Sussex Embroiderers Guild because the first had almost faded away. There is a pastel of Josephine, a treasure probably brought back from Vermont, a set of Edward Burne-Jones caricatures of each child sent at Christmas 1897, and a circular bronze relief of Elsie made by Henry Pegram in 1907. Another bedroom at the top of the main staircase, and opposite the study was one in which friends and relatives slept and which also accommodated John's regimental friends when they came to stay. The staircase itself is overhung by a seventeenth century Brussels tapestry depicting the Queen of Sheba. Above the half-landing is a very striking portrait by John Collier painted in 1900 when the family were still living at The Elms, and on the upper landing a wood-cut portrait by William Nicholson, for a series, *Twelve Portraits*, of famous personalities, created almost as soon as Rudyard came to Rottingdean. The two became firm friends and collaborated on *An Almanac of Twelve Sports*, for which Rudyard wrote the verses. Nicholson like the village so much that a few years later he bought the old rectory and renamed it The Grange. There is also a 'Spy' cartoon produced for the magazine Vanity Fair by Sir Leslie Ward. Nearby is a painting originally done for an illustration in *Puck of Pook's Hill* by André Castaigne, and presented by the artist as a token of admiration. A long-case clock with a rolling sailing vessel above the dial was made by Jonathan Williams of Bideford, in the late eighteenth century. It is a timely reminder of Kipling's schooldays at United Services College.

The ground floor is reached from the porch through a short corridor. The porch itself with AD 1634 encircled above, has scratched on its sandstone lintel, the initials of Rudyard, Carrie, Elsie and John, plus one other set of someone unknown. By the front door is the iron-work bell pull which once adorned the entrance to the Burne-Jones house in Fulham and which let Rudyard in to 'all felicity'. The Hall, panelled above the black and cream tiled floor has a magnificent fireplace with a Sussex fireback, in which Kipling would burn discarded manuscripts to ensure they didn't fall into the wrong hands. There is a delightful circular eagle-topped convex mirror. These features were transmuted to the 'House Beautiful' in the story '*They*'. The spy-windows from Carrie's office scan directly to the front door, an effective sentry post. On one occasion the normally placid Dudwell rose to engulf the Hall itself and Kipling aroused from slumber rushed to rescue valued rugs.

To the left of the hall just through the arch, the Parlour was the setting for enjoying gatherings of family and friends. If necessary the carpet could be rolled back as it surely was when they played with their dogs. Because the antiquity of the house couldn't allow them to introduce 'modern' furniture the chairs tended to be hard and uncomfortable to all but those who had grown up with the austerity of the Arts and Crafts movement, which had manifested itself in "The Mermaid" in North End House. Elsie found the style particularly disagreeable. The upholstered Knole sofa was not there initially. The log fire threw out too little heat and the Cordoba 'screen' made from left-over pieces from the dining room wallpaper would be expected to reduce the draughts flowing into the room. The fireplace is flanked by two nostalgic paintings, one of Rottingdean by Ambrose Poynter, and the other an anonymous watercolour of Rudyard Lake. A couple of Tiffany lamps bring a comforting golden glow to the room.

Opposite the Parlour is Elsie's Sitting Room which was, originally, the schoolroom for she and her brother, where in *A Centurion of the Thirtieth* John was kept back to do an 'impot', by Miss Blake, in reality Miss Blaikie. When Elsie was sixteen in 1912 it was transformed to her own room, which she enjoyed until her wedding twelve years later. It contains an Edwardian red lacquer bureau cabinet and has five of her grandfather's Indian themed watercolours.

On the other side of the Hall is the Dining Room, the most striking feature of which is the 'Cordoba' leather wall covering. The technique for making this luxurious dressed leather originated in Libya using goat-skins but it was taken up in Spain, even before the Moorish conquest, using sheep skin, the methods being refined by the conquerors. A favourite design was a theme of a swirling pattern of flowers, fruit and foliage among which animals and birds appear. The style reached its peak in the late seventeenth century, being produced not only in Spain but in the Netherlands as well. The silver foil covering was varnished to give a golden appearance. Carrie's diary records that in the month before the move to Batemen's they travelled to the Isle of Wight to buy the 'stamped Venetian leather', which they brought back in the car, rolled up like 'lino'. Ever formal they dressed for dinner even when alone, and usually eat bland food for health reasons. The highly spiced curries Rudyard had enjoyed in India were no longer acceptable to his digestion in later life, and Carrie was plagued with similar problems. Carrie always sat with her back to the fireplace, above which was a 'Virgin and Child' which they both disliked, but which remained in place because it had been a gift. Rudyard's short sight, sitting opposite his wife, prevented his seeing it with clarity. Lunch was served at 1.00 pm and dinner at eight. Tea might be taken there if there were guests staying or in the Hall. A silver tray commemorating the launch of H.M.S. Kipling by Elsie in 1939 is on a side table.

The Dining Room at Bateman's

Zam-Zammah

The Mill at Bateman's - for centuries grinding corn grown on the estate,

The walled garden at Bateman's

The Mill dates from the mid-eighteenth century, although it was probably the site of milling operations much earlier, although certainly not at the time of the Domesday survey as Kipling avowed in the poem *Puck's Song*. Having adapted the mill to produce electricity for the house almost as soon as they took up residence, it was restored to its original use between 1968 and 1975. Volunteers repaired the timber framework, overhauling the wheels and cogs, and installing a new water-wheel. Flour milled there is on sale to visitors. The mill features particularly in *Below the Mill Dam*. The adjacent cottages provided living quarters for the chauffeur and when the oast was converted, for the Secretary, Governess and the maid employed to look after them.

The Mill pond is almost circular, and played its part in the navigation of very early airliners flying between London and Le Bourget in Paris. Pilots, flying fairly low in those days knew that they were perfectly on course if they could identify a 'round pond, a square pond and six chimneys all in a row'. This would have been much appreciated by the author as he was most supportive of the early development of civil aviation.

The National Trust which benefited when Bateman's was handed over, received, also, when Elsie died, her home at Wimpole Hall and, of exceptional importance, the copyright of most of his works. This provided a very considerable income, which would end with the closure of the extended period raised from the initial 50 years to 70 years after his death in 1936. Copyright on all the works published in his lifetime was removed on January 1st, 2007.

Chapter 6

THE SUSSEX STORIES

The majority of those tales with a setting in the county are enfolded by the dual mantle of *Puck of Pook's Hill* and *Rewards and Fairies* and they have a common interest in the unrolling drama of our island story as witnessed in Sussex, either factually or imaginatively. Kipling himself was fascinated by those who lived through many millennia and so left their imprint, as a palimpsest, on the familiar scene of Weald and Down, coastal fringe and marsh. He constantly sought detail from those in his circle who knew most about the major periods, particularly Roman, Saxon and Norman, never wishing, as a conscientious journalist, to misrepresent much of the truth. Since his early overview of the sequence, much more archaeological detail has come to light, but in essence much of what he understood fits snugly within the currently more detailed panorama. Although the major events figure in the stories he was not averse to put an ingenious untruth for the sake of impact. A case in point is the introduction of a putative figure of a Harold who had not been killed at the end of the decisive battle of Hastings, but who, legend asserted, would survive to rebuild his kingdom. The collections are certainly masterpieces of great depth and beauty, projecting fragments of our history through the ages. He described the context in *Something of Myself*.

You see how patiently the cards were stacked and dealt into my hands? The Old Things of our Valley glided into every aspect of our outdoor works. Earth, Air, Water and People had been – I saw it at last – in full conspiracy to give me ten times as much as I could compass, even if I wrote a complete history of England, as that might have touched or reached our Valley.

Specifically with regards to *Rewards and Fairies* he showed how his mind worked in the preparation of the tales.

Yet since the tales had to be read by children, before people realised they were meant for grown-ups; and since they had to be a sort of balance to, as well a seal upon, some aspects on my 'Imperialistic' output in the past, I worked the material in three or four overlaid tints and textures, which might or might not reveal themselves according to the shifting light of sex, youth, and experience. It was like working lacquer and mother 'o pearl, a natural combination, into the same scheme as niello and grisaille, and trying not to let the joins show.

The two books, written slightly apart and as the children were growing up, introduce a comparatively new technique in the way that history is presented. His own John and Elsie, fictionalised as Dan and Una from their lion cub experiences at The Woolsack, are led to meet characters and events in English history through the medium of one who can transport them as time-travellers. Their courier is Puck, who from Shakespeare's time, was seen as a mischievous goblin or sprite. In *Weland's Sword* Kipling uses the acting of a scene from *A Midsummer Night's Dream* as their introduction to him.

The Theatre lay in a meadow called the Long Slip. A little mill-stream, carrying water to a mill two or three fields away, bent round one corner of it, and in the middle of the bend lay a large old Fairy Ring of darkened grass, which was the stage. The mill-stream banks, overgrown with willow, hazel and guelder-rose, made convenient places to wait in till your turn came; and a grown up who had seen it that Shakespeare himself could not have imagined a more suitable setting for his play. They were not, of course, allowed to act on Mid-summer Night itself, but they went down after tea on Midsummer Eve, when the shadows were growing, and they took their supper – hard-boiled eggs, Bath Oliver biscuits, and salt in an envelope – with them. **** Their play went beautifully. Dan remembered all his parts – Puck, Bottom, and the three Fairies – and Una never forgot a word of Titania – not even the difficult pieces where she tells the Fairies how to feed Bottom with "apricocks, green figs, and dewberries" and all the lines end in 'ies.' They were both so pleased that they acted it three times over from beginning to end before they sat down in the unthistly centre of the Ring to eat eggs and Bath Olivers. This was when they heard a whistle among the alders on the bank, and they jumped. The bushes parted. In the very spot where Dan had stood as Puck they saw a small, brown, broad-shouldered, pointy-eared person with a snub nose, slanting blue eyes, and a grin that ran right across his freckled face. **** The children looked and gasped. "We didn't expect anyone" Dan said. "This is our field". "Is it?" said their visitor sitting down. "Then what on Human Earth made you act 'Midsummer Nights Dream' three times over, on Midsummer Eve in the middle of a Ring, and under – right under one of my oldest hills in Old England ? Pook's Hill – Puck's Hill – Puck's Hill – Pook's Hill Its as plain as the nose on my face.

The spur for this idea came from an enjoyable family activity when, as Elsie later recorded 'we children and my father acted scenes from *A Midsummer Night's Dream*. Our stage was an old grass-grown quarry, and there my brother as Puck, myself as Titania, and my father as Bottom, rehearsed and acted happily'. That stage was certainly the overgrown circular hollow just up the lane opposite the front door of Bateman's from which the stone for the house had originally been quarried. Rudyard had ordered from London a pair of wings and an ass's head from a theatrical costumier to make the performance more authentic.

The actual location of Pook's Hill has long been a matter of debate amongst Kipling enthusiasts. The meaning of *pook* is generally defined as a conical stack of corn sheaves, although it has also been brought in to mean a 'spirit' or 'hobgoblin' sometimes even a malicious one. Shakespeare's sprite was much more helpful and exuberant and Kipling's version seems to follow the same pattern. In the Weald the hill named for him was given very specifically on the beautifully hachured first edition of the Ordnance Survey map produced at the beginning of the 19th century, but even before that there is a reference at virtually the same location. The *Sussex Weekly Advertiser* of December 11th 1786 refers to a sale of "a copyhold messuage consisting of two dwellings in good repair together with fourteen acres of very good land called Pookehill otherwise Pound Farm, well stocked with young thriving timber and pleasantly situated near Burwash Wheel." That spot on the Heathfield to Burwash road, just above Willingford, is now called Burwash Weald, the reference to a Catherine Wheel now transposed, just as the earlier Pook' Hill is now "Park Hill". (GR 645225) Kipling himself wrote to Charles Harper, an authority on coaching routes, that this was the original. But his Pook's Hill he translated to what is now Perch Hill (GR 666 222) only a mile from Bateman's and clearly visible from there. Even now there is no unanimity in accepting this location, but we were reminded by the late Ron King, a much respected Bateman's guide, that the Puck stories are fiction with a foundation of truth. Kipling would have been perfectly capable of placing it at a point more suitable to the story.

In the two books the stories are not arranged chronologically and so perhaps for the sake of clarity it would be expedient to discuss them in ascending time from prehistoric beginnings. Kipling chose the exact opposite in his verses of *Puck's Song* the first stanza being in Nelson's time and the last in Merlin's Isle. As usual he often inserts appropriate other poems before and after each tale. Although separated by an age gap of their original readers, it is probably best to treat *Puck* and *Rewards* as a single entity. There has always been considerable discussion as to the origin of the title *Rewards and Fairies* with even disagreement as to the pronunciation of 'rewards'. It is now accepted that the origin was within the eight verse lyric *The Fairies' Farewell* written by Bishop Corbet (1582 – 1635). The son of a gardener, well educated at Westminster and Christ Church, Oxford, he became Chaplain to James I and later Bishop of Oxford and then of Norwich. A generous witty and eloquent man he was popular at The Mermaid Tavern in Cheapside a meeting place of literary talent in the early seventeenth century. Naturally there are other Sussex tales in later collections, and to avoid the necessity of identifying the placement of each, a list is given at the end of the chapter.

Farewell, rewards and fairies, Good housewives now may say, For now foul sluts in dairies, Do fare as well as they; And though they sweep their hearths no less, Than maids were wont to do, Yet who, of late, for cleanliness , Finds sixpence in her shoe.

So clearly the sixpence left in the shoe is the 'reward'. Kipling peppered the stories with references to people, places and events which a century after publication may well seem a little obscure. Fortunately the pages of the brilliant Kipling Society website provides clarification in the New Readers' Guide, which can be found by clicking on 'Stories in their Settings'. The web address is www.kipling.org.uk The Sussex dialect meanings, included in the notes can be found separately in Appendix I in this book.

Kipling did venture into the Neolithic, with *The Knife and the Naked Chalk* when tools and weapons were knapped from the flint so abundant on the surface and on the beaches from the nodules eroded from the chalk, but which was worked, by experience, from flints mined from pits into the chalk because a freshly taken flint from layers *in situ* would yield a much sharper cutting edge. The period used overlaps with the Iron Age because Tyr was able to obtain metal weapons which helped his people prevail against the wolf pack. Living, as he did, in the heart of the Wealden iron industry, Kipling would know a great deal about the local sources of iron ore which from prehistoric times had fed the furnaces of a predominant industry until it moved to Ironbridge in the early 18th century. Furnace slag and pigs of iron were common on his own land, and the medieval industry is also included in the tales. An extract describing the landscape of the dry valleys around Rottingdean and the life of the shepherd, Ben Dudeney, is given in 'Downland Idyll'.

As stone gave way to bronze and bronze to iron, this becomes the focus of *Cold Iron*, the first story in the sequel volume. Iron was held in European folklore to have the power to drive away anything supernatural which was the reason for horse-shoes being fixed to stable doors to protect the animals inside. The fanciful story is of a foundling child adopted by Huon, King of the Fairies, but who must not touch iron, for if he does he will return to being human. Huon and his Lady Esclairmonde planned a wonderful future for him, and he learns to weave magic spells as he roams the hills with Puck. The lad finds a slave ring in the grass, snaps it round his neck and so is condemned to slavery in the real world. Little Lindens is a farm mentioned which is thought to be Little Batemans about half a mile north of Bateman's. Kipling also introduces Wayland Smith – the Teutonic equivalent of the Roman god, Vulcan, a supernatural smith who forged chain mail for the gods. A Neolithic burial chamber on the Berkshire Downs was named by the Saxons 'Wayland's Smithy' which tradition said that a horse tied there with a fee of sixpence, would be found shod when the rider returned the next day. It seems to be little coincidence that the pronunciation equates to 'Weland', the cunning smith who made swords for heroes in the first of the Puck stories. Rather neatly Weland's Ford is located at Willingford Bridge, which Kipling probably translated the Saxon origin as 'the ford of the people of Willa'. Puck then jumps ahead in time and talks of Hugh, the son of a local landowner who had undergone a novitiate in a French monastery before returning to one in Sussex. After chivalrous help to the ancient Weland, the smith forges a sword for him and his superior recognises that Hugh is not destined for a life of contemplation. This action took place not long before the Norman invasion and Hugh reappears with Sir Richard Dalyngridge in *Young Men at the Manor*.

Next chronologically Kipling came to Roman Britain, a period to which he was drawn, and the knowledge of which he created a phenomenal body of facts on which to draw. He was concerned with the prowess of the legions and the establishment of *Pax Britannica* as far as Hadrian's Wall. Roman Sussex was early on, after the Claudian invasion of AD 43, because of the collaboration of Claudius Tiberius Cogidubnus, a fairly peaceful prosperous area, although Kipling would have known nothing of the great palace at Fishbourne which was not really rediscovered until the 1960s. But he did know of *Anderita,* one of the forts of the Saxon Shore at Pevensey. At that time in the late 3rd century it was an ideally located position for the purpose because an oval shaped promontory protruded into a wide inlet, sea covered at high tide. Only a short moat needed construction to isolate it defensively as one of "The Forts of the Saxon Shore". Its Roman name, translated as "the Great Ford", refers to the fact that it was possible to cross the wide, but treacherous sands to the shore near Bexhill. It was from Anderita that Parnesius, *A Centurion of the Thirtieth,* set out to march his men north to the wall. The local capital was at *Noviomagus Regnensium,*(the new market of the Regni) sometimes given as *Reginorum,* and often spoken of as "Regnum", the city through which the centurion passed having crossed from his home on the Isle of Wight en route to his posting. Sussex was dotted with elegant villas, one of which was well known in Kipling's time, that at Bignor, adjacent to where Stane Street descends the face of the Downs to cross the wild brooks to the ridge of the Weald. He knew both his locations and his Roman history. It was Rudyard's cousin Ambrose Poynter who suggested the idea of writing of a story about the Roman period, and who thought of the name Parnesius for the Centurion. The ideas were mulled over with John Lockwood Kipling and with Uncle Ned, so clearly the concept came in Rottingdean and his father reinforced the necessity of checking references thoroughly. He owned a solid library but when in South Africa the public library of Cape Town provided suitable material for study. Parnesius describes his background as a Romano-British from the Isle of Wight, and the coincidence that Rudyard was staying at Freshwater with the Balestiers whilst his father was engaged with the Durbar Room at Osborne is inescapable. Parnesius's home was based on the recent excavations of an elegantly paved island villa at Brading. His subsequent career, after joining at the Regimental depot at *Clausetum* (Bitterne) took him to his posting at *Anderita* to join Legio XXX, *Ulpia Victrix*. Kipling however was not averse to introducing anomalies, for we know that that particular legion did not serve in Britannia, and indeed there was also a time discrepancy because the story is set in about 380 AD. Neither was the route he took with his Century likely, for there was no road through Burwash. Exit through the north gate at *Anderita* would not have been convenient because it was washed by the waters of Pevensey harbour. The group could, of course, have taken a small boat to the shoreline a few miles to the north, but one expects a Roman century to march. In the story Una first meets Parnesius alone, because her brother had been kept in by Miss Blake, to do an "impot", the schoolboy abbreviation of a punishment "imposition". The Centurion's posting to "the Wall" led to what might have been in Kipling's words "a leg-pull". He had given Parnesius command of the Seventh Cohort, and with an archaeological excavation undertaken at Corbridge in 1912 Kipling was sent a rubbing of a memorial tablet to that very unit which also showed the XXXth Legion. The fact that its seems likely that the initial "X" had been etched later, might confirm Rudyard's suspicions. It is surprising that, given his undoubted interest in Roman Britain, his whole output on the subject is confined to this story and *On the Great Wall* and *The Winged Hats*. A poem he wrote on the legionary theme is *The Roman Centurion's Song*, a moving account of how one who had served for so long in Britain pleaded not to be sent back to Rome after his lengthy service, for he felt that these islands were really his true home. There is more than an echo of the feeling that many British officers who had served the Raj so devotedly preferred to "stay-on" in the sub-continent.

The only purely Saxon story is *The Conversion of St. Wilfrid*. The Saxons who had provoked Romano-Britain, with their frequent raids, into creating the 'Forts of the Saxon Shore' before the legions were withdrawn in 410, began to settle some 60 years later. In 477 Æella and his sons, people of *Seaxe* from the German plain, became the first '*Sudseaxe*', the 'South Saxons' and so gave us the territorial name of 'Sussex'. The sequence of their gradual advance inland is clear from our place-names most of which define the landscape in which they lived and the agricultural practices they followed. But they were, for the most part, pagans. Their conversion to Christianity was the crusade of Wilfrid, Bishop of York. He recounts to Dan and Una of his time in Sussex and his friendship with Meon, a local chieftan, who has a pet seal called Padda. Eddi, (Eddius Stephanus) Wifrid's chaplain and later his biographer, believed that seals were demonic. Out in the sea on a fishing trip with Meon and Eddi, they are caught in a storm and are stranded on a rocky shore. Meon believes this to be a sign that he ought to accept Christ, but Wilfrid tells him that he should not abandon his old beliefs in a moment of crisis. They are rescued when Padda brings them fish and goes for help. Wilfrid (634 – 709) was one of the country's leading ecclesiastical figures who himself had a life of religious conflict, and worked in Sussex during his second exile. His conversion was to a richer and more tolerant form of Christianity. Kipling created a most wonderful Christmastide poem, *Eddi's Service*, set in a little chapel at Manhood End near the tip of the peninsula of Selsey – once 'seal-island'. Wilfrid, a Benedictine, founded a monastery there, long ago swallowed by marine encroachment. Later his community rose in the establishment of the diocese of Chichester.

His next target was the period on either side of the Conquest in 1066, so that both Saxons and Normans become figures in the landscape. The invasion by William Duke of Normandy was a fairly chancy operation, in which luck played its part for the invaders. Harold had been aware that his erstwhile colleague was preparing to seize the throne he thought rightfully his, but his own skilful interception plan had been thwarted by the fact that the invasion fleet was virtually becalmed on the coast of Normandy for a long time, and so being forced to accept that the defence force along the south coast had completed the period of conscripted service it owed. When he moved his fleet from a strategically superior base in the Isle of Wight it was destroyed by storm, which did lesser damage to the invasion longboats. Then not long before the invasion came Harold was forced to march his troops northwards in just four days in order to defeat another unrelated invasion force from Norway led by Harald Hadrada and Harold's own disaffected brother, Tostig. In doing so, successfully, he lost many of his own force. He was recovering in York after the Battle of Stamford Bridge when he learnt that William had landed at Pevensey. His hasty return to rally more troops meant that he was at a considerable disadvantage, and the Battle of Hastings could even then have turned ether way. At the end, after some ten hours of fighting, victory came to William. Kipling uses the period for some fanciful history and a superb analysis in the poems *Norman and Saxon* and *The Anvil* of the contrasting traits of character in the opposing peoples. *The Anvil* was first published in *A School History of England* published in 1911 in which Kipling collaborated with C. R. L. Fletcher. It is in the form of a chant in which the rhythmic 'hammered, hammered, hammered into line' depicts the clanging on an anvil. It reinforces Kipling's conviction that the defeat of the Saxon heptarchy produced a fusion into a powerful unity of strong government to our ultimate benefit.

The whole saga is depicted in the miraculous survival of The Bayeux Tapestry, an embroidered *tapisserie* commissioned by Odo, Bishop Bayeux and Williams half-brother for display at the consecration of his Cathedral in 1077. The events so graphically portrayed took place mainly in Sussex. But the message may well have been slightly distorted by its medium as a piece of Norman propaganda. The Saxon army formed up on a ridge above the valley across which the three-pronged Norman force had to advance. After the conflict William decreed that a monastery must be built on the slope in thanksgiving for victory. It became a site of great veneration for pilgrims until the Dissolution, but the town that grew around it was named Battle after *La Batailge* fought on the spot. One of William's chief supporters was William of Warenne, is introduced in the poem *The Land*.

In *Young Men at the Manor,* Puck introduces the children to Sir Richard Dalyngridge, a knight who rode his destrier into the battle. In the confusion of the Saxon flight, he loses his sword in combat with Hugh, who saves him from being killed by a remnant of Harold's army. Hugh takes him back to his manor but when the local baron, de Aquila, arrives he awards the manor to Sir Richard. Richard's friendship with Hugh brings followers of both sides to defend the valley. Once he sees that the partnership works de Aquila grants a neighbouring manor to Hugh who is once more entitled to buckle on his sword, and swears allegiance to Norman overlordship.

The Knights of the Joyous Venture opens some thirty years later. Hugh's sister, Aeluva, had married Sir Richard, but by now she had died, so the two friends decide to sail away together. Their voyaging to the coast of Africa brings a share in wealth which they hid on their return to de Aquila's castle at Pevensey, built within the walls of the ancient Roman fort.

Old Men at Pevensey takes us on to the very start of the twelfth century when Henry I pre-empted the throne three days after his brother William Rufus was killed, perhaps with Henry's connivance, in the New Forest. It was a time of great peril for their elder brother, Robert Curthose, who had inherited the Duchy of Normandy, invaded England, with scant justification, to seize the throne. Although supported by some nobles, others allied themselves to Henry and he made Robert relinquish the claim, in exchange for territory across the Channel. Robert's abuse of power led Henry to seize the Duchy after the battle of Tinchebrai in 1106 and he kept his brother prisoner for the rest of his life. Sir Richard and Hugh are at Pevensey castle built by De Aquila for Robert of Mortain, the conqueror's other half-brother, ready to protect the country from Robert's invasion. Their host is tricked into being ready to leave the castle but he is too wily and the messenger is seized. The castle would, originally have been an earth motte thrown up by the excavation of a moat, and topped by a pre-fabricated wooden keep, so the illustrations showing solid Norman stonework are somewhat anachronistic. The stone structure was not raised until the thirteenth century. In the story Kipling thought that such a castle would need a well and he wrote of one in the wall. Thirty years later archaeology revealed such a well, but as it was tidal and the water brackish, it would not have served for drinking purposes but as a flushing toilet.

In the same period *The Tree of Justice* focuses on the tribulations of the conquered Saxon population under the Norman yoke. Brutality and revenge feature in a darkly brooding tale told by Sir Richard of a period forty years after the battle. The children met him when they were looking for Hobden who was coppicing wood below Brightling beacon. A knight, granted land in Kent, had hanged the son of his forester and he himself was found a little later with three arrows through his leather jerkin. King Henry had decided to hunt deer at Pook's Hill before embarking for Normandy and Sir Richard was there to ensure good and safe sport for him. He understood that the King had hanged twenty-six Saxons at Salehurst to avenge the death of the Knight, a practice only too commonly repeated in the Nazi occupation of France. Sir Richard engages beaters, including ill-conditioned clerks and millers, to drive the deer towards the King's party, and some new knights taunted the Saxons about the prowess of Norman archers who had fired the opening flights of arrows at Hastings. Among the beaters is an old man dressed as a witless pilgrim who is revealed as King Harold still alive after his defeat. Old rumours ran in medieval times that he had survived and Kipling simply revived and modified that legend. It was, of course, nothing more than an unfulfillable dream, for Harold did perish at the end of the battle. There is a further story about Rahere the jester and how Hugh the Saxon is summoned by King Henry and reveals that the pilgrim is indeed Harold who is treated most courteously by the monarch. Soon Harold breathes his last against Hugh's shoulder.

The Treasure and the Law adds another century brining the story up to the time of the third of the Plantaganets, King John. Dan and Una meet Kadmiel an important Elder of the Jewish faith who tells them how, when the King was at odds with his Barons, a fellow Jew, Elias of Bury, had discovered the gold hidden in the castle by Richard and Hugh so long before. The Elder was determined that this hoard should not fall into the King's hand and so enable him to refuse their demands for a curb on the power of the monarchy. Kadmiel was able to enter the stronghold in disguise and remove the 'treasure'. Without additional funds John was forced to sign 'Magna Carta', considered as the first touchstone of English liberty. Thus as Puck relates Weland gave the Sword, The Sword gave the Treasure, and the Treasure gave the Law.

The Wrong Thing is a story in which Dan alone, with the village builder, Mr. Springett, meets the fictional master builder of the Tudor era, Harry Dawe. Dan learns of his intense pleasure in designing great architecture and of his soured relationship with a rival craftsman jealous of Hal's talent. Hal produces a painting to decorate one of Henry VII's ships but he is dissatisfied with the result which was all wrong. His rival Benedetto threatens to kill him one dark night. Hal tells him that he has just been elevated to the knighthood for some small service to the monarch, and that he was dubbed with a rusty sword, another wrong thing of the title. Their mutual animosity evaporates as the laugh at the irony of the situation.

Hal o' the Draft is a sequel to *The Wrong Thing* but published before it. The children meet Sir Harry Dawe, a fictitious character who was a great architect and craftsman who tells them of his restoration of the village church, St. Barnabas, (in fact St. Bartholemew's) and how, for some reason he seemed to have alienated the local people so that the work was not completed. Harry, or 'Hal' gained his nickname because he was ever at his drawings, had a good friend in Sebastian Cabot, who intended to sail to America as he had done with his father John. Although he had ordered cannons for his ship he was frustrated by delays and excuses for their delivery. Hal and Sebastian found that local gunfounders were actually providing them for a pirate, Sir Andrew Barton, and storing them secretly in the church. On advice from a local magistrate they collect, with the aid of the militia, the weapons from their hiding places, pretending that they were the armaments he had ordered. The conspirators escaped the retribution due to them. Clearly guns were contraband goods but this action took place long before the heyday of smuggling from the late seventeenth century. Kipling followed the tale with *A Smuggler's Song* as he was well aware of the activities of those in 'the trade' both in Burwash, where secret passages ran through the lofts of the houses and in Rottingdean where tunnels from the cliffs led to link with cellars beneath the High Street right up to The Green.

Dymchurch Flit is located on Romney Marsh, a unique landscape of reclaimed marshland behind the shingle foreland of Dungeness. Its eerie, mist enshrouded patchwork of sheepfolds and dykes exercised a powerful fascination on Kipling, a frequent visitor to Rye, a little of Sussex on its edge. Dymchurch is a small settlement between New Romney and Hythe, all three of which are now connected by a famous miniature railway. The story opens in an oast house on the Bateman's estate, where Hobden supervised the drying of the hops for use in the brewing of beer. Potatoes being baked by the fire with Hobden was the immediate concern of Dan and Una when Puck, as Tom Shoesmith joins them. He recounts how the religious intolerance and conflict of the 1530s, scared the little people, the fairies, or 'Pharisees' in Sussex dialect, who moved en masse onto the isolation of the marsh where they were never fully at ease. They sought advice from one of a well-known marsh family, the Widow Whitgift, and requested that she allow her two sons to take them across the channel. This they did but as one was blind and the other dumb they would never be able to tell anyone about it. Kipling concludes the tale with *A Three-Part Song,* showing he couldn't be sure which element of the landscape he loved the most – The Weald or the Marsh or the white chalk coast!

Gloriana, the name created by Edmund Spenser by which Elizabeth I was revered, receives the children with Puck in the port of Rye. She tells them of the painful and difficult decisions a monarch has to make. The fleet she sent to protect her American colonies from depredations by Philip of Spain is lost and she agonized as to whether she ought to have ordered the expedition. The children respond by asking her if there was any realistic alternative, with which the Queen agrees, thus salving her conscience. The visit to Rye, which she dubbed 'Rye Royal' came at the end of a 'progress' during which her hosts were expected to provide sumptuous feasts and spectacular entertainment. In Brickwall House, where she stayed, a few miles outside Rye, are still be seen a pair of high-heeled green damask shoes which she discarded there and which are noted in the story.

Simple Simon is also set in the time of Elizabeth, for it leads up to the remarkable victory over the Spanish Armada. Both children meet Simon Cheyneys, a leading citizen of Rye who owns a shipyard. Rye had been an important centre of shipbuilding from Saxon times, relying on the abundance of fine oak timber from the Weald. In his younger days Simon had sailed with Francis Drake to rescue Protestants from Spanish atrocity and thereafter they remain firm friends. After being injured by a cannon-ball he returned to Rye where he took over the family boatyard. With the approach of the Armada bent on the destruction of England, signalled all along the south coast by the firing of the beacons, Drake is on the heels of the Spanish fleet. Simon brings his old friend 'Frankie' fresh supplies and a vessel which can be used as one of the 'fire-ships' which helps to force the Armada on to Dutch shallows. There are some incidental events which inject an aura of sorrow.

A Doctor of Medicine exemplifies Kipling's interest in all medical matters and in this case the relationship, in the seventeenth century, between herbal cures and the influence of astrology. When playing hide and seek in the walled garden of Bateman's the children meet Nicholas Culpepper distinctively dressed in black coat and steeple-crowned hat. Nick Culpepper was a herbalist and apothecary whose family were Sussex folk. Their ancestral home, Great Wigsell, a house similar to Bateman's only seven miles away is brought into the tale. Nick, best known for his book *The Complete Herbal*, had been wounded in 1643 after which he suffered from tuberculosis, and he wrote a number of medical books. He tells Dan and Una how, during the Civil War, he had succeeded in ridding Burwash of 'the plague' caused by an infestation of rats. The plague reached England first in 1348, and recurrences occurred subsequently, the one in 1665 killing some 700,000. The interrelationship of the rat flea and the cause of the Black Death was not established until much later.

Brother Square-Toes carries the reader forward to the last decade of the eighteenth century. Although most of the action takes place across the Atlantic it starts along the coast between Rottingdean and Newhaven. Dan and Una have come from Bateman's to stay with Aunt Georgie at North End House. They walked down to the Gap where the bathing machines were stored ready for use beneath the low cliff. Kipling, with his usual eye for detail sets the scene.

It was almost the end of their visit to the seaside. They had turned themselves out of doors while their trunks were being packed, and strolled over the Downs towards the dull evening sea. The tide was dead low under the chalk cliffs, and the little wrinkled waves grieved along the sands up the coast to Newhaven and down the coast to long, grey Brighton, whose smoke trailed out across the channel
They walked to The Gap where the cliff is only a few feet high. A windlass for hoisting shingle from the beach below stands at the edge of it. The Coastguard cottages are a little farther on, and an old ship's figure head of a Turk in a turban stared at them over the wall.

Kipling was friendly with many of the officers of the coastguard, and they helped him run the Village Rifle Club. He knew how they patrolled the cliffline still on the watch for those running contraband goods, even though the 'trade' had diminished since its heyday in the late seventeenth and eighteenth centuries. On this occasion the children are introduced by Puck to Pharaoh Lee. He was a skilful smuggler with relatives on both side of the channel. They first heard him singing *The moon she shined on Telscombe Tye … She saw the smugglers riding by,* and he is still singing as he breasts the cliff. They discover that his fishing smack is moored in Shoreham, and that the family live a little inland on the old William Penn estate near Steyning, The Lees were of the Moravian faith and dressed in their fashion with plain brown coats, knee-breeches, broad brimmed hats and broad-toed shoes, which gave the name to the story. He related how when he was with his father grappling up contraband 'ankers' which had been thrown overboard from their lugger to avoid them being found whilst it was being searched by a revenue cutter. In the fog a French ship hits theirs and Pharoah was able to clamber through an open gun port. Being a French speaker he sailed with her, undetected, to Philadelphia. An important passenger is Ambassador Genêt, who hopes to persuade the Americans become allies against the British. The remainder of the story and its sequel takes place across the Atlantic and is thought to contain a most complete, understanding and moving story about George Washington that anyone had ever written.

The poem *Telscombe Tye*, from which Pharoah's snatch is taken is unusual in style. The word 'Tye' means a common or a large open field. The village of Piddinghoe mentioned in it, is just a little way up the Ouse valley from Newhaven.

In *Marklake Witches* Una alone meets Philadelphia Bucksteed the daughter of the Squire of Marklake, a village near to Burwash. The story dates to 1805, a year of significance in Napoleon's life, for he lost control of the seas at Trafalgar in October, but won a major victory at Austerlitz only two months later. Marklake may be the fictionalised name of Mark Cross, but is described as being near Dallington. Philadelphia, usually called Phil suffers from consumption, a scourge of the period, but does not know how serious a condition it is. She has a companion René Laennec, a French doctor captured by Phil's uncle off Belle Isle, who he treated for raging toothache. He would have been imprisoned with other Frenchmen in Rye, but the family arranged for him to stay at Marklake. Everyone, except Phil and Una, know that she does not have long to live and her nurse, Cissie, takes three stolen silver spoons to Jerry Gamm, the village witch doctor who has agreed to cure her with a charm. Phil finds out about this and confronts Jerry who realising that no charm could alleviate her suffering hands them back. He suggests, sensibly, that she ought to breathe deeply of the good air. But Jerry and René are friends and the Frenchman shows him the stethoscope he has invented, which they use on villagers only to be accused of witchcraft. Phil, hidden in a tree sees them arguing over the merits of the instrument and they argue fiercely only to stop when the Squire rides up. There are some amusing asides about the qualified, but incompetent Dr. Break. Phil's great dream is to oversee her father's household. He had ridden to Hastings to see an old military friend, the Colonel of the 33rd Foot, Sir Arthur Wellesley, later the Duke of Wellington, and to invite him to dine. Philadelphia had created a most acceptable menu and afterwards entertained her father and his guests to a harp recital to accompany a sad little song which seemed to predict her imminent departure from the world. The poem which follows *Marklake Witches* is the enchanting *The Way Through the Woods*, the origin of which was discussed in Chapter 3.

An Habitation Enforced brings the sequence to Edwardian England. A wealthy young American couple come to Sussex after a rest cure travelling through Europe necessitated by stress brought on by overwork. They arrive at Rocketts, an isolated farm on a neglected estate with a delightful Georgian house, with some superb features, but needing attention. They buy the estate so that George Chapin will have something to occupy him. His wife, Sophie, discovers a tombstone bearing her mother's maiden name. They had, by chance, returned to her ancestral home, and soon learn to find acceptance in local society. The story paints an idealised view of a perfectly stable way of life in which a traditional hierarchy is fully acceptable, but which so soon will be shattered for ever in the turmoil and legacy of the Great War. It is Sophie who is the energetic mainstay, perhaps a reflection of the relationship Rudyard had with Carrie. They bought Friars Pardon and five decaying farms and soon learnt to adapt to the unwritten obligations of the landed classes towards their tenants.

The Wish House although set mostly in the county does not emphasise the countryside as many of the other stories do. The central theme revolves around an old superstitious belief that it is possible for one who loves sufficiently to be able to bear the burden of pain suffered by their loved one. Dialogue between Grace Ashcroft, who had been in service in London, and her childhood friend Mrs. Fettley is in a broad Sussex dialect. It emerges that Grace visited a 'Wish House' where by mouthing your wish through the letterbox a 'token' inside would bring it to fruition. The object of her affection, Harry Mockler, a one-time lover who had abandoned her, suffered from various illnesses. The ulcerated leg which she found painful became worse when Harry was ill and just a shadow of his former self. Such belief in 'substitution' has had its adherents for many centuries.

The action in *Wireless* takes place at a chemist's shop in a seaside town, probably Brighton. The proprietor, Mr. Cashell, allows his nephew to experiment with the intricacies of radio telegraphy, the recent invention of Guglielmo Marconi. The narrator talks to the chemist's assistant, John Shaynor, who is consumptive. Although late in the evening the shop is still open, helping to provide prescriptions for a local influenza outbreak, and John is on duty because Mr. Cashell himelf is smitten upstairs. Kipling paints an accurate picture of the appearance and fragrances of a chemist's shop of the period, but he has really come to meet the younger Cashell. John's sweetheart, Fanny Brand, asks him to look after the shop while they go out for a walk. Returning alone from the bitter cold, the narrator gives John a Culpepper type cordial which soothes his rasping throat. Under the effect of the potion John lapses into a trance and writes portions of Keats verses. The narrator had been in earnest discussion with the radio enthusiast on a subject, which as Kipling, as a guest of the Royal Navy, had found fascinating. The narrator's focus soon transfers to John's writing and its Keatsian quality. At last they all return to the radio room and a gratified to hear Marconi signals between naval vessels off the Isle of Wight.

A curious tale, *Below the Mill Dam*, has the grey cat and the black rat, the mill and its waters talking to each other and reminiscing about the Spirit of the Mill from Domesday foundation, through medieval activity, right up to the use of the mill race to work a turbine to produce electricity. Angus Wilson, in what he transcribes, rather oddly, as "Beyond the Mill Dam" sees in it a satirical comment on the failure of high Toryism to adapt to a changing world. At the end of the story the cat notices that his friend, the Black Rat has been preserved by a taxidermist and exhibited in a glass case as an example of an endangered species by the engineer who installed the turbine. The story was written at the time Kipling developed a hydro-electric connection to the house with the help of Sir William Willcocks, who was famously described by the author as having been involved in "a trifling affair on the Nile".

Steam Tactics

Cars played an important part in a number of Kipling's short stories, but in respect of Sussex one above all others stands out as an account of some of the pleasures and pains confronted by dedicated 'automobilists'. The chief characters are based on two of the cars which he owned and which had given him an interest not only as a means of getting about but also a comprehensive knowledge of the developing science of motor engineering. These two cars play their part in a humorous adventure which takes Rudyard and his friends on a circular tour through the Weald. The cars themselves were a contrast in technology, the one a steam driven 'locomobile', the other an early example of a petrol driven machine. *Steam Tactics* was first published as a wire stitched, twelve page, ten cent edition by The Curtis Publishing Company of Philadelphia in 1902. It was later 'collected' as the sixth tale in *Traffics and Discoveries* in 1904. The cars were, therefore ones with which he was associated whilst living in Rottingdean. The steam car, in this case an American Locomobile Steamer, was a four-seater, surrey-bodied, affair. When working well a steamer could beat a petrol driven competitor handsomely for smooth, vibrationless and almost silent performance. But it was fit only for use as a fair weather runabout for smooth town streets rather than the uneven winding lanes of Sussex. To Kipling she was a 'Holy Terror' which kept on breaking down because of faulty pipes and the need to refill her water tank almost every twenty miles. Her foibles are noted in detail but as she was steam-powered she naturally appealed to the highly-skilled Engine-

Room Artificer Henry Salt Hinchcliffe of the Royal Navy, and his friend, the resourceful Petty Officer Emmanuel Pyecroft. Although she was steam driven she relied on petrol to heat tubes in the vertical boiler which occupied space beneath the back seat. The drive to the rear axle was by means of a chain and steering was effected by a lever pivoted near the driver's elbow. In the story Hinchcliffe says *"The blighted egg-boiler has steam up"*, and a little later *"Do you suppose that a man who earns his livin' by runnin' 30 knot destroyers for a parstime – for a parstime, mark you ! – is going to lie down before any blighted land-crabbing steam-pinnace on springs"*. It was as *"frail as a wicker-willow lunch basket"* with its boiler *"only seated on four paper-clips"*.

The rescue car in the story was based on a Lanchester Car, Number Sixteen, delivered to The Elms, by a new employee of the firm, Max Lawrence, brother to the two redoubtable ladies who had founded Roedean School. Carrie's diary records its arrival as June 5th, 1902, and it is this treasure which is cast as the 'Octopod', a black-dashed, tonneau-ed twenty-four horse powered one driven by the narrator's friend, 'Kysh'. The name Kipling gave to the car – Octopod – puzzled keen readers until J. M. S. Tomkins associated with an eight-legged horse of Nordic myth. Kysh may well have been based on Max Lawrence.

The story centres on the abduction of a policeman which had its foundation in truth. Fred and George Lanchester both attended a Rally of the Midland Automobile Club in 1902, with a luncheon party at the George Hotel, Solihull. The former drove a car on final test for a customer and George was in a car ready for delivery to the War Department. It was painted in glossy khaki and had the King's cipher emblazoned on one of the panels. During testing it had almost certainly exceeded the speed limit of 12 m.p.h. George asked Fred for his opinion of the car as so he climbed in with a passenger, Sidney Pinsent, a draughtsman employee. As he did so a police constable waiting nearby asked F. W. for his name and address. After some altercation, and within his rights to refuse giving his name, Fred drove off saying 'You can come and fetch it'. The PC scrambled over the side, bending one of the rear wings and scratching a pane with his boot. Instead of driving home Fred took the Stratford-upon-Avon road, and continued through Moreton-in-Marsh and Stow-on-the Wold. At each village they passed, the policeman stood up and shouted 'Stop him!' at which Pinsent also stood and shouted 'Are we right for – naming the next town ?' The passers-by signalled them straight on, assuming that the constable had commandeered the vehicle to chase a miscreant. Fred and Pinsent talked in French about what they ought to do. Driving at a speed over the limit Fred stopped beyond Stow and told the constable that having exceeded the limit he must stop for an hour so that the actual speed in m.p.h. could be reduced to within the legal limit. The officer was getting very nervous but after a while they agreed to take him back to Solihull. Arriving in Stratford they stopped for a meal at the Shakespeare Hotel, but as the policeman was on duty he couldn't be entertained. He had to remain outside and mind the car until the two motorists had finished their leisurely dinner. Back at Solihull Police Station at about 11.00 p.m. Fred returned the notebook in which the constable had asked him to write his name and address and enquired what offence had been committed. The officer replied 'Exceeding the speed limit between Olton and Solihull'. But I did not drive the car on that road, nor as my friend here is witness, was I in the car. Some other driver was in charge before I took her over. The constable escaped being charged with failing to report back at the correct time and no charge against Fred could be made.

The route taken through Sussex in the fictionalised escapade is clearly delimited by a series of place names, some of which are easily identifiable. The reality of the others was for long a matter of debate among members of The Kipling Society. The narrator overtakes the carrier, Agg, Hinch's cousin, on the road to the west of Cuckfield, running into Bromlingleigh (probably Bolney), and on to Pigginfold (Cowfold) for petrol. The road to the north, past the fictitious estate of Sir Michael Gregory, certainly based on Leonardslee, the garden, ponds and zoological park owned by Kipling's friend, Sir Edmund Loder, leads to Instead Wick (Lower Beeding). The constable who stops them for speeding at 23½ m.p.h. failed to produce identity documents and demanded to be taken to Linghurst (probably Horsham although that town is mentioned by name later on). The sailors communicate using a tapped morse code, rather then the French used in the Warwickshire reality, to agree a pretence of drunkenness. The narrator insists on seeing a warrant-card which the constable is unable to produce, and so claims that he can't accede to the demands of a possible blackmailer. When Kysh arrives on the scene, the prisoner is transferred to the Octopod so that the ailing steamer can be taken homeward. The roundabout journey continues through Ashdown Forest to Park Row (Forest Row) and Cramberhurst (Lamberhurst) before turning southerly towards the escarpment of the South Downs. The Long Man of Hillingdon (The Long Man of Wilmington) is passed although the 'little dorp' of Trevington (Jevington) is actually back towards the east. Cassocks (Hassocks) and Parsley Green (Partridge Green) lead on to Penfield Green (probably Henfield) before the adventure comes full circle and reaches the zoological park run by Sir Michael Gregory where Robert, the kidnapped constable, is released. A little sternward motoring is described when they encountered a 'hammer pond' in the estate woods, which is reminiscent of a description of such a hazardous stunt undertaken by a Lanchester when 'Banjo' Paterson was taken on a drive from The Elms. In Something of Myself Kipling writes:-

Then I bought me a steam-car called 'a Locomobile,' whose nature and attributes I faithfully drew in a tale called 'Steam Tactics.' She reduced us to the limits of fatigue and hysteria, all up and down Sussex.

It is fair to say that his frustration both with the foibles of the early car and the attitude of the law to speed is relieved by the humorous descriptions in the story.

"They"

Another story set snugly within the Sussex countryside also offers an opportunity to attempt to identify the location of the 'House Beautiful'. The description at the outset is easy to follow, so brilliantly does the narrator delineate the route, but the house which is the focus of the tale is impossible to locate because it is an amalgam of Bateman's and other properties and another garden set in the area to the north of the village of Washington at the inland end of the Findon gap. Washington is recorded as *that precise hamlet which stands godmother to the capital of the United States.* Thurston Hopkins tried, with lengthy description, to be really specific but his rather tenuous conclusions do not really convince.

A psychic tale, it comes into print, almost autobiographically because of the tragic loss of Josephine at the tender age of six. The nucleus of the story can be identified in a letter which John Lockwood Kipling wrote to Sallie Norton.

The house and garden are full of the lost child and poor Rud told his mother how he saw her when a door opened, when a space was vacant at table, coming out of every green dark corner of the garden, radiant and heartbreaking.

It is almost an exorcism on Kipling's part, no less poignant than the moving verses in *Merrow Down*. Although he detested the world of spiritualism because he recognised what a distressing effect it had on his own sister, here he focuses on ghostly children seen by an elderly, blind, heroine. He is enabled to share her vision of them because he has suffered a heartrending loss. As his car entered the garden he saw clipped yew sculpted horsemen and peacocks, which seem to have been transferred from actual examples at Ravello, a house at Rusthall, near Tunbridge Wells. The house is described as ancient with lichened and weather worn stone, mullioned windows and roofs of rose-red tile with slim brick chimneys. The hallway with a deep fireplace kept lit in case the spirit-children come in with cold toes, is pure Bateman's.

I waited in a still, nut-brown hall, pleasant with late flowers and warmed with a delicious wood fire. …. A child's cart and doll lay on the black and white floor where a rug had been kicked back. …. The red light poured itself along the age-polished dusky panels. …. An old eagle-topped convex mirror gathered the picture into its mysterious heart, distorting afresh the distorted shadows

The 'dream' children are linked with losses in the neighbouring village, and so there is a great deal more to the story. On his last of three drives to the house, the narrator, at tea in the firelight *felt his relaxed hand taken and turned between the soft hands of a child…. A brushing kiss fell in the centre of my palm – as a gift on which the fingers were, once, expected to close: as the all-faithful half-reproachful signal of a waiting child not used to neglect even when grown-ups were busiest – a fragment of the mute code devised very long ago.* As the door closed he realised that his daughter had come to him and that his hostess realised that it was so. The narrative also brings in quite an amount of detail in the farming of an estate similar in size to that of Bateman's.

"They" is preceded by verses called *The Return of the Children* – children freed from Heaven to come home again. 'They' was 'collected' in *Traffics and Discoveries* in 1904 and published separately in the following year, illustrated most charmingly by F. H. Townsend.

Railway Reform in Great Britain

An extraordinary little frolic of a story based on Kipling's experience as a regular rail traveller between Brighton and Victoria Station in London, whilst resident in Rottingdean. Then the railway operating the line was "The London, Brighton and South Coast Railway" (LBSCR) also known then as "the Brighton". Commander Alastair Wilson, a fine Kipling scholar and most knowledgeable about an enormous range of other topics, has noted that a fashionable hobby at that time was "Bashing the Brighton", and he was able also to fill in a number of other details about Kipling's acute observation. The line is transmuted to the Middle East, given an aura of an Arabian Nights tale, and the stations along the route given suitably ingenious eastern names. The London terminus boasted a fine glazed-tiled booking hall, so ornate that it had a mystic aura, sometimes drawing the word "religion" as a replacement for 'railway' in the LBSCR. The line ran First and Second Class carriages, with only rarely a Third Class for less affluent passengers. It had a reputation for treating its customers in a cavalier fashion in addition to chaotic unpunctuality. Well aware of these foibles Kipling aimed a precisely pointed salvo at the operation and its Board of Directors, the 'Afrit' of the story, some dozen 'merchants of the city'. There are humorous references to members of the Board in Arabic terms which might even identify specific wealthy industrialists such as Ali, the son of Abu-Bakr, a word-play on a firm of bakers, one of whom was certainly a director. Kipling also railed at the lack of control of those without the correct class of ticket invading the hallowed compartments of their superiors! Most of the coaches, apart from the 8.45 am 'up' and 5.pm 'down' had no corridors so once installed the passengers were a melange of professions and trades outside the possibility of a status check ! Kipling describes the engines as 'brazen', accurately, because they were painted in a bright yellow. Of the stations Bagdad is surely 'Brighton' because he uses the phrase *we lived among the valleys of Bagdad, merrily*. Indeed, additionally, the Prince Regent's Royal Pavilion there, with its domes and minarets has a glorious oriental flavour. Other stations include Tabriziz (Three Bridges), Raidill (Redhill), and Krahidin (Croydon) on the way to London. Lawaz (Lewes) 'Alisham (Hailsham) and Isbahan (Eastbourne) are on the coastway east, and Sha'ham (Shoreham) and Harundill (Arundel) on the route westward.

The tale appeared first in a copyright edition published by Doubleday, Page in 1901, was then in *The Fortnightly Review* the following month, and was collected in the Sussex Edition in *Uncollected Prose Part II* Volume XXX, in 1938.

Friendly Brook

Although one of only two 'murder stories' in the canon, it is less important for being the perfect study of country life in the early twentieth century and is clearly set in the Bateman's estate. The rising water of the brook and the description of the skill and care with which Jesse and Jabez size up the thick hedge for trimming is exquisite, setting the scene to perfection. Hobden was a 'hedger and ditcher' so the author had clearly tapped into his skill. There is perceptive comment that water levels in streams were raised considerably as a result of the asphalting of roads which increased run-off. The story is enigmatic as far as the death of Jim Wicksteed's tormentor. He was drowned in the 'friendly' brook when a rather rickety plank bridge collapsed. Was Jim responsible for making it less safe by 'gulling out' the earth beneath the supports. It was keenly debated in past discussion meetings of The Kipling Society with a majority feeling that he was 'not guilty'. The story is followed by *The Land* which traces graphically a fictional history of the Bateman's estate.

First published in the *Metropolitan Magazine* in March 1914, it was also printed in December of that year the *Windsor Magazine* before being collected in *A Diversity of Creatures in 1917.*

The Comprehension of Private Copper has only peripheral references to Sussex because he is a soldier fighting in the Boer War. But it is of interest for reference to his father who was a Southdown shepherd and his own brushes with authority in the shape of the Squire of Wilmington who caught him poaching rabbits in the Cuckmere valley. It is also of interest as an illustration of the way in which Kipling plucked names from his local community for use in his tales. The Coppers of Rottingdean were a well known and well respected family involved in agriculture for over three hundred years at the time Kipling was resident in The Elms. Another of Private Copper's company was named Moppet, another long-standing village family.

The Parable of Boy Jones is a fictionalised account of the activities of *A Village Rifle Club* which Kipling started in Rottingdean about which he wrote an article for *Spectator* in June 1901. This is printed in Appendix VI.

A typical 'Hobden' painted by Bob Copper

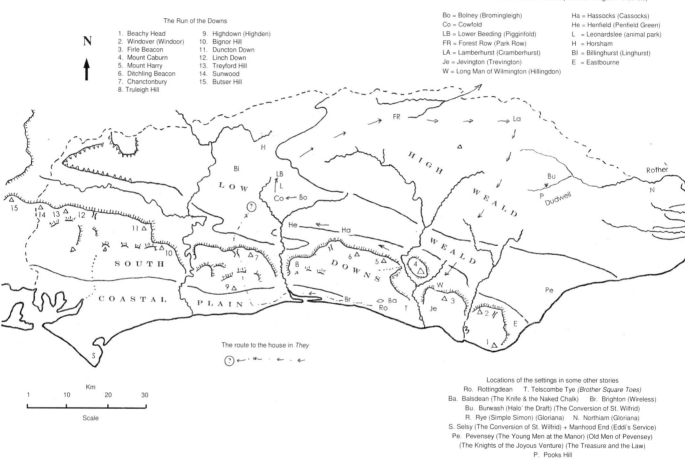

The Run of the Downs

1. Beachy Head
2. Windover (Windoor)
3. Firle Beacon
4. Mount Caburn
5. Mount Harry
6. Ditchling Beacon
7. Chanctonbury
8. Truleigh Hill
9. Highdown (Highden)
10. Bignor Hill
11. Duncton Down
12. Linch Down
13. Treyford Hill
14. Sunwood
15. Butser Hill

N

Steam Tactics
Possible route of the cars (Fictional villages in brackets)

Bo = Bolney (Bromingleigh)
Co = Cowfold
LB = Lower Beeding (Pigginfold)
FR = Forest Row (Park Row)
LA = Lamberhurst (Cramberhurst)
Je = Jevington (Trevington)
W = Long Man of Wilmington (Hillingdon)

Ha = Hassocks (Cassocks)
He = Henfield (Penfield Green)
L = Leonardslee (animal park)
H = Horsham
Bl = Billinghurst (Linghurst)
E = Eastbourne

The route to the house in *They*

Locations of the settings in some other stories
Ro. Rottingdean   T. Telscombe Tye *(Brother Square Toes)*
Ba. Balsdean (The Knife & the Naked Chalk)   Br. Brighton (Wireless)
Bu. Burwash (Halo' the Draft) (The Conversion of St. Wilfrid)
R. Rye (Simple Simon) (Gloriana)   N. Northiam (Gloriana)
S. Selsy (The Conversion of St. Wilfrid) + Manhood End (Eddi's Service)
Pe. Pevensey (The Young Men at the Manor) (Old Men of Pevensey)
(The Knights of the Joyous Venture) (The Treasure and the Law)
P. Pooks Hill
* Bateman's   <> The Elms

Km
1   10   20   30
Scale

Chapter 7

ARMAGEDDON

Throughout the first decade of the twentieth century Kipling warned an unheeding government of the need for vigilance and of a possible invasion threat not faced since the time of Napoleon. The message was clear in the poem *The Dykes* (1902) and in the story, *The Parable of Boy Jones* which fictionalized, in *Land and Sea Tales*, (1910) the story of his own rifle club. From 1905 onwards he had supported Lord Roberts who was pressing the case for conscription. As a result the liberal press branded them "warmongers" which entered into one part of the mythology surrounding him. For one who wrote "the wickedest of all evils is war" the charge is unsustainable. He believed in a thesis current from the time of Vegetius in the 4th century AD – "Qui desiderat pacem, praeparet bellum" (He who desires peace must prepare for war). In addition he recognized that considerable inefficiency permeated the Army and he did much to expose incompetence. With the advent of the Great War all Kipling's energies were devoted to doing what he could. He met it not with confidence or exultation but with grim fortitude and bleak prospect. His skill with words was engaged almost immediately. War was declared on August 4th in response to the breaking of a treaty obligation on the part of Germany with the outflanking invasion of Belgium. Ruddy's own hand in the diary for that day records "my cold possesses me - incidentally Armageddon begins." He was then staying at Rider Haggard's house, Kessingland Grange, near Lowestoft on the coast of Suffolk, which was very close to the shore. He was most interested to see naval vessels busily engaged along the coast and wrote to the Editor of the *Daily Express*, R. D. Blumenfeld, to ask him to get someone in the office to send him a daily telegram to keep him abreast of the fast moving events. As throughout the war German conduct showed utter disregard for international law, her own treaties, the position of non-combatants or even for common human decency. General von Schleiffen conceived a plan to outflank French defences by attacking through neutral Belgium, and although he had died two years earlier, his successor implemented the attack, but possibly without the total determination which his predecessor would have shown. Liege was under siege and the policy of *schrecklichkeit* (horror; frightfulness) was immediately activated. Belgium was to be terrorised into offering no resistance. Hostages were taken to ensure good civilian behaviour, and when this failed they were to be executed. During the month of August towns were obliterated and more than 6,000 civilians were shot or bayoneted, including women, children and even tiny babies. The German army indulged itself in an orgy of looting and burning. Many Belgians fled to Holland and young men were deported to work in Germany.

Horrified neutral reporters filed their stories across the world and their utter condemnation seems to have startled the German High Command into abandoning the pillage. Similar atrocities were repeated in World War II at Lidice, Oradour and even more extensively in the Ukraine. Kipling's reaction to the outrage was a poem published in *The Times* on Tuesday September 1st – *For All We Have and Are*. The fee for publication he asked should be passed to the Belgian Relief Fund. Later Kipling was to be pilloried for his excessive hatred of all things German!

As Carrie's diaries reveal Rudyard joined in the patriotic drive to recruit volunteers, conscription being politically unacceptable. He made speeches in a number of towns, including two in Brighton on September 7th, one of which had to be relayed to an overflow meeting. Men flocked to join the colours and his words were received rapturously. Two day later they welcomed at Bateman's a friend, Julia Catlin Depew, who having been forced to flee from Compiegne, brought with her reports of the outrages perpetrated by the advancing Germans. It seemed that many of the rumours, later dismissed as mere fabrications, had not, in fact, been exaggerated. Kipling's sense of revulsion at the atrocities spurred him to write a story *Swept and Garnished*, in which a German woman, ill in bed, has a vision of five Belgian children massacred by the advancing army.

He also made many visits to army units from Salisbury Plain and the New Forest to Aldershot, Crowborough and Sevenoaks and to a naval detachment at Crystal Palace, as well as visiting returning wounded troops. These travels gave him abundant material for a series of articles in *The Daily Telegraph* which were shortly to be published in a booklet *The New Army in Training*.

British civilians were now drawn into the conflict, for in January 1915 a virtually undefended population was being attacked by bombs dropped from Zeppelins. *Mary Postgate*, published in September 1915, is a tale which drew a charge of "wicked inhumanity and brutality" on Kipling's head. Mary is devoted to her charge, the orphaned nephew of her companion, Miss Fowler. He is killed while training with the R.F.C. Mary is in the garden, burning his books and toys having just witnessed the death of a small girl in the bombing of the village, when a badly injured German airman parachutes down close to her. A quiet peaceful spinster, whose upbringing would normally have evoked sympathy and help, shows no compassion whatsoever and she exults in his slow and painful death. Kipling ascribes neither praise nor blame for Mary's reaction. In addition to airborne attacks, German battle-cruisers bombarded Scarborough and Hartlepool with the loss of 150 lives. British Naval

Intelligence had, with the aid of a captured code book, been aware of this impending attack but, as with "Enigma" three decades later, it was decided not to intercept the attacking force and so alert the enemy to the fact that their code had been broken.

Ruthlessness was not confined to the land, for German U-boat commanders behaved just as outrageously. On May 7th 1915 the liner *Lusitania* was torpedoed with the loss of 1,201 lives, including 124 American citizens. Even this outrage was not sufficient to persuade the United States to enter the fray. Another U-boat captain, having inexcusably torpedoed a hospital ship, *Llandovery Castle*, then attempted to destroy the evidence by surfacing and machine-gunning the survivors in the lifeboats.

Sea Constables, first published in 1915, pursued a theme of retributive justice. Three "Wavy Navy" officers dining with a Royal Navy Lieutenant in a fashionable London hotel discuss their recent duties in keeping a watching brief on ostensibly neutral vessels within our territorial waters. Many of these were engaged in the indiscriminate sowing of mines and refuelling U-boats with diesel. These submarines bent on sinking our supply ships could thus avoid long and arduous voyages to their pens in Germany. In a tale which showed how scrupulously Britain observed international law it showed how it was still possible to gain revenge on the unofficial enemy. Kipling's, Admiralty sponsored, book of naval operations drew upon his own visits to the East Coast Harwich and Dover Patrols. *Sea Warfare* is a brilliant account of the very essence of the hardships endured, with stoic humour, by the crews of the converted trawlers pressed into willing and eager armed service of the Auxiliary Fleet whose task was to sweep mines from coastal waters. He also experienced, at first hand, and wrote of the cold uncertainty of life with "The Trade", our own submarine fleet. His previous honoured guest status with the Royal Navy had resulted, at the time of the Diamond Jubilee, in a brilliant and readable account of naval life in *A Fleet in Being*. In 1915, however, he had to supplement his own necessarily limited experience with official records.

Like all his friends John Kipling was eager to 'join up' in the state of general euphoria which seemed to believe that the conflict would be quickly won. He offered himself as a volunteer on August 10th in response to Kitchener's call, whilst Rudyard and Carrie were at Brown's Hotel on the way back home from Suffolk. He was rejected because of his poor eyesight, which precluded him from trying to get a commission. A week later, with his father in tow, he tried at Hastings and Maidstone but with the same result. Then Rudyard was persuaded to call for help from his old friend Lord Roberts to seek a nomination for a commission. Just three days after the Brighton speech Rudyard met the Field Marshal at Wellington Barracks. 'Bobs' was the Colonel-in-Chief of the Irish Guards, and agreed, even though John was only 17, to nominate him for officer training. John was quickly transformed, after due celebration and kitting out, as an officer cadet at Brentwood, before moving in mid-September to Warley Barracks in Essex. Although his father has on occasions been pilloried for encouraging John to enlist, it was a most unfair charge because it was what the boy wanted and because all his friends were enlisting. The emotional strain of these efforts and the fact that George Cecil, the son of a dear family had been reported missing, led to a rapid deterioration in Rudyards's health and it wasn't long before Carrie also succumbed. Having completed his training John, with a sporting car to carry him in style, John enjoyed a last few weeks of happy socialising, amidst the doleful news of other friends who had lost their lives. His car was a Singer, and in the rich correspondence kept up between father and son, Rudyard suggested that she should be called Caruso, who was also a great singer! Carrie was philosophical in face of the slaughter, saying that *the world must be saved from the Germans.* Following the death of Lord Roberts, Kitchener was appointed Colonel in Chief of the Irish Guards and on August 13th 1915 inspected the new battalion. Immediately afterwards John motored down to Bateman's for the last time. Carrie recorded that *He looks very smart and straight and grave and young, as he turns at the top of the stairs to say "Send my love to Daddo".*

Father reached war-torn France before his son because he had been invited, in his journalistic capacity, to write about French military preparations. These were published later as *France at War.* John crossed the Channel on his eighteenth birthday, and the letters between them carried on almost daily, Rud addressing him as 'Dear old man' and signing off as 'Dad', 'Daddo' or 'Your father'. John gave detailed descriptions of his progress through France and Rudyard was equally descriptive, on one occasion writing to say that he saw Kitchener review the troops. Between sorties Rud returned to the Hotel Brighton in the Rue de Rivoli so that John had an address for him. John's letters were full of comments about new experiences and about how all his men were bearing up under them. He had clearly taken to heart the need for officers, however young, to look after the welfare of the men under their command. Rudyard returned to Burwash by August 28th from where the correspondence continued, with the father adding family news to an explanation of how French troops used rabbit wire above their trenches to reduce the deadly effect of mortar bombs. It was amazing, considering the chaotic state of troop movements that the postal service was so well efficient, although on one occasion John lamented that not having received a letter for four days, nine were delivered simultaneously. John wrote fully of his experiences, sitting on a 'Field Court Martial', the strenuous effort needed for a 'Divisional Field day', the digging of trenches around the French ports, comments about the terrible rain coupled with a request for a genuine naval oilskin. Enclosure of a 'fiver' in early September was to cover little bills which came rolling in to Bateman's and to settle a debt at Dunhills, in Duke Street. It was all so casual that it was scarcely believable. The oilskin arrived as did edible goodies from well placed family friends. Perhaps the most poignant was the request for a replacement for a lost identity tag just a week before his first and only battle. The last letter was written at 5.30 p.m. on Saturday 25th September in which he speaks convincingly and optimistically of THE great effort to break though and end the war, the battle of Loos began. On the following afternoon, after a 15 hour march to the front, along roads clogged with wounded troops, they were allowed a couple of hours rest. At mid-morning on the 27th the 2nd Guards Brigade was ordered to attack Chalk Pit Wood, and the subalterns raised the morale of their men. Soon after 4.00 p.m. he led 'B' Company in the attack and shortly after 2nd Lieutenant John Kipling was mortally wounded, probably by a shell blast, although one soldier thought that he had been hit by a bullet.

Two days later his parents received some news that John had been wounded and had been left in a building which just afterwards was surrounded by Germans. Rudyard succumbed to gastritis and was very distressed. A few days later the heart-stopping telegram, so familiar by this time to so many, arrived with the news that John was missing. The Conservative Party leader Bonar Law came down on the same day to collect his daughter Isabel. Reportedly he reinforced the news causing Rudyard to utter a terrible cry of anguish. Like all those with influence the Kiplings started to try to find out more specific information, as others had already done by visits to the rear lines or by contacting those in power or talking with wounded soldiers from his regiment who had been repatriated. With his journalistic credentials it would have been easy for Rudyard to go back to France, but he decided not to do so. A Lance-Corporal in hospital in Hythe said that John had been able to lift the spirits of his men, and another in London claimed to have seen him receive a wound in the neck. H. A. Gwynne, a long-established friend, and the Editor of the *Morning Post* not only printed an over-fulsome piece about the Kiplings loss but also sounded the British Minister to the Vatican to see if any news had filtered through. They were deluged with condolences from the great and the good. Slight hope existed that he might have been taken prisoner. Swedish royalty promised to contact the Kaiser, and the Red Cross and diplomatic staff of the still neutral United States all tried, but of course, their efforts were in vain. Leaflets were dropped behind enemy lines asking for information about the son of the world renowned author. The dreadful void could not be closed with any hard fact. Indeed it was not for another eighty years that a Canadian researcher with the Commonwealth War

Graves Commission believed that he had discovered the whereabouts of John's remains, and a headstone was erected at St. Mary's A.D.S. (Advanced Dressing Station) The intriguing story of that attribution is wonderfully explored with most meticulous research, in a book *My Boy Jack?* by Tonie and Valmai Holt.   Their conclusion is that, regretfully, the case had not been proved.

Life at Bateman's could never be the same again, although the family was always pleased to see John's old friends and colleagues, one of whom was the son of Cormell Price.   The sorrow must have been compounded by the fact that, on occasions when the wind was in a certain direction, the barrage of the western front could be heard even in the peace of the Sussex weald.   Admittedly Kipling kept himself alive to the needs of his own war effort. In the spring of 1917 he was again reporting war, but this time on the Italian front.   He had as a companion an old friend of South African days, Percival Landon, and they were escorted to Udine, close by three war-torn sectors, all of which they visited.   Briefed by the Supreme Commander, General Luigi Cadorna and after meeting King Victor Emmanuel III, the pair were able assess the difficult terrain, where the roads looked as if they had been created by giants, and where Alpine troops had to climb rock chimney fissures carrying machine guns.   A farewell ceremonial band concert was held for them with typical Italian bravura and a backing group of heavy artillery.   The record was published, after appearing as five articles in *The Daily Telegraph*, as *The War in the Mountains*.   He wrote home to Carrie a number of letters, returned with the Diplomatic Bag, which encapsulate his personal experiences.   As with all his writings, his voluminous life-long letters are well worth reading.

That autumn Kipling was asked to serve on the Imperial War Graves Commission.   Lord Derby, Chairman of the Commission, having seen the list of Commissioners said "You must have R.K., the soldiers' poet."   Invited to serve by Fabian Ware he responded with alacrity and work on behalf of the fallen became from then on, a most significant part of his life.   The proposals of the Commission were not without critics, for the decision not to repatriate bodies was seen by some as bureaucratic and cruel.   Kipling, as a writer, with his personal grief and his wide knowledge of the funeral practices of other religions was able to explain all in a booklet for the public *The Graves of the Fallen*.   His work included collating information, planning cemeteries, hiring gardeners and Chairing the sub-committee responsible for registering the names of all identifiable bodies found on the battlefields.   When, later, with Winston Churchill as Chairman of the Commission, he was asked to speak to 150 MPs in order to stave off a Commons motion of censure.   His simple message won the day – "You see we shall never have any grave to go to.   Our boy was missing at Loos.   The ground is, of course, battered and mined past all hope of any trace of being recovered. I wish some of the people who are making this trouble realised how much more fortunate they are to have a name on a headstone in a named place."

Possibly, most important of all, was his responsibility for conceiving the inscriptions carved on headstones and memorial sculptures of the cemeteries. On the monolithic Stone of Remembrance he adapted words from Ecclesiasticus embracing the other faiths of those serving the King Emperor – "Their Names Liveth for Evermore." The simple uniform headstones of white Portland Stone bore details of the fallen and their regimental badge. For those who could not be identified it was inscribed with the simple, heartrending phrase "Known unto God". Such stone symbolism could not be introduced until the remains had been re-assembled and the first makeshift cemeteries with their wooden crosses in patches of mud or torn earth could be reordered. A conscious decision was made to create a garden, whilst the uniformly spaced headstones with leveled grass in front would convey the feeling of servicemen on parade. Many English gardeners were recruited and their efforts resulted in a very different style of cemetery to those in which the French or German dead lay. Lines from Rupert Brooke's poem *The Soldier* became especially poignant.

If I should die, think only this of me, That there's some corner of a foreign field, That is forever England

Wounded Indian troops were cared for in Brighton's Royal Pavilion and those who succumbed to their injuries were cremated on a burning *ghat* set on the Downs near Patcham, so that their own religious needs could be correctly observed. Later the domed monument, the *Chattri*, set on an octagonal base in an enclosed garden of remembrance, was dedicated by the Prince of Wales on February 1st 1921. Kipling was present and the inscription reads "To the memory of all the Indian soldiers who gave their lives in the service of the King-Emperor this monument, erected on the site where the Hindus and Sikhs who died in hospital in Brighton passed through the fire is, in grateful admiration and brotherly affection, dedicated". It remains a place of solemn and moving annual pilgrimage.

The culmination of Kipling's efforts for the war graves came in May 1922. Kipling persuaded His Majesty to make a tour of the cemeteries a sacred journey, for which he had written "*The King's Pilgrimage*". On the 11th Kipling changed into morning dress in a peasant cottage to be with the King who came to inspect a cemetery at Vlamertinghe in Belgium, a precursor for the speech which Kipling had written for his monarch to give at the

Indian Cemetery at Terlinchtun near Boulogne two days later. Rudyard and Carrie were full of praise for the way in which the King had delivered it. It was simple gratitude to those who had made the ultimate sacrifice.

Standing beneath this Cross of Sacrifice, facing the great Stone of Remembrance, and encompassed by the sternly simple headstones, we remember and must charge our children to remember, that as our dead were equal in sacrifice, so they are equal in honour.

In the course of my pilgrimage I have many times asked myself whether there can be more potent advocates of peace on earth than this massed multitude of witnesses to the desolation of war.

I hope that the existence of these visible memorials would serve to draw all peoples together in sanity and self-control, as it has already set the relations between Empire and our Allies on the deep-rooted basis of a common heroism and a common agony.

One of the most moving of all the short stories appeared in magazine form in 1917 and was collected in *Debits and Credits* in 1926. *"The Gardener"* has very specific echoes of his own loss and subsequent search as well as his work for the commission. Not a simple story, it first describes the nuances of English village life when Helen Turrell, with elaborate evasion, brings home the infant son of her late brother describing him as her nephew. It ends with her visit to find his grave in the vast uncompleted cemetery of Hagenzeele Third. She sees a gardener tending the plots who asks her who she seeks. She utters the well-used phrases about her nephew, but. her deception is immediately recognised by the gardener who says that he will take her to her son. The link with Mary Magdalene at Golgotha is unmistakable.

The other sacred task Kipling undertook was his own personal tribute to a lost son, in the form of a campaign history of the Irish Guards. John's name is to be found on the Burwash War Memorial just outside St. Bartholemew's Church in which there is a rounded memorial bronze tablet for him. The tablet was commissioned from Charles Wheeler on the recommendation of their old friend Herbert Baker, but its first appearance did not please the Kiplings, which they recorded as being ' a great failure' because of a fault, and so it had to be recast with a design improvement they thought necessary. Rud and Carrie commissioned Wheeler to cast a bust of John, which he completed. He told them it was ready for their approval, but they couldn't bear the emotion and so never came. Wheeler later destroyed the plaster model for it. The imposing War Memorial was unveiled by a much decorated war hero, Lord Horne in 1920. The Kiplings were criticised for missing the ceremony, rather unfairly, because, again, they simply couldn't bear the anguish of their own loss recorded on it. It is moving to know that the lantern above the war memorial is lit on the anniversary of the death of each of the 85 men on the Roll of Honour. It is moving to see close to John's name that of Alfred Isted, one of clan upon whom Hobden was based. For many years the man who volunteered to switch the lamp on was Albert Waterhouse, who had been dismissed as a garden boy at Bateman's for being late for work by Carrie. Kipling did, however, attend the dedication of the War Memorial at Etchingham, in which clearly, from the photograph of the ceremony, he took an important role.

Kipling worked painstakingly for a number of years on *The Irish Guards in the Great War* which was published in 2 volumes in 1923. It proved to be a masterpiece of military narrative and John Buchan reviewing the work wrote "No other book can ever be written exactly like this, and it seems likely to endure as the fullest document of war-life of a British regiment, compiled by a man of genius who brings to his task not only a quick eye to observe and a sure hand to portray, but a rare spirit of reverence and understanding".

It is impossible to do justice to Kipling's influence and to the words he wrote – reports, poems, stories and inscriptions. The bereaved of war will for ever be in his debt. There are many other tales; *On the Gate,* shows a wry humour at the confusion of Heaven's civil service with the inordinate increase in the numbers of those presenting themselves to St. Peter. His admiration for the men who guard us while we sleep and his awareness of our debt to them, with all their human failings, grew from his first encounters with the army in India. He was the first writer to present barrack and campaign life, with attendant terrors, anguishes and frustrations, to a civilian population. His championship of army and navy are frequently recalled whenever our troops are called upon to serve in yet another foreign field. The poppies of Flanders so movingly evoked in a poem by a Canadian Medical Officer, Lieutenant-Colonel John McCrae, *In Flanders Fields,* have come to symbolise the extent of the sacrifice of so many for the sake of the nation.

History repeated itself, for Rudyard foresaw the menace of the rise of the Third Reich and the usurping of his own beloved swastika, an ancient symbol of good fortune which had adorned his books. He noted the contrast between the fanatic nationalism injected into Hitler Youth and the downright pacifist disbelief in Britain that a threat existed. In Jubilee year of 1935 he spoke with careful deliberation to the Royal Society of St. George on May 6th. He gave a resumé of the staggering cost of the loss of a generation in the Great War and spoke of the lack of willingness on the part of the government to accept that a current danger existed.   He said, *Nevertheless the past year or so had given birth to the idea that our example of State – defended defenceless-ness had not borne much fruit, and that we had walked far enough along the road which was paved with good intentions.* It was a warning not well received, although he was not the only voice to carry it. Only three years earlier he had published a warning poem *The Storm Cone*, in which he warned *This is the tempest long foretold.* His prescience, as with more mundane matters, was exact yet he was regarded as an alarmist. The country was ill-prepared, and with a little foresight the horrors to come might have been lessened had he and a few others been heeded.

Chapter 8

ELITE MOTORING

The intermittent delight and frustration of pioneer motoring in Locomobile or Lanchester gave way in 1906 to the more extravagant comfort of the world of the Daimler, by way of a tested Siddeley. The dairy shows that in May 1906 a Daimler was being purchased and that it was used for local motoring in an around the Weald, and for a longer excursion to York. A letter to Cormell Price more than a year later recounts that John was delivered to St Aubyn's School in Rottingdean but rather plaintively that the Daimler, which had been christened Gunhilda, had to be returned "to her birthplace to have her innards repaired". In August 1908 surgically restored she took them northward to Hadrian's Wall where they met Baden-Powell. Ever seeking perfection, in November 1908 Rudyard wrote to John to tell him of a new car from the same stable, this time a 'Brighton Landaulette' which was supposed to move noiselessly. For the next year or more the new Daimler took them effortlessly around the country to visit wealthy relatives and friends and to look at Winchester where two who particularly interested Rudyard had lived. Both Jane Austen and Izaak Walton were associated with the city, and the latter, the author of *The Compleat Angler or the Contemplative Man's Recreation* whose famous work would have given Rudyard, a keen fisherman, much pleasure. They also visited a camp in the New Forest which was an experience for those enrolled in the embryonic Scout movement. Father and son also drove to Plymouth for a holiday aboard a friend's yacht.

But altogether new vistas opened up in March 1910 when the Kiplings were staying in the Pyreneean spa, Vernet-les-Bains, where Carrie took her annual restorative and fashionable treatment in sulphurated springwater. A chance encounter with Lord Montagu introduced Rudyard to the luxury of a marque to which he would in future be beholden. For Claude Johnson, the joint manger of Rolls-Royce, a company established in Derby in 1907, and who was, incidentally, the first secretary of the Royal Automobile Club, made an astutely attractive offer which Kipling found he could not possibly refuse. He explained that he was sending his car back to Paris empty but if Rudyard would care, he could have exclusive use at his disposition. This was a "Silver Phantom" which had *"all the power of the Horses of the Sun"* and an ex Royal Marine chauffeur, a breed of man in whom the author had the utmost confidence. It was an extensive meandering trip from Banyuls-sur-Mer, encompassing much of the delights of Provence, the Rhone valley and inland from the Côte d'Azur. They gathered narcissi, admired wisteria, and were entranced by the architecture of Roman cites, the beauty of the Papal city of Avignon, the stone grotesqueness of Les Baux, and the grandeur of Fontainebleau. He found the roads *straight, wide, level and perfect'*, a view which would be modified later with regard to the pavée of the towns. They found a new diversion where the long straight roads were paralleled by the chemin de fer and found enjoyment in racing the trains. Having arrived in Paris on April 1st 'tired and happy' they returned to Bateman's in their own car from Folkestone. In November CJ, known as the hyphen in Rolls-Royce, came to Bateman's to discuss the purchase of a new model, and soon after Rudyard had to hurry to Tisbury to visit his mother just before her death.

It seems that the new car, a dark green limousine landaulette, for which he had stipulated a body from Barkers, was damaged in a fire at the coach builders so that the order was delayed once and a second time because of the Coronation. Although being offered the loan of a replacement, Rudyard proved a somewhat irascible customer and Claude Johnson hoped he would transfer his custom to another firm so that he did not have to put up with his complaints any more. In March 1911 he asked for a car to be sent to Vernet and in the "Spectre" completed a 1,200 mile drive, around their favourite haunts in Provence. The return trip was marred by a collision near Paris, which he described in a placatory letter to C.J., as *a bad city inhabited by lunatics'*. The incident occurred because a Choisy-le-Roi tram suddenly moved on its tracks diagonally across the road. Some superb driving by a Roll-Royce employee, named Fleck, reduced the damage to a bent axle. Kipling was only sorry that he hadn't damaged the tram ! He recounted other amusing side effects of French sanitation, and it is to be hoped that Claude retained the letter as its value would have recompensed him in full for his earlier frustration.

It was the year in which he began his motoring notebooks, which included detailed distances covered, observations, anecdotes and some sketches. They were lost until, in the new millennium, they were discovered in an old desk-drawer at his publishers, Macmillans. It seems that they had originally been left with Thomas Mark, Kipling's editor, who could use them as a reference to check work in progress, and who retired in 1959. A miraculous survival for the desk in which they were placed had been moved three times as the publishers took on new premises. The six notebooks covered the years from 1911 until 1926. It was fortunate that they were deposited there because had they been returned to Elsie, after Carrie's death they would almost certainly have suffered the same fate as the diaries. Their unique record shows just how meticulous Rudyard was in noting his travels. He was a lover of France ever since his first visit to the Paris exposition with his father whilst still a schoolboy. The regularity of his motoring adventures emphasised just how much he was in thrall to the scale and beauty of the landscapes, to the gastronomic delights to be savoured, his respect for the hard working thrifty peasantry, and the heritage of its architecture. Not everything was always admirable for he acted as informal hotel and restaurant inspector, passing comments on to those he believed could make use of them, noting sub-standard sanitation and the way in which some restaurateurs could try to slip an extra franc on to *l'addition* for wine which had not been served. He noted wear and tear on tyres, always willing to experiment with the durability of different brands, and once complained bitterly how sunken tram-tracks made driving very risky.

His meticulous attention to detail proved most helpful to a youthful Lady Elizabeth Harris who found herself, full of trepidation, seated next to the great man at dinner at a House Party at Panshanger. He was the embodiment of charm and once he discovered that she hoped to drive a two-seater through France, promised to send her advice. In a letter from Bateman's, dated 25th October 1925, he suggested that the best route would be via Southampton to (Le) Havre because the ferry arrives early in the day and so allows time to try the car out on the way to Rouen. There one could obtain little aluminium butter-pots for use on roadside picnics. He then proposed a route through Les Andelys, where he recommended an hotel, Grand Cerf, and on to the beauty of Chartres Cathedral. Thence to Poitiers and Agoulême with the first sight of spring, and on to Bordeaux, which ought to be missed in favour of Arcachon for the route through the pines of the Landes, on a bad road though to Bayonne, Biarritz and "all sorts of adorable little places tucked under the Spanish Mountains". Rudyard included, most thoughtfully, his own annotated Michelin Guide, an essential item to carry. The daily mileages (actually kilometres) are carefully penned in. Lady Betty, as he addressed her was delighted to have such help from a real expert.

After the loaned car adventures in March and April 1911 they made a further trip to Normandy with the Aitkens. The new Green Goblin arrived in December and so in the spring of 1912, having sailed from Alexandria, they were met at Marseilles and then were driven to Albi and on to Bourges where he was due to talk business with A. P. Watt and Frank Doubleday. The new vehicle was named 'Duchess' and reportedly behaved herself exceptionally well, and in a letter to John he writes - *goes like a dream and is beautifully sprung. Never wish to sit in a better.* Back home it was possible even in April to drive to Andover with the top retracted. It was this car which made him declare that a Roll-Royce was the only car he could afford to run, because having paid £800 for her, he was given more than £200 more than that against the purchase of another new model. In the middle of 1913 a chauffeur of six years service was given the sack, because the new car needed a special type of man. The replacement, Eaves, met them at Bordeaux, in March 1914 and drove them through Provence and up the Rhône Valley, and back via Boulogne to Brown's Hotel. John and Elsie were encouraged to 'map read' the route but did not always make a very good job of it, to their father's disgust. It was to be the last of their French journeys until they were able to return, in sombre mood under very different circumstances after the war.

In 1914 a Ford was delivered for use as a local runabout, but a new Rolls costing £1350 was also added to the stable. It was a very busy period with John going to a 'crammer' in Bournemouth, much socialising and a notable speech about the Ulster question in Tunbridge Wells. Elsie was 'presented' at Court, an occasion marred somewhat by a suffragette demonstration, and Rudyard took a great interest in the potential of civil aviation. Soon after the declaration of war John took up his place at Warley Barracks, and a month later was the proud possessor of a red Singer, an event which prompted Rud, ever the humourist, to nickname it Car-uso, because it was a fine singer ! The car was well used on war business with visits to a number of army units spread across the southern counties, and to take him where he was to deliver impassioned recruiting orations. One other visit must have had especial nostalgia for in January 1915 he visited injured Indian troops housed at Brighton's Royal Pavilion. The desire all young men had to enlist meant that good candidates for a chauffeur's position were in short supply. An incident in London when his parents were driven to London to meet John left Rudyard seething because the driver missed a turning and drove towards recruiting tents. A few weeks later an indolent cart driver well over on the wrong side of the road approaching a bend caused a minor accident scarring the car. This resulted in a pungently phrased letter to the cart driver's employer, and a determination that the 'rule of the road' should be paramount. A year later the Kiplings decided in their words to 'put down' the cars for the duration.

Less than two months after the Armistice they were able to rejoice in the 'first drive for ages' on the day the bells of Burwash rang in the New Year. Most of September was taken up with a comprehensive tour though the Midlands and North and on to Scotland. Early in 1920 they returned to Rottingdean for Aunt Georgie's interment, and five months later they made what must have been a traumatic experience to visit Chalk Pit Wood where John had been lost. Even so they were able to offer comfort to an English party whose car had broken down. Subsequent motoring in France naturally involved, at least in part, his dedicated work as a Commissioner for the War Graves. Before they came to part with the 1914 car a new chauffeur, named Taylor, met them from a ship which had brought a convalescent Rudyard from Algiers to Marseille. Another Riviera and Provence tour saw them back to Bateman's via Dieppe, and Taylor must have given satisfactory service for he drove them for another ten years.   In June the old Rolls was sold for £200 more than they gave for it in 1914, but Rudyard regretted its departure for it was yet another link with John broken. It was replaced in June 1921 by "Esmerelda", the Fourth Duchess of Tours, a neat and appropriate name as Tours could refer to its purpose or to a favoured French town. She received her baptism in a drive to Scotland, where as well as delivering them safely to various friends and to the Oban Games, Rudyard inveighed against the reckless habits of 'Sunday Drivers'. It seems that nothing has changed ! Essential travel in England and further repeated visits to France followed. The most special one was to accompany His Majesty King George V on the Pilgrimage which Rudyard had devised for him. Rudyard noted with some satisfaction that the Roll-Royces hired for the official party did not match his own in splendour. An evocative moment came when Rudyard was waiting to greet the King at the Indian Cemetery near Boulogne for he spied an engraved headstone of 'Gunga Din – dooly bearer'. On the return trip an unusual incident happened when the Rolls became stuck on a small, but steeply sloping, hump-backed bridge. Villagers, employing a sturdy cart -horse, managed to pull her clear. Rudyard, never one to miss an opportunity to obtain local colour, chatted aimiably with the local peasantry over a cigarette, and observed modern *tricotteuse* at work. The following year, after some much needed surgery, they took passage from Tilbury to Toulon, with a stop in Gibraltar, for convalescence. His motoring diaries contain an enormous amount of comment on countryside, weather, shopping and people. His ingenuity with words turns mundane occurrences into a bewitching commentary, not only with regard to the motoring but also on the incidental excursions which they enjoyed. All the while his mind was active on his writing projects and on maintaining a considerable correspondence. Ever present on such tours was the need to keep abreast of the work of the Imperial War Graves Commission. On this trip it was to Villiers-Cotterêts to discuss with the Mayor, Dr. Moufflers, memorial stones to commemorate the Irish Guards. He was clearly sympathetic and Rudyard appreciated his help. Nearing Dieppe 'Esmerelda' 'lay down' by the roadside with a magneto problem. A telegram to R.R. ought to ensure a replacement in Newhaven, but they had to reach the French port relying on their own batteries. Their return home came a day after Cousin Stanley had taken up the Premiership for the first time.

This tour and the following one to Scotland are fully recorded in one of a series of articles which appeared in The Kipling Journal, under the general title *Lordly of Leather* between September 1982 and December 1985. (KJ Nos 223 – 236). One of the major reasons for the northward excursion was so that Rudyard could be installed, by the choice of the students, as Rector of St. Andrew's University. He was capped and gowned and drawn to the ceremony by some students. Field Marshal Earl Haig, his predecessor handed on the appointment and Rudyard responded by giving his Rectorial address. This was published as part of collection of speeches he had given over the years to distinguished gatherings in *A Book of Words* in 1928. Three days later he spoke at the University College, Dundee, his advocacy of full University status being greeted with delight. The return, in which Esmerelda performed superbly, included a charming reunion with Mary Blaikie and her family near Stamford.

1924 saw further drives to enjoy the Aldershot Tattoo, whilst guests of the Montgomerys and later to France again. But the highlight was the wedding, in October, of Elsie, an event which reinforced their isolation with the loss, to George Bambridge, of their only remaining child. The car had been refurbished by Hoopers for the celebrations. Subsequent years saw further restorative travels in France as well as attention to the work of the Commission. In 1927, after a rail journey from Lisbon to Biarritz, they were met by Taylor for a leisurely drive home, and a little later they were guests at Chequers, during Stanley's second Premiership. Increased popularity of motoring in France led Rudyard to the conclusion that the Riviera had become a *'noisy, smelly hell'*. In October they toured in Normandy and then met Elsie in Paris. After a final French tour for Esmerelda they ordered a replacement which was delivered in July, to Rudyard's great joy as the Phantom I had an improved chassis and 'all manner of new gadgets'. The greatest pleasure came from the fact that her acceleration was superb. The 0 to 60 mph syndrome had been initiated! Esmerelda, with ingenuity on the part of the Rolls-Royce sales department, was shipped to their Bombay branch. There she was bought by a religious sect to carry priests and a heavy effigy on an annual short pilgrimage. Devotees along the route shower her with coins and with a red powder, which could hardly improve her performance. Ever since she has been known, most appropriately, as the 'Holy Ghost'.

The new Phantom behaved impeccably in the autumn of 1928 with her owner greatly impressed by her unequalled performance as she toured Scotland. Highland scenery never failed to attune him to his mother's Scottish roots, and he even felt uneasy when travelling through Campbell country, the sworn enemies of the Macdonalds, since the massacre of Glencoe in 1692. He was even untroubled by the often appalling weather, shielded by the luxurious interior of his beautiful vehicle. On the journey home he felt that she was merely 'sleeping' at 60 m.p.h. This was the car which now graces Bateman's garage. He became alarmed by rash and selfish driving encountered on his journeys, and saw much evidence of its consequences in wreckage which often littered the roadside. A contributory factor was, as he saw it, increasingly slippery road surfaces. It wasn't long before he put his thoughts into the poem *Fox Hunting*, the last stanza of which goes:-

When men grew shy of hunting stag, For fear the law might try 'em, The car put up an average bag Of twenty dead per diem. Then every road was made a rink For Coroners to sit on; And so began, in skid and stink, The real blood-sport of Britain!

For reasons explained below the 1928 Roll-Royce was replaced, after a spell as motorless, by a lighter 25.h.p. model in mid-1932, for which a new chauffeur, Baskerfield, was employed. Some tentative excursions through midland England is all that could be managed, although he was pleased by the car's quiet manoeuvreability. As he was no longer allowed to undertake any long distance travel because of the poor state of his health, the South of France was the only option, and the Blue Train obliged. So with work on his autobiography, perhaps with an intimation that it needed urgent attention, the sparking plug of his motoring delight begins to glow less brightly.

The Roll-Royce which now adorns the old garage was Kipling's penultimate car. A 1928 Phantom I, 40/50 h.p. was purchased for £2,833.18.6. and delivered on July 11th. Originally green, with a cellulose coating with which it had been covered to reduce the possibility of scratch damage. It had an Open Fronted Limousine body by Hooper and Co., and its registration number was PN 1814. The "RR" symbol on the radiator is red, a style Sir Henry Royce himself changed to black a little later, to avoid a colour clash with the bodywork. Kipling sold the car in 1932 because the Road Tax for so powerful a model was too expensive. He replaced it with a lighter, less heavily taxed, model. After Kipling sold it in 1932 it passed though the half a dozen hands before being bought at auction by Jack Hayward O.B.E., a businessman and philanthropist whose benefactions included gifts towards the purchase of Lundy Island and the restoration of *S.S. Great Britain*. Having read an article in the *Daily Mail* in 1977 by Nigel Dempster who revealed the secret that Mr. Hayward who had bought the car, was a Kipling enthusiast, John Shearman, the Secretary of The Kipling Society approached him about its future. It was renovated by Sir Edward Caffyn, during 1979, at his Haywards Heath works, not without difficulty in finding correct inner tubes and other parts. As a result of John Shearman's discussions with Mr. Hayward it was transferred on permanent loan to The National Trust at Bateman's on Empire Day, 24th May 1982. Since then, in its air conditioned housing, it has delighted many thousands of motoring and Kipling enthusiasts.

Appendix I

SUSSEX DIALECT WORDS USED IN KIPLING'S STORIES

Kipling had a particular talent to incorporate Hindustani and Urdu words in his Indian stories and in the Soldier tales he used dialect so successfully that the reader felt that he could actually speak with a Cockney, North Country or Irish accent. In Sussex he soon became aware of the very specific and localised use of words which had common currency particularly among country people. He spoke with members of the rural community and soon their idiom became completely familiar to him. He was aided in this endeavour with a scholarly work published in Lewes, in 1875 by the Rev. W. D. Parish, called *A Dictionary of the Sussex Dialect*.

The use of these words is even more likely to baffle the reader more than a century after he first introduced them and so a Glossary of those which he put into dialogue would seem helpful. The Kipling Society recognised this need only four years after the Society was founded in 1927 and published, in four parts, as complete a selection as possible. The compilation was made for the Society by J. De Lancey Ferguson of the Western Reserve University, Cleveland, Ohio, and it is this which forms the basis of what follows. Some additional information and modifications have been added to these. Examples of where they have been used are shown by the title of the story (in italic script) and the collection in which that story is to be found capital letters. A list of the collected works is given at the end of the glossary.

ALLWITHER,
Adv.
in every direction
"Muddy waters ran allwither into the darkness"
Knights of the Joyous Venture (PPH)

ALONG
Adv.
about (a vague reference to time)
"Jenny's turn to walk in de wood nex' week along *They* (T &D)

ARY
Adj.
any
"She won't lie easy on ary wool-wain" *Hal o' the Draft* (PPH)

BACK-LOOKIN'S
n.
memories – in retrospect
I reckon you've your back-lookin's, too
The Wish House (D & C)

BACKWENT
backward
Adv. "She looks him up an' down, front an' backwent"
Friendly Brook (DC)

BAT
a stick (also used particularly for the vicious metal-tipped stick used by batmen to protect the tubmen who

carried the smuggled goods during the landing from an attack by customs officers)
"Take a bat (which we call a stick in Sussex) and kill a rat"
A Doctor of Medicine (R & F)

BEAZLE
Vb

to tire out - also BEZZLE
"He fair beazled him with his papers an' his talk"
Friendly Brook (DC)

BEE-SKEP

a bee-hive (made of raffia) which was also worn as a disguise by Rye smugglers
"Here comes my old white-top bee-skep"
Friendly Brook (DC)

BEHITHER
Conj.

on this side of
"Behither the small o' me ankle"
The Wish House (D & C)

BEHOVE
Vb.

to benefit
"We'd ha' jumped overside to behove him"
Simple Simon (R &F)

BELIEFT
Vb.

to believe
"They do say hoppin'll draw the very deadest; an' now I belieft 'em"
Dymchurch Flit (PPH)

BESOM
Vb.

utterly
"On besom black nights"
Simple Simon (R & F)

BEWL
Vb.

to whistle
"The wind bewling like a kite in our riggin's"
Simple Simon (R & F)

BINE

stalk
"Oh hop-bine yaller and woodsmoke blue"
A Three-Part Song (Verse)

BIVVER
Vb.

to shake or quiver
"Two kestrels hung bivvering and squealing above them"
The Knife and the Naked Chalk (R & F)
There is a Devon word "bever" and this version was probably invented by Kipling to suggest the rapid wing movement when a hawk is hovering in one spot looking for prey.

BLURT
Vb

to appear suddenly
"The boat we was lookin' for 'ud blurt up out of the dark"
Simple Simon (R &F)

BRISH
Vb.

to brush
"I've seen her brish sparks …out o' her hair"
Dymchurch Flit (PPH)

BRISHINGS

clippings
"This hay's full of hedge-brishings"
A Doctor of Medicine (R & F)

BRISHWOOD

brushwood
"Put the brishwood back again"
A Smuggler's Song (Verse)

BULT
Vb

to bolt (?)
"Bulting back and forth off they Dutch Sands"
Simple Simon (R & F)

BUNGER
an awkward performer – a bungler
"He's no bunger with a toppin' axe"
Friendly Brook (DC)

BURY
a burrow
"He'd thump ... like an old buck-rabbit in a bury"
Cold Iron (R & F)

CATERING
Vb.
to slant
"The Lashmar farms ... come caterin' across us"
An Habitation Enforced (A & R)

CHAM
Vb
to champ
"Moon be chawed and chammed his piece"
Simple Simon (R & F)

CHANCE-BORN
Adj.
illegitimate
"Then Mary is chance-born"
Friendly Brook (DC)

CONCERNED IN LIQUOR   slightly drunk
"The man wasn't drunk – only a little concerned in liquor, like"
Friendly Brook (DC)

CRY DUNGHILL
Vb.
to give up; to quit
"I've fair cried dunghill an' run"
Friendly Brook (DC)

DENE
a valley, usually a dry-valley
"In a deep dene behind me"
They (T & D)

The Saxon word "dene" is often used in place names, usually, now, spelled "dean" as in Rottingdean

DIK
a ditch or dyke
"The Marsh is justabout riddled with diks and sluices"
Dymchurch Flit (PPH)

DO
a success
"mostly they can make a do of it"
Brother Square-Toes (R & F)

DOLLOP
a large amount
"Tipped a dollop o' scalding water out o' the copper"
The Wish House (D & C)

DORTOIR
n.
a dormitory
(French) "He turned the keep doors out of dortoir"
The Old Men at Pevensey (PPH)

DOZEN
Vb.
To daze or stupify
"Baulked and dozened and cozened me at every turn"
Hal o' the Draft (PPH)

DRAFT
a drawing
"Called Hal o' the Draft because ... he was always drawing a drafting"
Hal o' the Draft (PPH)

DUNNAMANY
I don't' know how many
"Just tore the gizzards out of I dunnamany (churches)"
Dymchurch Flit (PPH)

DUNT
n. & vb
a dull thump; to strike with a dull sound
"Liddle bundles hove down dunt"
Dymchurch Flit (PPH)

EEND-ON
Adv.

straight ahead
"You'd think nothing easier than to walk eend-on acrost
Dymchurch Flit (PPH)

FARABOUT
Adv.

a long way round
"I dunno as I'd go farabout to call you a liar"
Dymchurch Flit (PPH)

FARDEN

n.

a fathing (a small copper coin worth a quarter of a penny)
"passed a farden in the mire"
Friendly Brook (D C)

FAVOUR
Vb.

to resemble
"The less she favoured any fashion o' pudden"
Simple Simon (R & F)

FINERY

an iron refinery
"The valley ... was full o' forges and fineries"
Hal o' the Draft (PPH)

FISK
Vb.

to run about
"To fisk and flyte through fern and forest"
The Old Men at Pevensey (PPH)

FLOG OUT
Vb.

to tire or make weary
"I felt a bit flogged out, like"
The Wish House (D & C)

FLYTE
Vb.

to flit or skip
See fisk above

FOREIGNER or FURRINER   an outsider
"A foreigner from the next parish"
An Habitation Enforced (A & R)

FROWTEN
Vb,

to frighten
"You've frowtened 'em (the bees)
The Vortex (DC)

GAFFER

a master
"Even the whale swallowed up Gaffer Jonah"
Hal o' the Draft (PPH)

GALLIWOPSE

a galley
"A Spanish galliwopse's oars creepin' up on ye"
Simple Simon (R & F)

GHYLL or GILL

a steep sided small ravine
"And the deep ghylls that breed"
Sussex (Verse)
"Twix' a liddle low shaw an' a great high gill"
A Three-Part Song (Verse)
The word "ghyll" was introduced during the Viking settlement of England and is rather more found in more northerly counties.

GOOD PIECE

food offered to fairies
"I saw ye throw the Good Piece out-at-doors"
Dymchurch Flit (PPH)

GOR-BELLIED
Adj.

fat-bellied
"A great gor-bellied Spanisher ... came rampin' at us" (in this case a ship)
Simple Simon (R & F)

GRUMMEL
Vb.

to grumble
"You can hear 'em (the ditches) bubblin's and grummelin'.
Dymchurch Flit (PPH)

GUB	a lump "Gubs of good oaken." *Simple Simon (R & F)*	**HOWK**	to dig (See under Hike above)
GULL *Vb.*	to seep away by force of running water "The brook had gulled out of the bank a piece." *Friendly Brook (DC)*	**HUGGLE** *Vb.*	to huddle or hunch up "A peevish greybeard huggled up in angle-edged drapery" *The Wrong Thing (R & F)*
HEAD-MARK	a characteristic of the head "You can still tell 'em by headmark" *An Habitation Enforced (A & R)*	**HURDLE** n. & vb.	a piece of wicker fence or to enclose within them "His head-piece all hurdled up in that iron-collar" *Friendly Brook (DC)*
HEAT-SHAKE	a puff or light gust of wind "A heat-shake o' wind will come up" *The Knife and the Naked Chalk (R & F)*	**HURLY-BULLOO**	hullaballoo ; disturbance "Then there just about was a hurly- bulloo" *Friendly Brook (DC)*
HEM *Adj.& n.*	a great deal ; a mild oath "You're a hem of a time makin' your mind" *Dymchurch Flit (PPH)*	**INTER-COMMON** *Adj.*	mutual "We sat on this bench sharing our sorrows inter-common" *Hal o' the Draft (PPH)*
HIKE *Vb.*	to move with a swing or a jerk "Dan hiked and howked with a boat- hook" *Knights of the Joyous Venture (PPH)*	**JUSTABOUT** *Adv.*	certainly; extremely ; altogether "I left St.Barnabas's a jewel just about a jewel" *Hal o' the Draft (PPH)*
HOB-UP *Vb.*	to rear "Children which they'd hobbed up for their lawful own" *Friendly Brook (DC)*	**KECKLE** *Vb.*	to kick up; to buckle "I've seen a scaffold-plank keckle" *The Wrong Thing (R & F)*
HOUSEN	houses (an archaic plural) "I hate housen in daylight" *Hal o' the Draft (PPH)*	**LITHER** *Adj.*	lithe ; slim "I counted the lither barrels of twenty serpentines" *Hal o' the Draft (PPH)*
HOUSE-LEEKED	overgrown with houseleek *(Sempervivium tectorum)* *An Habitation Enforced (A & R)*		

MASK
a complete covering (usually in mud or blood)
"His back was a mask where he'd slipped in the muck"
Friendly Brook (DC)

MIDDEST
amidst
"Twas right in the middest of a hot une night"
Brookland Road (R & F)

MIDDLING
Adv.
rather; very; or fairly (depending on context and tone of voice)
"I reckon you'll find her middlin' heavy"
Hal o' the Draft (PPH)

MORTAL
Adv.
very; extremely
"You've been mortal kind to me"
The Wish House (D & C)

MOWCH
Vb.
to loaf; to slouch; to mooch
"Jim comes mowchin' along with his toppin' axe"
Friendly Brook (DC)

MUCK-GRUBBER
a miser
"I never heard Jim was much of a muck-grubber"
Friendly Brook (DC)

MUCK ON
Vb.
to put on in haste
"The Spanisher kept muckin' on more an' more canvas"
Simple Simon (R & F)

MUCK-OUT
Vb.
to clean thoroughly
"I was obligin' Jim that evenin' muckin' out his pig-pen"
Friendly Brook (DC)

MUCKED UP
Adj.
confused; heavily laden
"A man forgets to remember when he's proper mucked up with work"
Simple Simon (R & F)

NAUN
nothing
"They didn't say naun to her"
Friendly Brook (DC)

NEXT-ABOVE-FOOL
one who is near to being a complete fool
"A man who can only do one thing, but he's next-above-fool to the man that can't do nothing"
The Wrong Thing (R & F)

NIGROMANCING
Vb.
conjuring; working black magic; (necromancy)
"She was honest-innocent of any nigromancing"
Dymchurh Flit (PPH)

ODD-FASHIONED
Adj.
odd; queer
"but our first twenty year or so she was odd-fashioned, no bounds"
Dymchurch Flit (PPH)

ODD-GATES
Adj.
odd; queer
"Won'erful odd-gates place – Romney Marsh"
Dymchurch Flit (PPH)

OUTGATE
Adj.
unusual
"My boy, he has her eyes and her outgate senses
Dymchurch Flit (PPH)

PAVISAND
Vb.
to strut
"Forth she come pavisanding like a peacock"
Simple Simon (R & F)

PHARISEES

fairies
"A passel o' no-nonsense talk ... about Pharisees"
Dymchurch Flit (PPH)

PIECE

a lunch – usually of bread and butter
"We was eatin' our pieces"
Friendly Brook (DC)

PIG-POUND

a sty; a pen for swine
"They filed out of the garden by the snoring pig-pound"
A Doctor of Medicine (R & F)

POACH

Vb.

to tread the ground into holes, as cattle do
"The ground about was poached and stouched with sliding hoof-marks"
Simple Simon (R & F)

POKE-HOLE

an out of the way corner
"We cleansed ... a hundred foul poke-holes"
A Doctor of Medicine (R & F)

POLT
Vb.

to strike hard; a driving blow
"Hop-poles and odd-end bats, all poltin' down together"
Friendly Brook (DC)

POMPION

a pumpkin ; a gourd "picture of Jonah and the pompion that withered"
The Wrong Thing (R & F)

PORTURE
Vb.

to sketch or draft
"I'll porture you a pretty, light piece of scroll-work"
The Wrong Thing (R & F)

PUDDLE
Vb.

to paddle; to splash
"We couldn't puddle about there in the dark"
Friendly Brook (DC)

PUTE
Adj.

pure; clear; thorough-going
"You and I chance to be pure pute asses"
Hal o' the Draft (PPH)

PUT-LOCK

a horizontal timber of scaffolding inserted in shallow holes in a wall
"I was at Torrigiano's feet on a pile of put-locks"
The Wrong Thing (R & F)

PUTTER
Vb.

to toddle
"As soon as he could walk, he'd putter forth with me"
Cold Iron (R & F)

RACKLE
Vb.

to rattle
"Passels o' liddle swords an' shields `raklin'"
Dymchurch Flit (PPH)

REMEDY

redress
"Thy Normans would slay him with out remedy"
Young Men at the Manor (PPH)

REYNOLDS

the fox (from Reynard)
"Oh, Mus' Reynolds! If I knowed all was inside your head"
The Winged Hats (PPH)

ROUNDEL

a circle; anything round
"The dark well of the old-fashioned roundel"
Dymchurch Flit (PPH)

RUGG
Vb.

to tug violently or forcibly
" 'Tis like a tooth. It must rage an' rugg till it tortures itself quiet on ye"
The Wish House (D & C)

RUMMEL
Vb.

to rumble
"The great Tide-wave rummelled along the wall"
Dymchurch Flit (PPH)

SALLY

A willow (presumably from "salix" the generic name of the plant)
"All they rubbishy alders and sallies"
Friendly Brook (DC)

SAY-SO

an assertion
"Do it lie in your mouth to contest my say-so?"
Simple Simon (R & F)

SCADDERING
Adj.

scattering
"I heard something in a scadderin' word- o'-mouth way"
Friendly Brook (DC)

SCRATT
Vb.

to scratch
"The woman scratted his face"
Cold Iron (R & F)

SCRATTLE

a feeble or skinny person
"I never reckoned the old scrattle 'ud risk her neck bone"
Marklake Witches (R & F)

SCUTCHEL UP
Vb.

to gather hurridly
"I've brought you what I could scrutchel up of odds and ends"
Simple Simon (R & F)

SEELY

Adj.

silly, in its old sense of simple (from Saxon "selig")
"Seely Sussex for everlastin' "
Hal o' the Draft (PPH)

SHAW

a small clearly delineated wood
"The valley was as full o' forges ... as a May shaw o' cuckoos"
Hal o' the Draft (PPH)

SHIRES

Counties of England other than Sussex, Surrey and Kent
"Frankie was born somewhere out west among the Shires"
Simple Simon (R & F)

SHRUCK
Vb.

to shriek
"Did you hear him shruck just now?"
They (T & D)

SINNIFICATION

significance
"If I was you, I'd take the sinnification o'the sign"
Hal o' the Draft (PPH)

SLEEPER

"Sleeper ? A doormouse do you say?"
The Tree of Justice (R & F)

SLEW

a wet place
"Sinks, slews and corners of unvisited
A Doctor of Medicine (R & F)

SLIDDER
Vb.

to slide or slip
"Benedetto ... sliddering up behind me"
The Wrong Thing (R & F)

SLOB
n.

tidal mud flats ; or thick mud
"We saw a man slouching along the slob"
The Conversion of St.Wilfrid (R & F)
"He cleaned off some o' the slob with a tussick of grass"
Friendly Brook (DC)

SLUBBER
to darken or obscure
"All slubbered with sleep"
The Old Men at Pevensey (PPH)

SOW
Vb.
to be hoggishly idle
"He had to get breakfast ... while she sowed it abed"
Friendly Brook (DC)

SPANG
Adv.
directly ; clear through
"We was all looking that she prod the fork spang through your breastes"
The Wish House (D & C)

SPATTLE
Adj.
a mottled effect
"Like jeweled images among the spattle of gay-coloured leaves"
Brother Square-Toes (R & F)

SPAULTY
n.
brittle; chipped or split
"A set of iron cramps ... never came to hand, or else they were spaulty or cracked"
Hal o' the Draft (PPH)

SPLUT
Vb
to split; to break
"Frankie had put in from Chatham with his rudder splutted"
Simple Simon (R & F)

SPOON
Vb.
to run before the wind
"She had the wind of us and spooned straight before us"
Simple Simon (R & F)

SPOON-MEAT
liquid food
"She couldn't more than suck down spoon-meat"
Friendly Brook (DC)

SQUABBY
Adj.
squat; thick-set
"The more I studied my squabby Neptunes the less I liked 'em"
The Wrong Thing (R & F)

SQUAT
a corruption or a fermentation
"You run too many chickens together ... an' you get a squat"
Dymchurch Flit (PPH)

SQUINTLINGS
Adv.
side-long; sideways
"He looked at me squintlings"
The Wrong Thing (R & F)

STATELIFIED
Adj.
dignified; impressive
"That was a statelified meeting to be hold"
Brother Square-Toes (R & F)

STILL
a lull; calm
"It was like a still in the woods after a storm"
Brother Square-Toes (R & F)

STOACH
Vb.
to trample the ground (as cattle do in wet weather)
"The ground about was poached and stoached with sliding hoof-marks"
Simple Simon (R & F)

STORM-COCK
the missel-thrush
"Whistles like a storm-cock through a sleet shower"
The Wrong Thing (R & F)

STUB
Vb.
to pluck a chicken clean
The Wish House (D & C)

SWAP
Vb.

to cut close; to trim
"Gaps used by every Hobden since a
Hobden swapped a hedge"
The Land (Verse)

SWARVE
Vb.

to silt up
"Next flood the brook'll swarve up"
Hal o' the Draft (PPH)

SWASH

a tidal channel
"Lost count of time among them black
gullies and swashes"
*The Knights of the Joyous Venture
(PPH)*

SWOP-HOOK

a reaping hook; a sickle
"A man had left his swop-hook ...
there
Cold Iron (R & F)

TACK

food; hard-tack is a ship's biscuit
"nothing to get from us save hard-tack
and a hanging"
Young Men at the Manor (PPH)

TARRIFY
Vb.

to terrify; also annoy or pester
"This Reformation tarrified the
Pharisees"
Dymchurch Flit (PPH)

"She was pickin' at me and tarrfyin'
me all the long day"
Marklake Witches (R & F)

THREDDLE
Vb.

to thread (as a needle)
"He ... threddled the longship through
the sea"
Knights of the Joyous Venture (PPH)

TIMBER-TUG

a heavy timber-wagon
"Did I ask Master Collins for his
timber-tug to haul beams?"
Hal o' the Draft (PPH)

TOD

a fox; a crafty person
"I warned the old tod"
Hal o' the Draft (PPH)

TOKEN

an apparition
"A token is a wraith of the dead, or,
worse still, of the living"
The Wish House (D & C)

TOT

a bush: tuft
"Hid our horses in a willow-tot"
Hal o' the Draft (PPH)

TOTTLY
Adj.

shaky
"My legs were pretty tottly"
Brother Square-Toes (R & F)

TOWL
Vb.

to give tongue; to bray
"A couple of (beagles) towling round
the kitchen-garden after the laundry
cat"
The Treasure and the Law (PPH)

TRAIPSE
Vb.

to trudge
"I seed a stranger come traipsin' over
the bridge"
Friendly Brook (DC)

TRINKLE
Vb.

to trickle
"People had no more than begun to
trinkle back to town"
A Priest in Spite of Himself (R & F)

TUTT-MOUTHED
Adj.

having protruding lips
"Just an outrageous, valiant,
crop-haired, tutt-mouthed boy"
Simple Simon (R & F)

TWO-THREE MINDED doubtful
Adj. "Plenty good men .... was two-three minded about the upshot"
Simple Simon (R & F)

UPSIDES even with; on the same level
Adj. "We must be upsides with'em for the honour of Bristol"
Hal o'the Draft (PPH)

USUALS normal condition
"The man come again ... in his usuals"
Friendly Brook (DC)

VAMBRISH to fleck
Vb. "A great smoky pat vambrished with red gun-fire"
Simple Simon (R & F)

VIVERS fibres
"The vivers of her roots they hold the bank together"
Hal o' the Draft (PPH)

WATER-LET a drainage ditch
"Diks an'sluices, an' tide-gates an' water- lets"
Dymchurch Flit (PPH)

WAY-WASTE unused land by the roadside
"A grass way-waste that cut into a summer-silent hazel wood"
They (T &D)

WEATHER-TENDER sensitive to the weather
Adj. "My woman was won'erful weather-tender"
Dymchurch Flit (R & F)

WERISH weak or insipid
Adj. "This Oxfordshire plague ... was of a werish, watery nature"
A Doctor of Medicine (R & F)

WILDISHER someone from the wilds
n. "Her folk come out of the ground here, neither chalk or forest, but wildishers"
An Habitation Enforced (A & R)

In Parish's Dictionary the word "wild" is specifically used for the "Weald" so it means in the Kipling context one who lives in the Weald.

WITHINSIDES inwardly
Adv. "That thought shrivelled me withinsides"
The Wrong Thing (R & F)

WOODLUMP a woodpile
"I was going to toss the man over his own woodlump"
Cold Iron (R & F)

WOPS a wasp
"It's too early for wopse-nestes"
Cold Iron (R & F)

YERK to goad; to thrust
Vb. "He would yerk us in the ribs with his scabbarded sword"
Young Men at the Manor (PPH)

THE COLLECTIONS IN WHICH THE ABOVE TALES APPEAR

(A & R)	Actions and Reactions
(DC)	A Diversity of Creatures
(D & C)	Debits and Credits
(PPH)	Puck of Pook's Hill
(R & F)	Rewards and Fairies
(T & D)	Traffics & Discoveries

LANDSCAPE AND PLACE NAMES IMPORTANT IN KIPLING'S SUSSEX

ANDERITUM (ANDERITA)

The name for the Roman fort of the Saxon Shore which later became to be known as Pevensey. It was from here that Parnesius, who met Una in the wood in the Dudwell valley, led his century northwards to the Wall. The name actually mean "the great ford" because in Roman and Norman times the indented harbour behind was the coastline. At low tide it was possible, if one knew the intricacies of mud, sand and tide, to cross to what is now Bexhill on foot.

ASHDOWN FOREST

A large forested area in the High Weald whose name is derived from a hill overgrown with Ash trees. It was granted by Edward III to his son, John of Gaunt in 1372 and was a Royal Hunting domain for over 300 years.

BATTLE

The place where the Battle of Hastings was fought. The name is derived from the Norman French "La Batailge". An alternative name for the battle is "Senlac" which is derived from the Old English "sandy watercourse". The prefix "sandy" is probably derived from the rusty iron-stained appearance of the water, fancifully thought to be bloodied from the wounds of the combatants.

BEACHY HEAD

The dominant, 536', cliff which terminates the South Downs above Eastbourne. Kipling refers to it in the poem *Sussex*. The name is derived from the Norman French *beau chef,* 'beautiful headland' and so the word 'Head' is really superflous.

BULVERHYTHE

A small haven, three miles to the east of Hastings, where a valley draining from Battle Abbey ran into the sea.. It was where the Norman invasion fleet moored after the original landing at Pevensey.

BURWASH

The village which features in many of the stories, and whose church, St.Bartholemew's features as St. Barnabas, rebuilt by Hal o'the Draft. Pronounced "Berrish" locally the name is derived from "a stubble field near a fortified place". There is, however no trace of such a 'burh' or earthwork now.

BURY

In Sussex place-names the word, pronounced "berry" means a stronghold from the Old English *Burh* and is incorporated in other names such as Burpham – pronounced "Burfham", meaning a settlement beside a stronghold.

CHANCTONBURY RING

"The ringed head" noted in *They* was planted by Charles Goring, son of the Wiston estate, in 1760. He nurtured the young beeches by carrying water up to them and was rewarded in his old age by seeing the clump approaching maturity. It was a much admired, widely seen, landmark until, sadly, it was destroyed by the hurricane of 1987. It was an earthworked Bronze Age site and had, later, a rural Roman temple. It takes its name from the fortified site, 'burh' or 'bury', near the 'brushwood thicket farmstead' Chancton.

COMBE

An Old English word for a valley. It is often associated with the fretted indentations on the edge of the chalk scarp.

DEW POND

A man made circular pond which collects rainwater and was used from the eighteenth century to water the flocks of sheep which roamed the Downs.
"Only the dew-pond on the height, unfed that never fails".
Sussex (Verse)

DOWN

Derived from the Saxon word "dun" meaning "hill", the Downs are the rounded chalk uplands of Southern England. The ones Kipling knew best were the South Downs stretching from Wiltshire and Hampshire through Sussex to the great cliff at Beachy Head.

"On the Downs, in the Weald, on the Marshes" Very Many People (Verse)

DRY-VALLEY

Because under normal circumstances the chalk absorbs water, it seems strange that these waterless valleys were once obviously eroded by running surface water. They were actually carved out during the Pleistocene glaciation when the chalk was frozen solid to a considerable depth. Melt-water during occasional warm spells could drain down the surface and acts as an erosive agent. Kipling refers to them as *our broad and brookless vales* in the poem *Sussex.*

DUDWELL

The river in the valley which passes through the Bateman's estate. The name is derived from Dudda's spring. The small stream was used by the children for adventuring in their canoe. I was also occasionally liable to flood. The action of *Faithful Brook* is set on it, and it powered the Mill.

DYMCHURCH

A small coastal town on the shore of Romney Marsh. It held the Court Room for the Lords of the Level to meet while planning the drainage of the area lying behind the shingle foreland of Dungeness.

FORGE PONDS and HAMMER PONDS

Many of the deep ghylls draining the High Weald were dammed in order to build a head of water to power machinery used in the medieval iron industry. They drove ore-crushers, and bellows to force air into the blast-furnaces, and to lift and drop the great hammers to shape the iron. When the industrial revolution made them superfluous because iron was then smelted by use of coal rather than charcoal, the former derelict landscapes were transformed by the creation of garden features around them for wealthy landowners.

HEFFLE CUCKOO FAIR

Heffle was the local pronunciation of Heathfield. The Fair, held annually on April 14th was when the oldest lady in the town let a cuckoo out of her basket. *(The Treasure and the Law)*

HITHE (HYTHE)

An old port town near the eastern end of Romney Marsh. It was one of the Cinque Ports, the charters of which gave trading rights in return for maritime service when necessary. *(Dymchurch Flit)*

LEONARDSLEE

An estate at Lower Beeding where Sir Edmund Loder converted a series of hammer-ponds into an exquisite garden. It has a favourable micro-climate for some exotic plants to flourish. At one time Sir Edmund kept a menagerie of animals. It was the inspiration for one of the locations in *Steam Tactics*.

LEWES

The county town of East Sussex. Its overlordship was given by the Conqueror to William de Warrenne, who built the twin-keep castle as well as the Cluniac Priory of St. Pancras. He is introduced as one of the owners of Bateman's in the poem *The Land*. The name may be derived from the pre-Roman term 'us' meaning water.

LONG MAN OF WILMINGTON

An enigmatic chalk hill-figure about which there is no academic agreement as to origin. Numerous theories have been championed, ascribing it pre-historic, Roman, Saxon and medieval. As it is in a combe on the flank of Windover Hill which was a pre-eminent site in Neolithic and Bronze Age times it seems reasonable to think that it could have been carved then. Incredibly the designers realised that as it was on a steep slope it needed elongation to make it appear correctly proportioned from ground level. It is 240' tall and the male figure is holding to poles, neither of which ever carried a spear-head. The grass, cut through to chalk, once removed would have had to be cleaned annually to prevent obscurity. Its outline was later delineated in white brick to avoid the annual chore. The figure is mentioned in the poem *Sussex*, and as the Long Man of Hillingdon in *Steam Tactics*.

MANHOOD END
Appears in *Eddi's Service* where stood his chapel. It is so called because the spot marked the limit of the Manhood Hundred, a Saxon administrative unit. The hundred was gifted to the Bishop of Chichester, St.Wilfrid, by King Cadwalla in 683. Eddi was one of his four companions and is traditionally associated with it. The word 'Manhood' means "the wood owned by the community".

MARLPIT
A natural chalky-clay was used before the days of modern fertilizers to spread over sandy, acid soils in order to improve both texture and fertility. Pits from which the material was extracted were common in Sussex.

MARTELLO TOWERS
The numbered circular defensive towers which extend round the coast from Aldeburgh in Suffolk as far as Seaford were erected to counter a possible Napoleonic invasion. The curved walls were expected to have the ability to deflect cannon-shot, a characteristic noted in such a shaped fort on Cape Mortella in Corsica. The design impressed English military architects but the "o" and the "a" were transposed by an Admiralty clerk and so they became "Martello". Mortella, meaning "myrtle" is a common landscape name in the Mediterranean.

NORTHIAM (NORGEN)
Brickwall House was the home of many generations of the Frewen family. Queen Elizabeth I visited there en route to inspect her ships at Rye. (*Gloriana*)

OAST-HOUSE
A circular building, usually of brick, in which hops were roasted. The word oast is derived from the Latin for "searing heat".
"Marched off to roast potatoes at the oast-house". *Dymchurch Flit (PPH)*
A pair of oast houses may be seen at Bateman's, which, when Kipling bought the property, had been used for drying the hops from the fields close by.

PETT LEVEL
Between the sandstone cliffs of the Fairlight area and beneath the bluff on which Winchelsea is built lies the beginning of the great marsh area. Pett Level extends to the river which flows through Rye to the sea.

PEVENSEY
Is associated with a number of tales centred on the Norman land, gifted to Earl Robert of Mortain, half-brother to the Conqueror within the walls of the Roman fort, Anderita. His successor Richer de Aquila, raised the castle after 1101. Pevensey is pronounced locally 'Pemzee' and is derived from *Pefen's ea* (Pefen's river or water).

PEVENSEY LEVELS
The ancient harbour area lying beween Pevensey and Bexhill gradually silted up, a process hastened by the efforts at reclamation in medieval times. Drainage ditches carried the small rills flowing from the rising land behind to the sea, the shoreline of which extended southward. The maze of channels were well known to locals, and so was the territory of the smuggling gangs in the eighteenth and early nineteenth centuries.

PIDDINGHOE
The round towered Saxon church is surmounted by a golden sea-trout. Kipling brings it into the poem *Sussex* erroneously as a 'begilded dolphin'. The old local pronunciation was 'Piddenhoo' and means "the spur of land belonging to Pyddi's people".

POOK'S HILL
The location is discussed fully in the text.

ROMNEY MARSH
A flat ill-drained area between Rye and Winchelsea in the west to Romney and Hythe in Kent. The Royal Military Canal was created below the old cliff-line to act as a water defence against possible seaborne invasion in Napoleonic times. It has a maze of dykes and drains and was for centuries the pasturage for sheep, the wool of which was smuggled across the channel by the "owlers". It has such a special, other-worldly, aspect that it was regarded locally as a continent on its own. "I've heard say the world's divided like into Europe, Ashy, Afriky, Ameriky, Australy, an' Romney Marsh". *(Dymchurch Flit)*

ROTTINGDEAN
The village in which Kipling settled in 1897. Its name reflects its Saxon origin, meaning the valley (dean) of the people (ingas) of Rota. Rota would have been the first tribal elder to have settled there. The children Dan and Una return to spend time there on holiday from Bateman's in *The Knife and the Naked Chalk*.

RYE
The ancient ("antient", locally) port, once an island at the confluence of the rivers Eastern Rother, Tillingham and Brede. Since its heyday the shoreline has retreated some distance through reclamation and longshore drift so that Kipling could define it a "*" port of stranded pride*" in the poem *Sussex*. The name is derived from *atter eye* meaning "at the island". The name was reduced to "Rye" and its importance as one of the Cinque Ports diminished as the water receded.

SELSEY BILL (SELSEA)
The much eroded headland at the western end of the county. It is the setting for *The Conversion of St. Wilfrid*. It means "Seal's Island".

SENLAC
See above under "Battle"

TELSCOMBE TYE
Telscombe is a small village above the Ouse valley. Its "tye" or common-land stretches to the cliffs at modern Telscombe, between Saltdean and Peacehaven. Its name is used in a poem, the first line of which is *"The moon she shined on Telscombe Tye"* in *Brother Square-Toes*.

VECTIS
Mentioned in *A Centurion of the Thirtieth*, this is the Roman name for the Isle of Wight.

WASHINGTON
The farmstead of Wassa's people, is a village some ten miles north of Worthing. It is noted in both *Brother- Square Toes* and in *They*. In the latter Kipling describes it as the hamlet *that stands Godmother to the capital of the United States*.

THE WEALD
The area enclosed by the escarpments of the North and South Downs. It has varied landscapes, clay vales, sandstone ridges and a high plateau. Its name, meaning "forest" in Old English, relates to the woodland which covered most of the area originally. Andredesweald, the earliest name referred to the Roman fort of Anderida has been shortened to the present name. The largest patches of remaining woodland are Ashdown Forest and St. Leonard's Forest, although there are numerous smaller patches. Much of the woodland was consumed in the charcoal burners furnaces which provided fuel for the medieval blast furnaces of the iron industry.

WELANDS FORD and WILLINGFORD BRIDGE
On the Dudwell not far from Bateman's. They are one and the same spot.

WINCHELSEA
A town planned by Edward III which replaced Old Winchelsea destroyed by the force of the sea in 1287. The new town with a rectilinear street plan was on a ridge well out of reach of the storms. *(Dymchurch Flit)*

Appendix III

The poems of most significance referred to within the text of *Kipling's Sussex*

THE POEMS

A Charm

Take of English earth as much
As either hand may rightly clutch.
In the taking of it breathe
Prayer for all who lie beneath.
Not the great or well-bespoke,
But the mere uncounted folk
Of whose life and death is none
Report or lamentation.
Lay that earth upon thy heart
And thy sickness shall depart!

It shall sweeten and make whole
Fevered breath and festered soul.
It shall mightily restrain
Over-busied hand and brain.
It shall ease thy mortal strife
'Gainst the immortal woe of life,
Till thyself, restored, shall prove
By what grace the Heavens do move.

Take of English flowers these –
Spring's full-facèd primroses,
Summer's wild wide-hearted rose,
Autumn's wall-flower of the close,
And, thy darkness to illume
Winter's bee-thronged ivy bloom.
Seek and serve them where they bide
From Candlemass to Christmas-tide,
For these simples, used aright,
Can restore a failing sight.

These shall cleanse and purify
Webbed and inward-turning eye;
These shall show thee treasure hid,
Thy familiar fields amid:
And reveal (which is thy need)
Every man a King indeed!

A Smuggler's Song

If you wake at midnight,
and hear a horse's feet,
Don't go drawing back the blind,
or looking in the street,

Them that ask no questions isn't told a lie.
Watch the wall, my darling,
while the Gentlemen go by!
Five and twenty ponies,
Trotting through the dark –
Brandy for the Parson,
'Baccy for the Clerk;
Laces for a lady, letters for a spy,
And watch the wall, my darling,
while the Gentlemen go by!

Running round the woodlump
if you chance to find
Little barrels, roped and tarred,
all full of brandy-wine,
Don't shout to come and look,
nor use 'em for your play.
Put the brishwood back again –
and they'll be gone next day!

If you see the stable-
door setting open wide;
If you see a tired horse
lying down inside;
If your mother mends a coat
cut about and tore;
If the lining's wet and warm –
don't you ask no more!

If you meet King George's men,
dressed in blue and red,
You be careful what you say,
and mindful what is said.
If they call you "pretty maid,"
and chuck you 'neath the chin,
Don't you tell where no one is,
nor yet where no one's been!

Knocks and footsteps round the house –
whistles after dark –
You've no call for running out till
the house dogs bark.
Trusty's here, and *Pincher's* here,
and see how dumb they lie –
They don't fret to follow when
the Gentlemen go by!

If you do as you've been told,
   'likely there's a chance,
You'll be give a dainty doll
   all the way from France,
With a cap of Valenciennes,
   and a velvet hood –

A present from the Gentlemen,
   along o' being good!
Five and twenty ponies.
   Trotting through the dark –
Brandy for the Parson,
   'Baccy for the Clerk.
Them that asks no questions isn't told a lie –
   Watch the wall, my darling,
   while the Gentlemen go by!

The Burial
1902
(C. J. Rhodes, buried in the Matoppos, April 10th 1902)

When that great Kings return to clay,
   Or Emperors in their pride,
Grief of a day shall fill a day,
   Because its creature died.
But we – we reckon not with those
   Whom the mere Fates ordain,
This Power that wrought on us and goes
   Back to the Power again.

Dreamer devout, by vision led
   Beyond our guess or reach,
The travail of his spirit bred
   Cities in place of speech.
So huge the all-mastering thought that drove –
   So brief the term allowed –
Nations, not words, he linked to prove
   His faith before the crowd.

It is his will that he look forth
   Across the world he won –
The granite of the ancient North –
   Great spaces washed with sun.
There shall he patient take his seat
   (As when the death he dared),
And there awaits a people's feet
   In the paths that he prepared.

There, till the vision he foresaw
   Splendid and whole arise,
And unimagined Empires draw
   To council 'neath his skies,
The immense and brooding Spirit still
   Shall quicken and control.
Living he was the land, and dead,
   His soul shall be her soul.

A Tree Song
(A.D. 1200)

Of all the trees that grow so fair,
Old England to adorn,
Greater are none beneath the Sun,
Than Oak, and Ash, and Thorn.
Sing Oak, and Ash, and Thorn, good sirs,
(All of a Midsummer morn!)
Surely we sing no little thing,
In Oak, and Ash, and Thorn!

Oak of the Clay lived many a day,
Or ever Æneas began.
Ash of the loam was a lady at home.
When Brut was an outlaw man.
Torn of the Down saw New Troy Town
(From which was London born);
Witness hereby the ancientry
Of Oak, and Ash, and Thorn!

Yew that is old in churchyard mould,
He breedeth a mighty bow.
Alder for shoes do wise men choose,
And beech for cups also.
But when you have killed,
and your bowl is spilled,
And your shoes are clean outworn,
Back ye must speed for all that ye need,
To Oak, and Ash, and Thorn!

Ellum she hateth mankind, and waiteth
Till every gust be laid,
To drop a limb on the head of him
That anyway trusts her shade.
But whether a lad be sober or sad,
Or mellow with ale from the horn,
He will take no wrong when he lieth along
'Neath Oak, and Ash, and Thorn!

Oh, do not tell the Priest our plight,
Or he would call it a sin;
But – we have been out in the woods all night,
A-conjuring Summer in!
And we bring you news by word of mouth –
Good news for cattle and corn –
Now is the Sun come up from the South,
With Oak, and Ash, and Thorn!

Sing Oak, and Ash, and Thorn, good sirs
(All of a Midsummer morn)!
England shall bide till Judgement Tide,
By Oak, and Ash, and Thorn!

Cuckoo Song

Tell it to the locked up trees,
Cuckoo, bring your song here!
For Spring to pass along here!
Tell old Winter, if he doubt,
Tell him squat and square – a!
Old Woman! Old Woman!
Old Woman's let the Cuckoo out
At Heffle Cuckoo Fair – a!

March has searched and April tried –
'Tisn't long to May now,
Not so far to Whitsuntide
And Cuckoo's come to stay now!
Hear the valiant fellow shout
Down the orchard bare – a!
Old Woman! Old Woman!
Old Woman's let the Cuckoo out
At Heffle Cuckoo Fair – a!

When you heart is young and gay
And the season rules it –
Work your works and play your play
'Fore the autumn cools it!
Kiss you turn and turn about,
But my lad, beware a!
Old Woman! Old Woman!
Old Woman's let the Cuckoo out
At Heffle Cuckoo Fair – a!

A Three-Part Song

I'm just in love with all these three,
The Weald and the Marsh and the Down countree,
Nor I don't know which I love the most,
The Weald or the Marsh or the white Chalk coast.

I've buried my heart in a ferny hill,
Twix' a liddle low shaw an' a great high gill.
Oh hop-bine yaller an' wood-smoke blue,
I reckon you'll keep her middling true!

I've loosed my mind for to out and run
On a Marsh that was old when King's begun.
Oh, Romney Level and Brenzett reeds,
I reckon you know what my mind needs!

I've given my soul to the Southdown grass,
And sheep-bells tinkled when you pass.
Oh, Firle an' Ditchling an'sails at sea'
I reckon you keep my soul for me!

Alnaschar and the Oxen

There's a pasture in a valley where
the hanging woods divide,
And a Herd lies down and ruminates in peace;
Where the pheasant rules the nooning,
and the owl the twilight tide,
And the war-cries of our world die out and cease.

Here I cast aside the burden that
each weary week-day brings
And, delivered from the shadows I pursue,
On peaceful, postless Sabbaths
I consider Weighty Things –
Such as Sussex Cattle feeding in the dew!

At the gate beside the river where
the trouty shallows brawl,
I know the pride that Lobengula felt,
When he bade the bars be lowered
of the Royal Cattle Kraal,
And fifteen miles of oxen took the veldt.
From the walls of Bulawayo in
unbroken file they came
To where the Mount of Council cuts the blue . . . .
I have only six and twenty,
but the principle's the same
With my Sussex Cattle feeding in the dew!

To a luscious sound of tearing,
where the clovered herbage rips,
Level-backed and level-bellied watch 'em move –
See those shoulders, guess that heart-girth,
praise those loins, admire those hips,
And the tail set low for flesh to make above!
Count the broad unblemished muzzles,
test the kindly mellow skin
And, where yon heifer lifts her head at call,
Mark the bosom's just abundance 'neath

the gay and clean-cut chin.
And those eyes of Juno, overlooking all!
Here is colour, form and substance!
I will put it to the proof
And, next season, in my lodges shall be born
Some very Bull of Mithras,
flawless from his agate hoof
To his even-branching ivory, dusk-tipped horn.
He shall mate with block-square virgins –
kings shall seek his like in vain,
While I multiply his stock a thousandfold,
Till an hungry world extol me,
builder of a lofty strain
That turns one standard ton at two years old!

There's a valley, under oakwood,
where a man may dream his dream,
In the milky breath of cattle laid at ease,
Till the moon o'ertops the alders,
and her image chills the stream,
And the river-mist runs silver round their knees!
Now the footpaths fade and vanish;
now the ferny clumps deceive;
Now the hedgerow-folk possess their fields anew;
Now the Herd is lost in darkness,
and I bless them as I leave,
My Sussex Cattle feeding in the dew!

Army Headquarters

Ahasuerus Jenkins of the "Operatic Own",
Was dowered with a tenor voice
of *super*-Santley tone.
His views on equitation were,
perhaps, a trifle queer,
He had no seat worth mentioning,
but oh! he had an ear.

He clubbed his wretched company
a dozen times a day;
He used to quit his charger in a parabolic way;
His method of saluting was the joy of all beholders;
But Ahasuerus Jenkins had
a head upon his shoulders

He took two months at Simla when
the year was at the spring,
And underneath the deodars eternally did sing.
He warbled like a *bul-bul* but particularly at
Cornelia Agrippina, who was musical and fat.

She controlled a humble husband,
who, in turn, controlled a Dept.
Where Cornelia Agrippina's human
singing-birds were kept
From April to October on a plump retaining-fee
Supplied, of course, *per mensum*,
by the Indian Treasury.

Cornelia used to sing with him,
and Jenkins used to play;
He praised unblushingly her notes,
for he was false as they;
So when the winds of April
turned the budding roses brown,
Cornelia told her husband: -
"Tom, you mustn't send him down."

They haled him from his regiment,
which didn't much regret him;
They found for him an office-stool,
and on that stool they set him
To play with maps and catalogues
three idle hours a day,
And draw his plump retaining-fee –
which means his double pay.

Now, ever after dinner,
when the coffee-cups are brought,
Ahasuerus waileth o'er the grand pianoforte;
And, thanks to fair Cornelia,
his fame has waxen great,
And Ahasuerus Jenkins is a Power in the State!

Delilah

Delilah Aberyswyth was a lady –
  not too young –
With a perfect taste in dresses
  and a badly bitted tongue,
With a thirst for information,
  and a greater thirst for praise,
And a little house in Simla
  in the Pᶒrehistoric Days.

By reason of her marriage
  to a gentleman in power,
Delilah was acquainted with
  the gossip of the hour;
And many little secrets,
  of the half-official kind,
Were whispered to Delilah,
  and she bore them all in mind.

She patronized extensively
  a man, Ulysses Gunne,
Whose mode of earning money
  was a low and shameful one.
He wrote for certain papers which,
  as everybody knows,
Is worse than serving in a shop
  or scaring off the crows.

He praised her "queenly beauty"
  first; and later on he hinted
At the "vastness of her intellect"
  with compliment unstinted.
He went with her a-riding,
  and his love for her was such
That he lent her all his horses –
  and she galled them very much.

One day, THEY brewed a secret
  of a fine financial sort;
It related to Appointments,
  to a Man and a Report.
'Twas almost worth the keeping, -
  only seven people knew it –
And Gunne rose up to seek the truth
  and patiently ensue it.

I was a Viceroy's Secret, but –
  perhaps the wine was red –
Perhaps an aged Councillor
  had lost his aged head –
Perhaps Delilah's eyes were bright –
  Delilah's whispers sweet –
The Aged Member told her what
  "twere treason to repeat.

Ulysses went a-riding,
and they talked of love and flowers;
Ulysses went a-calling,
and he called for several hours;
Ulysses went a-waltzing,
and Delilah helped him dance –
Ulysses let the waltzes go,
and waited for his chance.

The summer sun was setting,
and the summer air was still,
The couple went a-walking
in the shade of Summer Hill.
The wasteful sunset faded out
in turkis-green and gold,
Ulysses pleaded softly, and . . .
that bad Delilah told!
Next morn, a startled Empire
learnt the all-important news;

Next week the Aged Councillor
was shaking in his shoes.
Next month I met Delilah and
she did not show the least
Hesitation in affirming that
Ulysses was a "beast".

We have another Viceroy now,
those days are dead and done –
Off, Delilah Aberyswith
and most mean Ulysses Gunne!

My Boy Jack
1914 – 18

"Have you news of my boy Jack?"
Not this tide.
When d'you think that he'll come back?"
Not with this wind blowing, and this tide.

"Has any one else had word of him?"
Not this tide.
For what is sunk will hardly swim,
Not with this wind blowing, and this tide.

"Oh, dear, what comfort can I find?"
None this tide,
Nor any tide,
Except he did not shame his kind –
Not even with that wind blowing, and that tide.

The hold your head up all the more,
This tide,
And every tide;
Because he was the son you bore,
And gave to that wind blowing and that tide.

"For All We Have and Are"
1914

For all we have and are,
For all our children's fate,
Stand up and take the war.
The Hun is at the gate!
Our world has passed away
In wantonness o'erthrown,
There is nothing left to-day
But steel and fire and stone!

Though all we knew depart,
The old Commandments stand:-
"In courage keep your heart,
In strength lift up your hand,"

Once more we hear the word
That sickened earth of old:-
"No law except the Sword
Unsheathed and uncontrolled."
Once more it knits mankind,
Once more the nations go
To meet and break and bind
A crazed and driven foe.

Comfort, content, delight,
The ages' slow-bought gain,
They shrivelled in a night.
Only ourselves remain

To face the naked days
In silent fortitude,
Through perils and dismays
Renewed and re-renewed.
Though all we made depart,
The old Commandments stand:-
"In patience keep your heart,
In strength lift up you hand."

No easy hope or lies
Shall bring us to our goal,
But iron sacrifice
Of body, will and soul.
There is but one task for all –
One life for each to give.
What stands if Freedom fall?
Who dies if England live?

Eddi's Service
(A.D. 687)

Eddi, priest of St.Wilfrid
In his chapel at Manhood End,
Ordered a midnight service
For such as cared to attend.

But the Saxons were keeping Christmas,
And the night was stormy as well.
Nobody came to the service,
Though Eddi rang the bell.

"Wicked weather for walking,"
Said Eddi of Manhood End.
"But I must go on with the service
For such as care to attend."

The altar-lamps were lighted, -
An old marsh-donkey came,
Bold as a guest invited
And stared at the guttering flame.

The storm beat on at the windows,
The water splashed on the floor,
And a wet, yoke-weary bullock
Pushed in through the open door.

"How do I know what is greatest,
How do I know what is least?
That is My Father's business,"
Said Eddi, Wilfrid's priest.

"But three are gathered together –
Listen to me and attend.
I bring good news, my brethren!"
Said Eddi of Manhood End.

And he told the Ox of a Manger
And a stall in Bethlehem,
And he spoke to the Ass of a Rider,
That rode to Jerusalem.

They steamed and dripped in the chancel,
They listened and never stirred,
While, just as though they were Bishops,
Eddi preached them The Word.

Till the gale blew off on the marshes
And the windows showed the day,
And the Ox and the Ass together
Wheeled and clattered away.

And when the Saxons mocked him,
Said Eddi of Manhood End,
"I dare not shut His chapel
On such as care to attend."

A ruined chapel was to be found near the point of the Selsey Peninsula at a spot marking the limit of the Hundred of Manhood, hence the title. The name 'Manhood' meant that it was a communally owned woodland. It lay within the 'hundred', an ancient administrative unit, which was in the liberty of the Bishop of Chichester, granted by King Cædwalla to St. Wilfrid in 683. Eddi was one of the four companions of St.Wilfrid and is traditionally associated with Manhood End.

The poem precedes The Conversion of St. Wilfrid, the eighth story in Rewards and Fairies.

Merrow Down

I

There runs a road by Merrow Down –
A grassy track to-day it is,
An hour out of Guildford town,
Above the river Wey it is.

Here, when they heard the horse-bells ring,
The ancient Britons dressed and rode
To watch the dark Phoenicians bring
Their goods along the western road.

Yes, here, or hereabouts, they met
To hold their racial talks and such –
To barter beads for Whitby jet,
And tin for gay shell torques and such.

But long and long before that time
(When bison used to roam on it)
Did Taffy and her Daddy climb
That Down, and had their home on it.
Then beavers built in Broadstonebrook
And made a swamp where Bramley stands;
And bears from Shere would come and look
For Taffimai where Shamley stands.

The Wey, that Taffy called Wagai,
Was more than six times bigger then;
And all the tribe of Tegumai
They cut a noble figure then!

II

Of all the Tribe of Tegumai
Who cut that figure, none remain, -
On Merrow Down the cuckoos cry –
The silence and the sun remain.

But as the faithful years return
And hearts unwounded sing again,
Comes Taffy dancing through the fern
To lead the Surrey spring again.

Her brows are bound with bracken-fronds,
And golden elf-locks fly above;
Her eyes are bright as diamonds
And bluer than the sky above.

In moccasins and deer-skin cloak,
Unfearing, free and fair she flits,
And lights her little damp-wood smoke
To show her Daddy where she flits.

For far – oh very far behind,
So far she cannot call to him,
Comes Tegumai alone to find
The daughter that was all to him.

My Rival

I go to concert, party, ball –
What profit is in these?
I sit alone against the wall
And strive to look at ease.
The incense that is mine by right
They burn before her shrine;
And that's because I'm seventeen
And she is forty-nine.

I cannot check my girlish blush,
My colour comes and goes.
I redden to my finer-tips,
And sometime to my nose.
But She is white where white should be,
And red where red should shine.
The blush that flies at seventeen
Is fixed at forty-nine.

I wish I had her constant cheek:
I wish that I could sing
All sorts of funny little songs,
Not quite the proper thing.
I'm very gauche and very shy,
Her jokes aren't in my line;
And, worst of all, I'm seventeen
While she is forty-nine.

The young men come, the young men go,
Each pink and white and neat,
She's older that their mothers, but
They grovel at her feet.
The walk beside Her 'rickshaw-wheels –
None ever walk by mine;
And that's because I'm seventeen
And she is forty-nine.

She rides with half-a-dozen men
(She call them "boys" and "mashes"),
I trot along the Mall alone;
My prettiest frocks and sashes
Don't help to fill my programme-card,
And vainly I repine
From ten to two A.M.   Ah me!
Would I were forty-nine.

She calls me "darling," "pet," and "dear,"
And "sweet retiring maid."
I'm always at the back, I know –
She puts me in the shade.
She introduces me to men –
"Cast" lovers, I opine;
For sixty takes to seventeen,
Nineteen to forty-nine.

But even She must older grow
And end her dancing days,
She can't go on for ever so
At concerts, balls and plays
One ray of priceless hope I see
Before my footsteps shine;
Just think, that She'll be eighty-one
When I am forty-nine.

Norman and Saxon

"My Son," said the Norman Baron,
    "I am dying, and you will be heir
To all the broad acres in England that
    William gave me for my share
When we conquered the Saxons at Hastings,
    and a nice little handful it is
But before you go over to rule it
    I want you to understand this:-

"The Saxon is not like us Normans,
    His manners are not so polite.
But he never means anything serious till
    he talks about justice and right.
When he stands like an ox in the furrow
    with his sullen set eyes on your own,
And grumbles, 'This isn't fair dealing,'
    my son leave the Saxon alone.

"You can horsewhip your Gascony archers,
    or torture your Picardy spears;
But don't try that game on the Saxon;
    you'll have the whole brood round your ears.
From the richest old Thane in the county to the
    poorest chained serf in the field,
They'll be at you and on you like hornets,
    and, if you are wise, you will yield.

"But first you must master their language,
    their dialect, proverbs and songs,
Don't trust any clerk to interpret when
    they come with the tale of their wrongs,
Let them know that you know what they're saying;
    let them feel that you know what to say.
Yes, even when you want to go hunting,
    hear 'em out if it takes you all day.

They'll drink every hour of daylight and poach
    every hour of the dark.
It's the sport not the rabbits they're after
    (we've plenty of game in the park).
Don't hang them or cut off their fingers.
    That's wasteful as well as unkind,
For a hard-bitten, South-country poacher
    makes the best man-at-arms you can find.

"Appear with your wife and the children at
    their weddings and funerals and feasts.
Be polite but not friendly to Bishops;
    be good to all poor parish priests.
Say 'we,' 'us' and 'ours' when you're talking,
    instead of 'you fellows' and 'I.'
Don't ride over seeds; keep your temper;
    and *never you tell 'em a lie.*

Puck's Song

See you the ferny ride that steals
Into the oak-woods far?
O that was whence they hewed the keels
That rolled to Trafalgar.

And mark you where the ivy clings
To Bayham's mouldering walls?
O there we cast the stout railings
That stand around St.Paul's.

See you the dimpled track that runs
All hollow through the wheat?
O that was where they hauled the guns
That smote King Philip's fleet.

(Out of the Weald, the secret Weald,
Men sent in ancient years,
The horse-shoes red at Flodden Field,
The arrows at Poitiers!)

See you our little mill that clacks,
So busy by the brook?
She has ground her corn and paid her tax
Ever since Domesday Book.

See you our stilly woods of oak,
And the dread ditch beside?
O that was where the Saxons broke
On the day that Harold died.

See you the windy levels spread
About the gates of Rye?
O that was where the Northmen fled,
When Alfred's ships came by.

See you our pastures wide and lone,
Where the red oxen browse?
O there was a City thronged and known,
Ere London boasted a house.

And see you, after rain, the trace
Of mound and ditch and wall?
O that was a Legion's camping-place,
When Caesar sailed from Gaul.

And see you marks that show and fade,
Like shadows on the Downs?
O they are the lines the Flint Men made,
To guard their wondrous towns.

Trackway and Camp and City lost,
Salt Marsh where now is corn –
Old Wars, old Peace, old Arts that cease,
And so was England born!

She is not any common Earth,
Water or wood or air,
But Merlin's Isle of Gramarye,
Where you and I will fare!

Recessional
1897

God of our fathers, known of old,
Lord of our far-flung battle-line,
Beneath whose awful Hand we hold
Dominion over palm and pine –
Lord God of Hosts, be with us yet,
Lest we forget – less we forget!

The tumult and the shouting dies;
The Captains and the Kings depart:
Still stands thy ancient sacrifice,
An humble and a contrite heart.
Lord God of Hosts, be with us yet,
Lest we forget – less we forget!

Far-called, our navies melt away;
On dune and headland sinks the fire:
Lo, all our pomp of yesterday
Is one with Nineveh and Tyre!
Judge of the Nations, spare us yet,
Lest we forget – lest we forget!

If, drunk with sight of power, we loose
Wild tongues that have not Thee in awe.
Such boastings as the Gentiles use,
Or lesser breeds without the Law –
Lord God of Hosts, be with us yet,
Lest we forget – lest we forget!

For heathen heart that puts her trust
In reeking tube and iron shard,
All valiant dust that builds on dust,
And guarding, calls not the to guard,
For frantic boast and foolish word –
Thy mercy on Thy People, Lord!

Sussex
1902

God gave all men all earth to love,
But since our hearts are small,
Ordained for each one spot should prove
Belovèd over all;
That as He watched Creation's birth,
So we, in godlike mood,
May of our love create our earth
And see that it is good.

So one shall Baltic pines content,
As one some Surrey glade,
Or one the palm-grove's droned lament
Before Levuka's Trade.
Each to his choice, and I rejoice
The lot has fallen to me
In a fair ground – in a fair ground –
Yea, Sussex by the sea!

No tender-hearted garden crowns,
No bosomed woods adorn
Our blunt, bow-headed, whale-backed Downs,
But gnarled and writhen thorn –
Bare slopes where chasing shadows skim,
And, through the gaps revealed,
Belt upon belt, the wooded, dim,
Blue goodness of the Weald.

Clean of officious fence or hedge,
Half-wild and wholly tame,
The wise turf cloaks the white cliff edge
As when the Romans came.
What sign of those that fought and died
At shift of sword and sword?
The barrow and the camp abide,
The sunlight and the sward.

Here leaps ashore the full Sou'west
All heavy-winged with brine,
Here lies above the folded crest
The Channel's leaden line;
And here the sea-fogs lap and cling,
And here, each warning each,
The sheep-bells and the ship-bells ring
Along the hidden beach.

We have no waters to delight
Our broad and brookless vales –
Only the dewpond on the height
Unfed, that never fails –

Whereby no tattered herbage tells
Which way the season flies –
Only our close-bit thyme that smells
Like dawn in Paradise.

Here through the strong and shadeless days
The tinkling silence thrills;
Or little, lost Down churches praise
The Lord who made the hills:
But here the Old Gods guard their round,
And, in her secret heart,
The heathen kingdom Wilfrid found
Dreams, as she dwells, apart.

Though all the rest were all my share,
With equal soul I'd see
Her nine-and-thirty sisters fair,
Yet none more fair than she,
Choose ye your need from Thames to Tweed,
And I will choose instead
Such lands as lie 'twixt Rake and Rye,
Black Down and Beachy Head.

I will go out against the sun
Where the rolled scarp retires,
And the Long Man of Wilmington
Loos naked toward the shires;
And east till doubling Rother crawls
To find the fickle tide,
By dry and sea-forgotten walls,
Our ports of stranded pride.

I will go north about the shaws
And the deep ghylls that breed
Huge oaks and old, the which we hold
No more than Sussex weed;
Or south where windy Piddinghoe's
Beguilded dolphin veers
And red beside wide-bankèd Ouse
Lie down our Sussex steers.

So to the land our hearts we give
Till the sure magic strike,
And Memory, Use, and Love make live
Us and our fields alike –
That deeper than our speech and thought,
Beyond our reason's sway,
Clay of the pit whence we were wrought
Yearns to its fellow clay.

God gives all men all earth to love,
But since man's heart is small,
Ordains for each one spot shall prove
Beloved over all.
Each to his choice, and I rejoice
The lot has fallen to me
In a fair ground – in a fair ground –
Yea, Sussex by the sea!

Telscombe Tye
(Authorship questionable)

The moon she shined on Telscombe Tye
On Telscombe Tye at night it was
She saw the smugglers riding by.
A very pretty sight it was.

Three Dunkirk boats was standing in,
To run a proper load of it,
O' brandy, 'baccy, lace and gin
An' half Newhaven knowed of it.

King George's customs men had not
The proper understanding of it.
They thought Newhaven was the spot
Intended for the landing of it.

An'so they watched Newhaven close
An'Piddinghoe that's nigh to it.
An' that was how the joke arose,
As all can testify to it.

The moon she shined on Piddinghoe,
At ten o'clock at night it was
King George's customs men rode through,
As was their lawful right it was.

The moon she shined along the Ouse,
An' showed an' no mistaking it,
That half the men o'Piddinghoe
Was in the horsepond soakin' it.

With water splashing up their legs
An' talking low an' soft, of course
They looked like they was liftin' kegs
Which they had never even set o'course.

The customs men they had no doubt
They'd sunk the Dunkirk lot in it,
An' so they says "You rake it out
An' show us all you've got in it.

The Absent-Minded Beggar

When you've shouted "Rule Britannia",
when you've sung "God Save the Queen",
When you've finished killing
Kruger with your mouth,
Will you kindly drop a shilling
in my little tambourine
For a gentleman in *khaki* ordered south?
He's an absent-minded beggar,
and his weaknesses are great –
But we and Paul must take
him as we find him-

He is out on active service,
wiping something off a slate –
And he's left a lot of little things behind him!
Duke's son – cook's son – son of a hundred kings –
(Fifty thousand horse and foot going to Table Bay!)
Each of 'em doing his country's work
(and whose to look after their things?)
Pass the hat for your credit's sake,
And pay – pay – pay !

There are girls he married secret,
asking no permission to,
For he knew he wouldn't get it if he did.
There is gas and coals and vittles,
and the house-rent falling due,
And it's more than rather likely there's a kid.
There are girls he walked with casual.
They'll be sorry now he's gone,
For an absent-minded beggar they will find him,
But it ain't the time for sermons
with the winter coming on.
We must help the girl that Tommy's
left behind him!
Cook's son – Duke's son – son of a belted Earl –
Son of a Lambeth publican – it's all the same to-day!
Each of 'em doing his country's work
(and whose to look after the girl?)
Pass the hat for your credit's sake,
And pay – pay – pay!

There are families by thousands,
far too proud to beg or speak,
And they'll put their sticks and
bedding up the spout,
And they'll live on half o' nothing,
paid 'em punctual once a week,
'Cause the man that earns the wage is ordered out.
He's an absent-minded beggar,
but he heard his country call,
And his reg'ment didn't need to send to find him!
He's chucked his job and joined it –
so the jobs before us all
Is to help the home that Tommy's left behind him!
Duke's job – cook's job – gardener, baronet, groom,
Mews or Palace or paper-shop,
there's someone gone away!
Each of 'em doing his country's work
(and whose to look after the room?)
Pass the hat for your credit's sake,
and pay – pay –pay.

Let us manage so as,
later, we can look him in the face,
And tell him – what he'd very much prefer –
That, while he saved the Empire,
his employer saved his place
And his mates (that's you and me)
looked out for *her.*
He's an absent-minded beggar and
he may forget it all,

But we do not want his kiddies to remind him
That we sent 'em to the workhouse while
their daddy hammered Paul,
So we'll help the homes that Tommy
left behind him!
Cook's home – Duke's home –
home of a millionaire,
(Fifty thousand horse and foot going to Table Bay!)
Each of 'em doing his country's work
(And what have you got to spare?)
Pass the hat for your credit's sake,
and pay – pay – pay.

*(Paul, is, of course Paul Kruger, the ageing President of
the Transvaal)*

The Anvil
(Norman Conquest, 1066)

England's on the anvil – hear the hammers ring-
Clanging from the Severn to the Tyne!
Never was a blacksmith like our Norman King –
England's being hammered,
hammered, hammered into line!

England's on the anvil!
Heavy are the blows!
(But the work will be a marvel when it's done)
Little bits of Kingdoms cannot
stand against their foes.
England's being hammered, hammered,
hammered into one!

There shall be one people – it shall serve one Lord –
(Neither Priest nor Baron shall escape!)
It shall have one speech and law,
soul and strength and sword.
England's being hammered, hammered,
hammered into shape!

The Architect's Alphabet

A was an Architect; B were his Brains,
C was the Chaos he wrought when he used 'em,
D was the dissolute course of his Drains
E was the End of the people who used 'em,
F were the Fools who allowed him to build.
G his Gehennas of brickbats and lime
H were his Houses, bacteria filled
I am the poet who left them in time
J were his Joists – but they
broke with the rats on 'em

K his Kements (I adhere to this spelling)
L were his Leadings –
you couldn't swing cats on 'em
M was the Mildew that clove to each dwelling,
N was his Notion of saving expense
O were the Odds it would cost like all Tophet
P (Please insert for the sake of the sense)
Q were his Quantities, P was his Profit
R were his Roofs which were waterlogged rafts,
S for they Sagged (S is also his sinks)
T the Tornadoes he told us were draughts
U were his Usual Unspecified stinks
V was the Vengence I Vowed on the head of him
W for Wrong and Waiting and Waste
X is King Xerxes (God knows I have need of him!)
Y and a Yataghan (wielded with taste)
Z are Zymotic diseases, a host of 'em
Ambo's my architect, I have got most of 'em!

(This verse was written in the late 1890's in the margin of a notebook belong to his friend and distinguished architect, Herbert Baker. Ambo was Ambrose Poynter, Kipling's cousin who had recently enlarged the upper windows of The Elms in Rottingdean.)

Gehenna was a valley of sacrifice near Jerusalem, for which Tophet is an alternative name. A Yataghan is a long unsheathed Turkish dagger and Zymotic refers to moulds caused by fermentation.

The Destroyers
1898

The strength of twice three thousand horse
That seek the single goal;
The line that holds the rending course,
The hate that swings the whole:
The stripped hulls, slinking through the gloom,
At gaze and gone again –
The Brides of Death that wait the groom –
The choosers of the slain.

Offshore where sea and skyline blend
In rain, the daylight dies;
The sullen, shouldering swells attend
Night and our sacrifice.
Adown the stricken capes no flare –
No mark on spit or bar, -
Girdled and desperate we dare,
The blindfold game of war.

Nearer the up-flung beams that spell
The council of our foes;
Clearer the barking guns that tell
Their scattered flank to close.
Sheer to the trap they crowd their way
For ports from this unbarred.
Quiet and count our laden prey,
The convoy and her guard!

On shoal with scarce a foot below,
Where rock and islet throng,
Hidden and hushed we watch them throw
Their anxious lights along.
Not here, not here your danger lies –
(Stare hard, O hooded eyne!)
Save where the dazed rock-pigeons rise
The lit cliffs give no sign.
Therefore - to break the rest you seek,
The Narrow Seas to clear –
Hark to the siren's whimpering shriek –
What midnight terror stays
The bulk that checks against the spray
Her crackling tops ablaze?

Hit, and hard hit ! The blow went home,
The muffled, knocking stroke -
The stream that overruns the foam –
The foam that thins to smoke –
The smoke that chokes the deep aboil –
The deep that chokes her throes
Till, streaked with ash and sleeked with oil,
The lukewarm whirlpools close!

A shadow down the sickened wave
Long since her slayer fled:
But hear their chattering quick-fires rave
Astern, abeam, ahead!
Panic that shells the drifting spar –

Loud waste with none to check –
Mad fear that rakes a scornful star
Or sweeps a consort's deck.

Now, while their silly smoke hangs thick,
Now ere their wits they find,
Lay in and lance them to the quick –
Our gallied whales are blind!
Good luck to those that see the end,
Good-bye to those that drown –
For each his chance as chance shall send –
And God for all! *Shut down!*

The strength of twice three thousand horse
That serve the one command
The hand that heaves the headlong force,
The hate that backs the hand:
The doom-bolt in the darkness freed,
The mine that splits the main;
The white-hot wake, the 'wildering speed –
The Choosers of the Slain!

The Glory of the Garden

Out England is a garden
that is full of stately views,
Of borders, beds and shrubberies
and lawns and avenues,
With statues on the terraces and
peacocks strutting by;
But the Glory of the Garden lies
in more than meets the eye.

For where the old thick laurels grow,
along the thin red wall
You find the tool- and potting-sheds
which are the heart of all;
The cold-frames and the hot-houses,
the dungpits and the tanks,
The rollers, carts and drain-pipes,
with the barrows and the planks.

And there you'll see the gardeners,
the men and 'prentice boys
Told off to do as they are bid and
do it without noise;
For except when seeds are planted
and we shout to scare the birds,
The Glory of the Garden it abideth not in words.

And some can pot begonias and
some can bud a rose,
And some are hardly fit to trust
with anything that grows;
But they can roll and trim the lawns
and sift the sand and loam,
For the Glory of the Garden occupieth all who come.

Our England is a garden,
and such gardens are not made
By singing: - "Oh, how beautiful!"
and sitting in the shade,
While better men than we go out
and start our working lives
At grubbing weeds from gravel-paths
with broken dinner-knives.

There's not a pair of legs so thin,
there's not a head so thick.
There's not a hand so weak and white,
nor yet a heart so sick,
But it can find some needful job
that's crying to be done,
For the Glory of the Garden glorifieth every one.

Then seek your job with thankfulness
and work till further orders,
If it's only netting strawberries or
killing slugs on borders ;
And when you back stops aching
and your hands begin to harden,
You will find yourself a partner
in the Glory of the Garden.

Oh, Adam was a gardener,
and God who made him sees

That half a proper gardener's work
is done upon his knees.
So when your work is finished,
you can wash your hands and pray
For the Glory of the Garden,
that it may not pass away!
And the Glory of the Garden it shall never pass away!

The King's Pilgrimage
1922

Our King went forth on pilgrimage
His prayers and vows to pay
To them that served our heritage
And cast their own away.

And there was little show of pride,
Or prows of belted steel,
For the clean-swept oceans every side
Lay free to every keel.

And the first land he found,
it was shoal and banky ground –
Where the broader seas begin,
And a pale tide grieving at the
broken harbour-mouth
Where they worked the death-ships in.
And there was neither gull on the wing,
Nor wave that could not tell

Of the bodies that were buckled
in the life-buoy's ring
That slid from swell to swell.

All that they had they gave – they gave ;
and they shall not return,
For these are those that have no grave where any heart
may mourn.

And the next land he found,
it was low and hollow ground –
Where once the cities stood,
But the man-high thistle had been master of it all,
Or the bulrush by the flood.

And there was neither blade of grass,
Nor lone star in the sky,
But shook to see some spirit pass
And took its agony.

And the next land he found,
it was bare and hilly ground –
Where once the bread-corn grew,
But the field were cankered
and the water was defiled,
And the trees were riven through.

And there was neither paved highway,
Nor secret path in the wood,
But had borne its weight of the broken clay
And darkened 'neath the blood.

Father and mother they put aside,
and the nearer love also-
An hundred thousand men that died
whose graves shall no man know.

And the last land he found,
it was fair and level ground
About a carven stone,
And the stark Sword brooding
on the bosom of the Cross
Where high and low are one.

And there was grass and the living trees,
And the flowers of the spring,
And there lay gentlemen from out of all the seas
That ever called him King.

'Twixt Nieuport sands and the eastward lands
where the Four Red Rivers spring,
Five hundred thousand gentlemen
of those that served their King.

All that they had they gave – they gave –
In sure and single faith
There can no knowledge reach the grave
To make them grudge their death
Save only if they understood
That, after all was done,
We they redeemed denied their blood
And mocked the gains it won.

The Land

When Julius Fabricius,
Sub-Prefect of the Weald,
In the days of Diocletian
owned our Lower River-field,
He called to him Hobdenius –
a Briton of the clay,
Saying: "What about that River-piece
for layin' in to hay?"

And the aged Hobden answered:
"I remember as a lad
My father told your father that
she wanted dreenin' bad'
An' the more that you neeglect her
the less you'll get her clean,
Have it jest *as* you've a mind to,
but, if I was you, I'd dreen."

So they drained it long and crossways
in the lavish Roman style –
Still we find among the river-drift
their flakes of ancient tile,
And in drouthy middle August,
when the bones of meadow show,
We can trace the lines they followed
sixteen hundred years ago.

The Julius Fabricius died as even Prefects do,
And after certain centuries,
Imperial Rome died too.
Then did robbers enter Britain from
across the Northern main
And our Lower River-field was won
by Ogier the Dane.

Well could Ogier work his war-boat – well could
Ogier wield his brand –
Much he knew of foaming waters –
not so much of farming land,
So he called to him a Hobden of
the old unaltered blood,
Saying: "What about that River-piece;
she doesn't look no good?"

And that aged Hobden answered:
"'Tain't for *me* to interfere,
But I've known that bit o' meadow
now for five and fifty year.
Have it *jest* as youv'e a mind to,
but I've proved it time on time,
If you want to change her nature
you have got to give her lime!"

Ogier sent his wains to Lewes,
twenty hours' solemn walk,
And drew back great abundance of the cool,
grey, healing chalk.
And old Hobden spread it broadcast,
never heeding what was in't. -
Which is why in cleaning ditches,
now and then we find a flint.

Ogeir died. His sons grew English –
Anglo-Saxon was their name -
Till out of blossomed Normandy
another pirate came;
For Duke William conquered England
and divided with his men,
And our Lower River-field he
gave to William of Warenne.

But the brook (you know her habit) rose
one rainy autumn night
And tore down sodden flitches of
the bank to left and right.
So, aid William to his Bailiff as
they rode their dripping rounds:
"Hob, what about the River-bit –
the Brooks got up no bounds?"

And that aged Hobden answered:
"Tain't my business to advise,
But you might ha' known
'twould happen from the way the valley lies.
Where ye can't hold back the water
you must try and save the sile.
Hev it jest as you've a *mind* to,
but, if I was you, I'd spile!"

They spiled along the water-course
with trunks of willow-trees,
And planks of Elms behind 'em
and immortal oaken knees,
And when the spates of Autumn
whirl the gravel-beds away
You can see their faithful fragments,
iron-hard in iron clay.

*   *   *   *   *   *

Georgii Quinti Anno Sexto, I,
who own the River-field,
Am fortified with title-deeds,
attested, signed and sealed,
Guaranteeing me, my assigns,
my executors and heirs
All sorts pf powers and profits which -
are neither mine nor theirs.

I have rights of chase and warren,
  as my dignity requires.
I can fish – but Hobden tickles.
  I can shoot – but Hobden wires.
I repair, but he reopens, certain gaps,
  which men allege,
Have been used by every Hobden since
  a Hobden swapped a hedge.

Shall I dog his morning progress
  o'er the track-betraying dew?
Demand his dinner-basket into
  which my pheasant flew?
Confiscate his evening faggot
  under which my conies ran,
And summons him to judgement?
  I would sooner summons Pan.

His dead are in the churchyard –
  thirty generations laid.
Their names were old in history
  when Doomsday Book was made;
And the passion and the piety
  and prowess of his line
Have seeded, rooted, fruited in
  some land the Law calls mine.

Not for any beast that burrows,
  not for any bird that flies,
Would I lose his large sound council,
  miss his keen amending eyes.
He bailiff, woodman, wheelwright,
  field-surveyor, engineer,
And if flagrantly a poacher –
  'tain't for me to interfere.

"Hob, what about that River-bit?"
  I turn to him again,
With Fabricius and Ogier
  and William of Warenne,
"Hev it jest as you've a mind to, *but*" –
  and here he takes command.
For whoever pays the taxes
  old Mus' Hobden owns the land.

The Mother-Lodge

There was Rundle, Station Master,
  An' Beazeley of the Rail,
An' 'Ackman, Commissariat,
  An' Donkin o' the Jail;
An' Blake, Conductor-Sergeant,
  Our Master twice was 'e,
With 'im that kept the Europe-shop,
  Old Framjee Eduljee.

Outside – 'Sergeant! Sir! Salute! Salaam!'
Inside – 'Brother,' an' it doesn't do no 'arm.
We met upon the Level an' we parted on the Square,
An' I was Junior Deacon in my Mother-Lodge out there!

We'd Bola Nath, Accountant,
An' Saul the Aden Jew,
An' Din Mohammed, draughtsman
Of the Survey Office too;
There was Babu Chuckerbutty,
An' Amir Singh the Sikh,
An' Castro from the fittin'-sheds,
The Roman Catholick!

We 'and't good regalia,
An' our Lodge was old an' bare,
But we knew the Ancient Landmarks,
An' we kep' 'em to a hair;
An' lookin' on it backwards
It often strikes me thus,
There ain't such things as infidels,
Excep', per'aps, it's us.

For monthly, after labour,
We'd all sit down and smoke
(We dursn't give no banquets,
Lest a Brother's caste were broke!

An' man on man got talkin'
Religion an' the rest,
An' every man comparin'
Of the God 'e knew the best.

So man on man got talkin'
An' not a brother stirred
Till mornin' waked the parrots
An' that dam' brain-fever bird;
We'd say 'twas 'ighly curious,
An' we'd all ride 'ome to bed,
With Mo'ammed, God an' Shiva
Changin' pickets in our 'ead.

Full oft on Guv'ment service
This rovin' foot 'ath pressed,
An' bore fraternal greetin's
To the Lodges east an' west,
Accordin' as commanded,
From Kohat to Singapore,
But I wish that I might see them,
In my Mother-Lodge once more!

I wish that I might see them,
My Brethren black an' brown,
With the trichies smellin' pleasant
An' the hog-darn passin' down;

An' the old khansamah snoring'
On the bottle-khana floor,
Like a Master in good standing
With my Mother Lodge once more.

Outside – 'Sergeant! Sir! Salute! Salaam!
Inside – 'Brother,' an' doesn't do no 'arm,
We met upon the Level
an' we parted on the Square,
An' I was Junior Deacon in my
Mother-Lodge out there!

(*The Level* in Freemasonry, part of a Lodge's regalia, symbolizes the equality of all Freemasons, whilst the *Square* symbolizes honourable conduct. A Mother-Lodge is the one in which a mason is initiated. *Ancient landmarks* are the 25 leading principles of the craft, and Labour represents the ceremonials which take place when a Lodge meets. 'Trichies' were cigars from Trichinopoli, and *hog-darn* the cigar lighter. A 'Khansamah' is a house-steward, or butler, and 'bottle-khana' , the pantry.)

The Way Through the Woods

They shut the road through the woods
Seventy years ago.
Weather and rain have undone it again,
And now you would never know
There was once a road through the woods
Before they planted the trees.
It is underneath the coppice and heath,
And the thin anemones.
Only the keeper sees
That, where the ring-dove broods,
And the badgers roll at ease,
There was once a road through the woods.

Yet, if you enter the woods
Of a summer evening late,
When the night-air cools on the trout-ringed pools
Where the otter whistles his mate,
(They fear not men in the woods,
Because they see so few)
You will hear the beat of a horse's feet,
And the swish of a skirt in the dew,
Steadily cantering through
The misty solitudes,
As though they perfectly knew
The old lost road through the woods. ***
But there is no road through the woods.

"The Power of the Dog"

There is sorrow enough in the natural way
From men and women to fill our day;
And when we are certain of sorrow in store,
Why do we always arrange for more?
Brothers and Sisters, I bid you beware
Of giving your heart to a dog to tear.

Buy a pup and your money will buy
Love unflinching that cannot lie –
Perfect passion and worship fed
By a kick in the ribs or a pat on the head.
Nevertheless it is hardly fair
To risk your heart for a dog to tear.

When the fourteen years which Nature permits
Are closing in asthma, or tumour, or fits,
And the vet's unspoken prescription
To lethal chambers or loaded guns,
Then you will find – it's your own affair –
But . . . you've given your heart to a dog to tear.

When the body that lived at your single will,
With its whimper of welcome, is stilled (how still!)
When the spirit that answered your every mood
Is gone – wherever it goes – for good,
You will discover how much you care,
And will give your heart for a dog to tear.

We've sorrow enough in the natural way,
When it comes to burying Christian clay.
Our loves are not given, but only lent,
At compound interest of cent per cent.
Though it is not always the case, I believe,
That the longer we've kept 'em,
the more do we grieve:
For, when debts are payable, right or wrong,
A short-time loan is as bad as a long -
So why in – Heaven (before we are there)
Should we give our hearts to a dog to tear?

The Roman Centurion's Song
(Roman occupation of Britain, A. D. 300)

Legate, I heard the news last night
– my cohort ordered home
By ship to Portus Itius and thence by road to Rome.
I've marched the companies aboard,
the arms are stowed below:
Now let another take my sword.
Command me not to go!

I've served in Britain forty years,
from Vectis to the Wall.
I have none other home than this, nor any life at all.
Last night I did not understand,
but, now the hour draws near
That calls me to my native land,

I feel that land is here.
Here where men say my name was made,
here where my work was done;
Here where my dearest dead are laid –
my wife – my wife and son;
Here where time, custom, grief and toil,
age, memory, service, love,
Have rooted me in British soil.
Ah, how can I remove?

For me this land, that sea, these airs,
those folk and fields suffice.
What purple Southern pomp can match
our changeful Northern skies,
Black with December snows unshed or
pearled with August haze –
The clanging arch of steel-grey March,
or June's long lighted days?

You'll follow widening Rhodanus till
vine and olive lean
Aslant before the sunny breeze
that sweeps Nemausus clean
To Arelate's triple gate ; but let me linger on,
Here where our stiff-necked
British oaks confront Euroclydon!

You'll take the old Aurelian Road
through shore-descending pines
Where blue as any peacock's neck,

the Tyrrhene Ocean shines,
You'll go where laurel crowns are won,
but - will you e'er forget
The scent of hawthorn in the sun,
or bracken in the wet ?

Let me work here for Britain's sake –
at any task you will –
A marsh to drain, a road to make
or native troops to drill.
Some Western camp (I know the Pict)
or granite Border keep,
Mid seas of heather derelict, where our old
messmates sleep
.
Legate, I come to you in tears –
My cohort ordered home !
I've served in Britain forty years.
What should I do in Rome ?
Here is my heart, my soul, my mind –
the only life I know.
I cannot leave it all behind.
Command me not to go!

(Portus Itius was a port used by the Romans in the region of Boulogne; Rhodanus is the River Rhone; Nemausus is Nimes; Arelate is Arles; Euroclydon is the North-east wind; The Aurelian road ran from Genoa to Rome, and the Tyrrhenian Sea (rather than ocean) occupies the area between Italy, Sicily and Sardinia.)

"Very Many People"
1926

On the Downs, in the Weald, on the Marshes,
I heard the Old Gods say:
"Here come Very Many People:
"We must go away.

"They take our land to delight in,
"But their delight destroys.
"They flay the turf from the sheep-walk.
"They load the Denes with noise.

"They burn coal in the woodland.
"They seize the oast and the mill.
"They camp beside Our dew-ponds.
"They mar the clean-flanked hill.

"They string a clamorous Magic
"To fence their souls from thought,
"Till Our deep-breathed Oaks are silent,
"And Our muttering Downs tell nought.

"They comfort themselves with neighbours.
"They cannot bide alone.
"it shall be best for their doings
"When We Old Gods are gone."

Farewell to the Downs and the Marshes,
And the Weald and the Forest known
Before there were Very Many People,
And the Old Gods had gone!

The Run of the Downs

The Weald is good, the Downs are best –
I'll give you the run of 'em, East to West.
Beachy Head and Winddoor Hill,
They were once and they are still.
Firle, Mount Caburn and Mount Harry
Go back as far as sums'll carry.
Ditchling Beacon and Chanctonbury Ring,
They have looked on many a thing,
And what those two have missed between 'em,
I reckon Truleigh Hill has seen 'em.
Highden, Bignor and Duncton Down
Knew Old England before the Crown'
Linch Down, Treyford and Sunwood
Knew Old England before the Flood;
And when you end on the Hampshire side –
Butser's as old as Time and Tide.
The Downs are sheep, the Weald is corn,
You be glad you are Sussex born!

Appendix IV

A CHRONOLOGY of the years in SUSSEX

Please note that initials are used for the main characters throughout the text.

1871 JLK treats the family to a seaside holiday, on the recommendation of the Burne-Jones, in Littlehampton. Rudyard delighted in making sandcastles – precociously attempting a replica of the Tower of London which he had seen illustrated in Harrison Ainsworth's novel. Enjoyed donkey rides and watching the acrobats. Trips to Arundel and Chichester. He is taken from there to Lorne Lodge, the home of the Holloways, which he saw as 'Forlorn Lodge' and 'The House of Desolation' in Southsea. He and Trix appear, semi-autobiographically as 'Punch' and 'Judy' in *Baa, Baa, Black Sheep*.

1882 After leaving United Services College RK stays with Aunt Georgie at North End House, Rottingdean before leaving for India to begin his work as sub-editor on the *Civil and Military Gazette* in Lahore.

1897 After leaving the rather depressing Rock House in Torquay and abortive house-hunting in Kent the family move to stay with Aunt Georgie at North End House in Rottingdean. As Carrie is expecting a child the Burne-Jones leave the house for the confinement. The gift of a tandem arrived from S.S. McClure. John is born on August 17th *under what seemed every good omen*. In the meantime the village celebrated the Diamond Jubilee and RK wrote *Recessional*. He had earlier been a guest on trials of a destroyer and wrote also *The Destroyers*. Worked on *The White Man's Burden* and on editing some of the *Just So Stories* begun in Brattleboro. JLK and RK guests of Capt Bayly on H.M.S. Pelorus and experience manoeuvres of the Channel Squadron which are chronicled in *A Fleet in Being*. House hunting in Dorset and at Hastings comes to nothing and RK rents The Elms for 3 guineas a week. Working on *Stalky and Co.* With RK, J. M. Barrie, Cormell Price and the B-J's enjoy a long downland walk.

1898 With William Nicholson RK provides the verses for *An Almanac of Twelve Sports*. He published *The Day's Work*, twelve stories written in Vermont and *A Fleet in Being*, reprints from his articles in *The Times* and *Morning Post*. In January to Cape Town and Rhodes sends him to Khama's Country where he saw "the great grey-green greasy Limpopo River". Back to Rottingdean in April. Ned Burne-Jones dies. After a vigil in which RK takes part his ashes are set in the west wall of St. Margaret's. Rudyard entertains his children and their friends with recitations of *Just So Stories*.

1899 In January the family sailed to the U.S.A. and most suffered from a virulent form of 'flu. Not long after their arrival in New York Josephine dies and Rudyard is so gravely ill that he can't be told of the loss of his beloved daughter for several weeks. The family returned to England in June, with JLK and Frank N. Doubleday – "effendi". RK sits to Philip B-J in The Elms, and the portrait becomes one of the most popular. He is introduced to the joys of pioneer motoring when Alfred Harmsworth comes down to ask for a poem for the troops fighting the Boers. *The Absent-Minded Beggar* became incredibly successful and raised almost a third of a million pounds. In December RK is offered a KCB but declined the honour.

1900 In South Africa from January to the end of April. Various driving adventures around Sussex. His love of the Sussex countryside is used to brilliant effect in introductions to short stories, such as *"They"*. When house-hunting they see Bateman's for the first time but found it let for a year. Occupied with *Kim* and with Rifle Club/Volunteer matters. Return to Cape Town in Dec and to The Woolsack.

1901 In Africa until May. The first car he owned arrived on June 18th, beautiful to look at, but *"as a means of propulsion a nickel-plated fraud"*. In October Rhodes visits The Elms as, later, does "Banjo" Paterson, the Australian poet. Worked on various tasks including Motoring verses.

1902 In South Africa until May, during which time RK is much taken up with the death of Cecil Rhodes. Back home as their car is "out of order" they went by train to Etchingham and then by fly to Burwash. This time the purchase agreed. Price £9,300 with 30 acres. On June 1st news of Peace arrived in Rottingdean and Aunt Georgie had to be protected from locals who objected to her banner. A Lanchester, "Jane Cakebread", arrives and so much motoring. On 10th July last *Just So* proofs sent off. By 29th Bateman's purchase complete. And in August *Steam Tactics* describes car adventures. Move to Bateman's on 2nd September. In October to Rye for lunch with Henry James who delights in the fact that RK's car is taken with a "cataleptic trance". Work starts on the installation of the water turbine at the mill race to light the house.

1903 Again in South Africa at Woolsack. Arrive home in May and *"Bateman's looks divine"*. *The Five Nations* is published in October, and the following month he is offered KCMG which is also declined. Christmas is spent at sea en-route to The Woolsack.

1904 Return at end of April. The Governess Miss Blaikie arrives. In June a replacement Lanchester "Amelia" is delivered but proves unsatisfactory. RK winds up the Rifle Club. The Dunstervilles stay but CK doesn't like Mrs. D. Other visitors include Conrad and Gwynne. Rottingdean Drill Shed removed to Burwash for use as a reading room. *Traffics and Discoveries*. Works on Puck tales among others – consults Sussex Records Office. In December he buys Dudwell farm for £7,000. Again off to S. Africa.

1905 Works with Herbert Baker on the Rhodes Memorial in Cape Town. Return in April. A pony, "Stella", arraived for the children. In July working on the Centurion stories. Travelled in summer to stay with various friends. In Sept Jameson comes but looks *"ill and wretched"*. Dines in Oxford with Rhodes Trustees and Scholars. Again to S. Africa.

1906 Completes the last Puck story at The Woolsack. Returns in May and writes the Puck verses. Buying a Daimler. He supported Roberts in the National Defence League. In June demolition of Dudwell Mill. Death of Agnes Poynter – a well loved aunt. In August RK consults a garden designer about a new layout. In September *Puck of Pook's Hill* is published and he is beginning the sequel *Rewards and Fairies*. There is a Liberal landslide which upsets RK. Again to S. Africa.

1907 Return in April. In June they visit Bodiam frequently. RK is given Honorary Doctorates at Durham and Oxford and becomes a Fellow of Magdalene, Cambridge. John goes to school – St. Aubyns in Rottingdean and Elsie goes a-milking. In September a great trip to Canada where treated with great respect with a train at disposal. (Medicine Hat among many other places) Home in November in time to have Nobel Prize for Literature offer. Ceremonies in Stockholm muted because of death of King. The prize money is used for the garden.

1908 Again to S.Africa, Visits the Rhodes Memorial. No further return to S.A. because of increasing Boer control. Return in May and sees John who is homesick. They start a stamp collection. In August they tour the north, and Bateman's is featured in *Country Life*. To Switzerland for New Year – Engleberg – first of many annual visits.

1909 To Italy – then Paris and home. Concern over investments because of Liberal Budget. Touring in southern England. In October Dudwell floods up to the south door. Alice K ill.

1910 In Switzerland and then through France by train to Vernet-les-Bains where Carrie has sulphur bath treatment. Back in a borrowed motor. In August a flower show at Bateman's leaves them "devastated". After more English touring he goes to an "Aeration" meeting in Folkestone.
Rewards and Fairies published which carries "If-". In November Alice Kipling dies at Tisbury and sister Trix has a third major breakdown.

1911 J.L.K. died at Clouds near Tisbury. In February, March & April touring in France. Opens a small rifle range. In June they are guests in The Abbey for the Coronation of George V. In August again in France. But work continues unabated, and guests continue to be entertained at home. To Switzerland after Christmas.

1912 To Italy – return in April and works on Ulster verses - much socialising with important people. Speaks at Wellington College – John's school. In August taken up with meeting various regiments and watching manoeuvres. Travel to west country - U.S.C. becomes I.S.C. and moves to Windsor. In November saw flying machines at Aldershot. Back to Engelberg after Christmas but Rudyard very tired.

1913 In Feb to Egypt via France. Back in April and they see *The Harbour Watch* at The Royalty . Well received. He builds a cottage "Keylands" on the estate for Perceval Landon. Again goes off on Army and R.F.C. manoeuvres. Later to Kessingland, Rider Haggard country.

1914 In Switzerland. Returns to protest against home rule bill. He makes a speech to 10,000 Unionists on the common at Tunbridge Wells. The attack on the Liberals is resented by many. War declared on 4th August – *"incidentally Armageddon begins"*. RK begins his war effort by writing up his impressions of the services. German atrocities "schrecklikeit". 6,000+ civilians shot out of hand in Belgium. *For All We Have and Are.* In September John joins the 2nd Battalion , The Irish Guards. Commission secured by Roberts. All work on aid for refugees from Belgium. Visits to the wounded in hospital. All his energy thereafter directed to doing what he can for the war effort. Articles on Army and Navy which are collected into booklets – recruiting speeches – visiting troops -

1915 Working on *Sea Constables* and *Mary Postgate* In June Bateman's was offered for use as a hospital – but was declined. August – in France as a war correspondent. John not far away but after Rud's return from visiting Dover and Harwich naval patrols a telegram arrives at Bateman's to say John is missing. In spite of vain hopes he had been killed at Loos on September 27th.

1916 Many of John's friends call. *Sea Warfare.* In May makes an official visit to the Italian Front, which results in *The War in the Mountains.* After the Kitchener Memorial Service in St. Paul's *Recessional* is sung in the Abbey. Works from Admiralty sources on Battle of Jutland.

1917 Asked to write the Regimental History of The Irish Guards. U.S. enters war. *A Diversity of Creatures.* They hear the heavy gunfire from across the channel. He is asked, as the soldiers' poet, to serve on the Imperial War Graves Commission to which thereafter he devotes a great deal of time and effort in so many ways; catalogue; inscriptions; cemetery design; the Grave of the Unknown Soldier in Westminster Abbey. Jameson invites him to select Rhodes Scholars. Jameson dies.

1918 German p.o.w's working at Bateman's. *The Graves of the Fallen; Epitaphs of War.* The news of the Armistice reaches Burwash on the 12th by the ringing of the bells of St. Bartholemew's. Dines at the Palace by Royal Command to meet the President of the U.S.A. Carrie enraged by a caller from the Ministry of Agriculture who tells her how to farm her land. Rud discusses the "text for all Altars" with the Prince of Wales, which is accepted.

1919 Able to drive again – to Scotney. Distressed by the death of his old friend – Roosevelt. Death of Isted – the model for Hobden. *The Years Between.* Motor touring revived.

1920 *Letters of Travel.* Aunt Georgie dies. Her funeral *"A simple beautiful service"* in St Margaret's Rottingdean. Ashes placed in west wall with those of Ned. Takes Carrie to see Lorne Lodge. Spoke to 150 MP's at

Churchill's request to stave off a motion of censure re war graves. Conferment of Ll.D. at Edinburgh. They visit Chalkpit Wood and many other cemeteries. On 24th October Burwash Memorial is dedicated. Rud was asked to speak but could not face the ordeal, so Lord Home does so. Christmas Day – "much pleasure but no joy".

1921 To Brighton to join The Prince of Wales at the dedication of the Chattri. To Algiers, returning in May through France. Purchased a Rolls-Royce Silver Ghost, which is used for the next seven years. First major trip in new car to Scotland. In winter to France again where he is lionised by French Society. In December he is offered the O.M. by the King for services to literature and for the unique position his works occupy in the Empire. Declined.

1922 Visit to Gibraltar and Spain. In May with King George V at cemeteries in Belgium (Vlamertinghe) near Ypres and France (Terlinchten) where the King delivers the speech which RK has written. The interview he had given to Clare Sheridan (daughter of the Frewens) at Bateman's the year before gave a greatly distorted account of his supposed anti-American feeling. Considerable ill-health.

1923 Speech to Royal College of Surgeons. Much socialising – Downing Street and the Palace. Illness of the cook necessitates their going to an hotel in Brighton. Sea voyage to Toulon. In April *The Irish Guards in the Great War* is published to acclaim. John Buchan writes that it is "the fullest document of the war life of a British Regiment, compiled by a man of genius who brings to his task not only a quick eye to observe and a sure hand to portray, but a rare spirit of reverence and understanding". Becomes Rector of the University of St. Andrews.

1924 O.M. re-offered but again declined. In October Elsie marries George Bambridge and R & C dread losing their daughter to compound the emptiness of Bateman's. In November RK writes *Alnaschar and the Oxen* in praise of his Sussex cattle.

1925 Returns from a tour in France feeling very depressed. Loss of family (Aunt Louie) and friends (Rider Haggard, Lord Milner), Ill while in France.

1926 His health still causes concern. Touring in France till May. Worried by the General Strike. FND gives him a wireless set. In July he receives the Royal Literary Society's Gold Medal. They are charmed by a pageant from *Rewards and Fairies* at Rushlake Green. *Debits and Credits* published in September and is very well received.

1927 Visit to Brazil aboard RMS *Andes*. Return through Lisbon and France. His articles on the trip are collected in *Brazilian Sketches*. Christmas in France.

1928 On January 16th a Pall Bearer at Thomas Hardy's funeral. March to May Sicily, Italy and France. On return bought a new Rolls – a dark green Phantom (now in the garage but dark blue). His speeches are collected in *A Book of Words*.

1929 Receives the copy of *Kim* which stopped a bullet from killing Maurice Hammoneau. He insist that it and the Croix de Guerre goes to Hammoneau 'fils' to whom he is godfather. Boat to Egypt and then to Jerusalem.

1930 *Thy Servant a Dog*. To West Indies but Carrie ill and she is taken to hospital in Bermuda. Return via Halifax, Nova Scotia. On 4th August he was to have spoken at Dud Corner Cemetery at Loos but was overcome with emotion.

1931 Again in Egypt and Palestine. Then France. Angered by Cousin Stan's apparent shift to Socialism. Much illness and discussion of selling the car.

1932 *Limits and Renewals*. Cecily Nicholson joins as Private Secretary – acting in a similar capacity to Elsie after Rud's death. (Later her reminiscences are published in The Kipling Journal). He writes the King's Christmas broadcast.

1933 A Paris doctor finally diagnoses Rud's trouble as a duodenal ulcer. Helps to alleviate the pain. Prepares the King's Speech for South Africa House. Speaks to the Canadian Authors Society. (A recording is available). King's Christmas broadcast again.

1934 Treatment for Carrie at various spas. RK declines Legion d'Honneur.

1935 Assists with various film productions of his stories by British and American studios. An additional Just So story *Ham and the Porcupine* is written for Princess Elizabeth's Gift Book. In August he begins to write *Something of Myself*, the title having been suggested by Sir Alfred Webb-Johnson. They visit Wimpole Hall after the Bambridges have decided to buy the estate.

1936 They plan to go to Cannes but at Brown's Hotel, on January 13th, RK haemorrhages and is rushed to the Middlesex where Webb Johnson operates. Peritonitis sets in and he dies on January 18th two days before the death of the King. On Jan 20th he is cremated at Golders Green and his ashes are taken to St Faith's Chapel in Westminster Abbey. The King lies in State in Westminster Hall. RK's ashes are interred in Poet's Corner in Westminster Abbey on January 23rd. Carrie dies at Bateman's in 1939 having bequeathed the estate to The National Trust. The Kipling Papers which Elsie inherited are eventually placed by the Trust at the University of Sussex Library.

Appendix V

The list of Sussex Stories

Kipling's Stories which have an element of Sussex in them.

First Published in a Magazine

An Habitation Enforced	(A & R)	*Century Magazine*	Aug.1905
Below the Mill Dam	(T & D)	*Monthly Review*	Sept.1902
Brother Square Toes	(R & F)	*Delineator*	July 1910
Centurion of the Thirtieth, A	(P o PH)	*Strand*	May 1906
Cold Iron	(R & F)	*Delineator*	Sept.1909
Comprehension of Private Copper, The	(T & D)	*Strand*	Oct.1902
Conversion of St.Wilfrid, The	(R & F)	*Delineator*	Jan.1910
Doctor of Medicine, A	(R & F)	*Delineator*	Oct.1909
Dymchurch Flit	(P o PH)	*McClure's*	Sept.1906
Friendly Brook	(D o C)	*Metropolitan Mag*	Mar.1914
Gloriana	(R & F)	*Delineator*	Dec.1909
Hal o' the Draft	(P o PH)	*Strand*	Aug.1906
Knife and the Naked Chalk, The	(R & F)	*Harper's Magazine*	Dec.1910
Knights of the Joyous Venture, The	(P o PH)	*Strand*	Mar.1906
Marklake Witches, The	(R & F)	*Harper's Magazine*	Dec.1910
Old Men at Pevensey,	(P o PH)	*Strand*	Apr.1906
Parable of Boy Jones, The	(L & ST)	*The Rifleman*	July 1910
Railway Reform in Great Britain	Sussex Edition Vol XXX		1938
Simple Simon	(R & F)	*Delineator*	June 1910
Steam Tactics	(T & D)	*Windsor Magazine*	Dec.1902
They	(T & D)	*Scribner's Magazine*	Aug. 1904
Treasure and the Law, The	(P o PH)	*Strand*	Oct.1906

Tree of Justice, The	(R & F)	*Delineator*	Feb.1910
Weland's Sword	(P o PH)	*Strand*	Jan.1906
Wireless	(T & D)	*Scribner's Magazine*	Aug.1902
Wish House, The	(D & C)	*MacLean'sMagazine*	Oct.1924
Wrong Thing, The	(R & F)	*Delineator*	Nov.1909
Young Men at the Manor	(P o PH)	*Strand*	Feb.1906

(A & R) Actions and Reactions	1909
(D & C) Debits and Credits	1926
(D o C) Diversity of Creatures	1917
(L & ST) Land and Sea Tales	1923
(P o PH) Puck of Pook's Hill	1906
(R & F) Rewards and Fairies	1910
(T & D) Traffics and Discoveries	1904

Appendix VI

The Rudyard Kipling Archive

With the death of Elsie Bambridge, Kipling's daughter bequeathed her magnificent property, Wimpole Hall in Cambridgeshire to the National Trust, just as her mother had done with Bateman's in 1939. Within that offer to the nation came an archive of a mass of material relating to her grandparents, to her father's life and work and to those of their relatives, in particular the Baldwins, the Macdonalds and the Balestiers. The material was deposited at the University of Sussex in 1978, having been collected and sorted by Elsie with the help of one of Kipling's secretaries, Cecily Nicholson. They have proved an incomparable asset to scholars concerned with an extraordinarily varied life of one who was at times regarded as one of Britain's greatest sons. John Burt, one of the librarians, was the first of the staff to be responsible for the accumulated material, held in the Manuscripts Section. Under his aegis came a massive volume of letters to and from family, friends and associates, drawings and paintings made by Rudyard's father and himself, newspaper articles, literary manuscripts, and the transcription by Charles Carrington of Mrs. Kipling's diaries before they were destroyed. To these must be added photographs, business and legal documents, adaptations for stage and screen of various works, as well as Visitors' Books. There is a wealth of family photographs from the various places in which they lived and transcripts and tape recordings of Kipling's broadcasts.

To the main collection a number of additions have been made over the years. The Baldwin Papers were loaned by the Countess Baldwin on Bewdley and may be viewed by permission of Lord Baldwin. The Carrington Papers relate to the massive amount of work C. E. Carrington undertook as the official biographer. The Beresford and Dunsterville letters complete the trio of school friends at United Services College, Westward Ho! Other collections have been acquired when papers belonging to those who worked for or were associated with the family came on to the market. Of special interest are those from the estate of Mary Blaikie, Governess to Elsie and John who remained a family friend for so many years. The Parker collection includes letters relating to her employment, first as Nanny and later as Secretary, as well as drafts of letters and typescripts which she had no permission to remove. The Lewis Collection and the Macdonald Papers also have special significance. Some have been bought from funds and others have been acquired through the generosity of anonymous benefactors. Those wishing to discover the detailed nature of the archive are invited to turn to the website at (www.sussex.ac.uk/library/speccoll). In 2002 the University of Sussex published a book concerned with all the special collections, naturally including The Rudyard Kipling Archive. It was compiled and edited by Neil Parkinson and is entitled *Poets and Polymaths – Special Collections at the University of Sussex*.

A small collection owned by the Borough of Brighton was at one time on display in The Grange in Rottingdean when it was operated as the Toy Museum. Unfortunately it was dispersed without the Rottingdean Preservation Society having an opportunity to include it in the Kipling Room set up by the Society in the property it took on as The Grange Museum and Art Gallery. This material related particularly to Kipling's residence in the village.

Appendix VII

A VILLAGE RIFLE CLUB

A letter to The Spectator
Also printed in The Sussex Edition Vol XXX
1901

We were born, with many others, in the Black Week of '99; and the story of our adventures would fill a book. It Is enough for the world to know that the Marquis[1], the Squire[2], and the Farmer[3] gave us leave to lay out a thousand-yard range over their broad Downs; that the Range was made and passed to National Rifle Association specification, that we number, perhaps, sixty working members, and hope to become fair shots. You may see us any week-end, strolling down by ones and twos to the little loft where the Lee-Enfields live, under the eye of the Sergeant-Instructor[4]. Six months ago we should have handled a rifle as a bachelor handles a baby, but now we know the vices and virtues of all our twelve. Gorman, of the Electric Light Works, picks out Number Nine (a free-thinking old lady, near sighted, and hard mouthed) with a disparaging grunt. Number Seven of the light pull is his favourite, but Andrews the carpenter has just taken her, 'Never mind,' says Hawkins the gardener, lengthening the sling of Number Two, 'you can change on the ground with Andrews.' 'M' yes,' says Gorman, 'after Andrews has gone and got her fouled. She throws up like a pump when she's fouled - Seven does.'

Last autumn, we would marvellously tie ourselves up in our slings; but skirmishing-drill once, and range-work twice at least a week, has wonted us lo the heft and balance of the long rifles. The accepted fashion is to sling our gun across our back, shove both hands into our pockets, and progress at ease. The range is not fifteen minutes' walk from the village, Hawkins hurries on ahead. He has carnations to pot this afternoon, but is taking advantage of a spare minute to get off half his allowance (each man has ten rounds free a week) at two hundred. Our time, of course, is not all our own; but the Sergeant knows our business engagements pretty closely and takes urgent cases first. 'Jimmy the Crack'' (he that won the prize rifle at the spring competition) passes us with the cheerful news that the new regulation Bisley[5] target is in use, - a seven-inch bull at two hundred. We do not need to be told that there is also a roaring north-easter on the Downs, It catches us a razor catches a rough face; purring and scraping over the thyme-studded turf the moment we leave the village street. A mile away, very clear in the sun-glare, the lathy youngsters of the local training-stable[6] are dancing in their body-cloths as they file towards Windy Height Barn. The trainer's son, on a hot three-year old who gallops alone, comes sidling and frisking behind us. He is a very good shot in process of being made. The three-year old (also being made) bucks at the sight of the rifles, which he has not seen more than twenty times, and makes pretence of flight The boy catches him neatly on the first bound and laughs. 'Comin' down this evenin'? somebody calls out. He nods. 'Bad for your hand, if he pulls much isn't it?' 'Ye-es, but he won't pull'. He turns his youngster on to the dry turf and gets off at a stretching canter. 'Don't wonder we don't hit 'em when they're riding away - the Boers[7] - much,' says a bad shot meditatively, as horse and rider grow small across the green. We discuss this point as we breast the slope above the Squire's kennels[8], and just below East Hill. Some one delivers himself of the final argument. 'Young Carroll, *he* told us that at long range it doesn't matter about hittin' 'em so much. The thing is, *he* said, to pick up the range of the next ridge quick enough, and to keep on sprayin' it down near enough an' long enough to make 'em lie quiet.'

'Young Carroll' was a farmer's son who served a year in the South African Light Horse, returned to his native village, *en route* for the Argentine, and out of his extended experience - for he had over a dozen big affairs to his credit - gave us valuable tips. Our Downs are precisely like the veldt, in that as soon as you have crowned one ridge your are deadlily commanded by the next. For instance, here we are on the top of East Hill and all the range is spread below us. A thousand yards to the east, at the bottom of the three-hundred foot hummock that Nature has so kindly built for a stop-butt, the windmill-targets flicker and wheel against their dun-sod backing; a line of gorse in bloom marks the Two-hundred range; a black tarred shed where we keep our oddments at the Five-hundred firing point. Behind that Six, Seven, Eight, and Nine rise one above the other step fashion from the smooth turf. They command every inch of the ground, and except at the Two-hundred all shooting is a little downhill. It looks big enough in all conscience, this treeless, roadless, fenceless cup of green on the edge of the English Channel. And yet from the hill behind the butts, where the red flag streams, to where we stand, cannot be more than fifteen hundred yards; and that would mean most open order if bullets were coming the other way. Young Carroll and two or three other warriors have taught us to consider these things. Already we have learned to look at the scattered furze-patches among the sheep-walks with an eye to more than rabbits, and to think over the value of little dimples and wrinkles in what to a stranger would show for level ground.

At the Two-hundred we find our much-advertised Bisley bull, not more conspicuous that the head of a bonnet-pin. Hawkins and Yeo the chemist are hammering at it. The tricky wind, focused in the bottom of the valley, playfully pats and twitches their rifles, as a kitten pats a cork. We, waiting to get our hand steady after the run down, chuckle while shot after shot drives right and right again. 'You won't laugh in a minute,' says the

Sergeant grimly, 'Try your last three from the shoulder, Mr. Yeo.' That is Yeo's strong point He jumps up relievedly and pumps in a bull and two magpies[9]. Hawkins, after five shots returns to his carnations. The business of gardening teaches one to wait on the weather. Hawkins will further 'pot' that bull tomorrow when it may not be so gusty. Gorman and Number Nine get down alongside of young Nutley, that was a gardener's boy, but is becoming a man and a shot. 'This wind'll about suit her' says Andrews with a wink, as Gorman's cheek cuddles the stock. 'Hold!' cries the Sergeant, and there is a roar of laughter. We are rather a doggy community. Billy, Babette, and Tim are lying down beside their owners, but the markers have taken Flossie into the trench, and that impudent little beast has escaped and is sitting precisely under the bulls-eye. The breech-bolts clack as Gorman and Nutley rise to their knees; our red flag goes up and the Sergeant's whistle cuts across the wind. Out crawls a marker, but Flossie has disappeared behind the sod-banks. The marker cannot see what we would be at, for our voices are carried away by the gale, and so re-signals the last shot. 'Oh, get up and tell him, Ted' says Gorman. Young Nutley uncoils himself and flings his long arms abroad. He is the star of our signalling class which the Coastguard were teaching all last winter. He semaphores 'Dog' twice. Flossie is caught and dragged down; the red flag falls, and Number Nine rewards Gorman with a magpie, - perfect elevation too. She must be feeling well today, - the old beast!

To Gorman succeeds Lauder of the Coastguard, - trim, alert and brown. He gets in his five rounds Navy fashion; fitting the rough ground as though he were poured in to it. He and Purvis are full members of the Club. They can make or mend anything from a new wind flag to an old target; and their uniforms give us a pleasant air of official responsibility. The Admiralty decree that Coastguards shall fire so many rounds a year, but do not supply a range. They serve out tins stuffed with cordite chips, which they call 'reduced charge' cartridges. A rude target is then painted on the cliffs, and our Coastguards blaze off at two hundred yards; using the seven-hundred yard sight! (If this should meet the eye of the Admiralty, they may be interested to know that - for a consideration - we should be most happy to open the range to neighbouring Coastguards.) For the next hour or so we cut in and out like men at whist. Lauder gives place to Scott, the baker's son; Scott is followed by Keeley, son of a farmer; then comes Fane, the blacksmith's assistant; Anderson, the butcher; a mechanic or two; a member from Brighton (he has cycled over five miles in the teeth of this wind, but shoots none the less closely); and half-a-dozen others. A man from Burma, on sick leave, his fingers itching for the feel of a trigger again; the Vicar,[10] an Australian, and the schoolmaster make up the gallery,

'No more for the Bisley bull?' says the Sergeant, 'Then go back to six hundred. The wind's dropping. In Flags! Quick!' 'Please, Sergeant, mayn't I try a shot at six hundred?, says a man newly emancipated from the Morris tube[11]. We do not allow men to begin even at two hundred till they are dismissed their tube-course in the village drill-shed. 'Not yet,' is the answer. 'We'll give you another turn at the Two-hundred first. You had beginner's luck today.' The man obeys without protest (you are not encouraged to argue with our Sergeant), but follows up the range, for the sight and the talk of the game lay strong hold on him. Even our substitute postman (our permanent man is at the Front), who has not yet fired twenty shots with the Morris tube, spends his rare leisure here, listening and looking and learning. One can pick up knowledge for the asking, when the light is good, and the experts come down and lie down and demonstrate.

Over the hill, his rifle cased, walks Vansittart, a man of leisure, with a dozen years' experience of shooting, - all at the service of the Club, He attends our days as though it were his one business in life, and his advice to the colts is invaluable. He drops beside young Dixon, who has just slipped away from the frieze of huge farm-horses filing home against the skyline to the left. We have hopes of Dixon the farm-hand, for he has good knowledge of the lights and shadows under which he spends most of his life. He has never missed a drill or a shoot, or spoken an unnecessary word, since the Club began. The wind at the firing-point has fallen, but it still trickles up and down the valley in heart-breaking fashion. Vansittart's eye is on the wind-flag, which we others are apt to regard as mere ornament, and he follows the changes with some seventh sense denied to beginners. Then he falls back with young Keeley and two or three others, to whom the mystery of wind-allowance is not so black as it once was, - and they work it all out together at ease on the turf. The Sergeant checks each shot, explains, suggests, and, on occasion, casts himself down alongside to show by example. Hear his wisdom: - 'It wasn't the rifle's fault; give her to me. There you are! The direction's perfect, but you've been dropping your muzzle.' It is absurdly easy to get a bull when you have mastered the Sergeant's secret. He tells it to one concerned in these very words: 'You hang too long, and when you hang, you wobble. Never mind when she's going off, - keep your eye on the aim. Don't drop your muzzle, and don't pull at her. Press her! Press her!' Or thus; -'Left again! Oh, you drive - that's what it is. Your left's your master-hand. Try not to give that near-side jerk when you loose off. She'll throw to the near on her own account.'

This is to Maxwell, our local flyman,[12] who with the trainer's son, has hurried up in the garments of his calling. The box-cloth gaiters twitch uneasily as he strives to overcome a professional instinct to pull to the near.

Oddly enough, the trainer's son, though his hands are yet red from the reins (the three-year-old *did* pull after all!), shoots as straight as a die. Then Jimmy the Crack lies down to fight it off with Gorman, who, having unloaded Number Nine on an innocent friend, has been lying low for Jimmy all the afternoon. Jimmy comes to us from the high veldt, so to speak, - from a little lonely village in the Downs, where there may have been rabbits. At any rate he can shoot. He said the other day before some twenty of us:- 'If a man smokes or drinks he is no good at this game.' Then he turned on his belly and drove home bulls to clinch the sermon. A thousand tracts could not have taught us more. But Gorman in the blue jean overalls has the level eye and steady hand of the mechanician, and in a few weeks there should not be much to choose between him and Jimmy.

Last of all - he has business in London all the week, and comes down specially early on Saturdays to do his turn - young Foster, son of the local innkeeper, bicycles over the hill. Vansittart snaps his sight down and turns to watch. This is important, for Foster, Gorman, and Jimmy may represent us if ever we dare to enter for the *Spectator's* prize at Bisley, The light softens as the day and the wind go down together, the Channel recovers its unbroken blue, and the young thyme gives out the first true smell of summer. We are all quiet now, except Tim, the terrier, digging a field-mouse with squeakings somewhere on the edge of a wheatfield. 'Get back from behind the sights!' The Sergeant raises a warning hand. We tiptoe backwards and squat like partridges. They are proud-stomached men, these three cracks. They are not grateful, as some others, for a chance-won magpie. If they get an inner even, they scowl and the sergeant scowls, and they ask why they 'dropped' so badly. 'Bull, Gorman! Foster, bull – five! – Jimmy – high oh, high! Inner, high, right! Gorman, inner! Hold a minute till I get my glasses. That was bad Gorman, remember the light's changing every minute. Foster – bull again! *Good!* Now Jimmy, your last!' ….. It is a hang-fire – a bad one, too and you can hear our quick indrawn 'Ah!' of sympathy as Jimmy's last goes away to the right.

This ends the regular work, and the Club sits on the faulty cartridge, giving its opinion of Dum-dums and Service ammunition with entire lucidity. A member hands in a new rifle – his very own - to be shot for sighting; and while the Sergeant puts her through her paces, and a couple of us gamble for cartridges (five shots at six-hundred; loser to pay for the whole packet), the Committee, cleaning out its rifles, discussed the terms of a challenge that has come in from Newhaven Volunteer Engineers. We know nothing of their record – though we have all taken to reading the scores of local clubs, a fact which country editors should note- but we fear the worst. 'Oh, take 'em on,' says the Vicar. 'They won't do more than beat us. What do you think Sergeant?' The Sergeant smiles but guarantees nothing. He led us to victory against an Essex Volunteer team. He sees to it that we turn out the best eight we have, and the rest is with Allah's wind and sun and cloud. 'Ye-es, take 'em on,' says the Sergeant, and packs away the spare ammunition. The red flag slides down besides the butts, and we stroll home by two's and threes through the everlasting English twilight, explaining, arguing, chaffing, and reshooting every shot.

This game has enlarged the skirts of our understanding. Whether we like it or not, we must when we back our sights, for instance, learn a little neat-handedness; when we meet a visiting team we must entertain them as men of the world: when we use the verniers[13] we must think with an approach to precision; and when we wish to describe what is the matter with our shooting we must speak to the point and quickly. Our mistakes are our own, - pitilessly signalled from the trenches on the echo of each shot. If we lose our tempers, the target will not answer back; we cannot impress the unseen markers by our rank, wealth, or achievement in the world without. They will credit us precisely with what we make, - neither more nor less; and our companions at the firing point, who now know us very well, will do the same. We cannot patronise anyone except a rank duffer fresh from the Morris tube (and *he* may beat our head off in a month); we dare not tell or act a lie; and if we have a weakness for excess in any shape, the score book will check us off as scientifically as a German penologist. Unlike cricket, football, lawn-tennis or fives, any man can play the game; for here, no more than on the high veldt, will the discreet bullet tell its billet whether the despatcher was old, unlovely, poor, weak, or ill-clad.

There are those who say: 'Ah, but wait till this war fever dies down, and the men will get tired of coming down to fire off a gun.' One hears very little of war fever on the range, and the wonder (infinitely pathetic in grown men) of being allowed to fire and handle a real live rifle departed long ago. We are enjoying the game for its own sake; because it is sane, and healthy, and quiet (infinitely quieter than a cricket match), does not knock our daily work to pieces, or necessitate drinks before, during, and after; because it wakes up in us powers whose existence we never dreamed of till now; and because it opens to us a happy new world of interests and idea, - things that men need as urgently as inland cattle need salt.

But if only the range could be open on Sunday!

1. The Marquis of Abergavenny
2. Mr. Beard
3. Mr. Brown
4. Sgt. Johnson
5. Bisley, near Bagshot, in Surrey was the home of all Rifle Shooting competition.
6. The stable was at The Dene, the long building beside the west side of the pond.
7. The Boer War had been waging since October.
8. The kennels were for the hounds of the Brookside Harriers
9. A 'magpie' outside the bull is so called because of the way the triangular marker, black on one side and white on the other, when turned to signal, resembles a magpie's markings.
10. The Vicar was the Rev. Frederick Tower
11. A Morris tube fits into the barrel of a standard .303 rifle to reduce the bore to .22
12. The 'flyman' drove the horse-cab
13. The finely drawn scale which folds on to the rifle

The Boer War

The war came about as the culmination of almost a century of dispute between the expansion of Dutch settlers and British involvement in Southern Africa which was initiated during the Napoleonic Wars. The Afrikaners were Dutch Calvinists who believed in white supremacy and so when, in 1834, the British abolished slavery, the Great Trek was triggered to take the *boers* – farmers–, with their slaves, across the Orange and Vaal rivers beyond the British colony's frontiers. Friction and conflict persuaded Gladstone to restore internal self-government to the Boers although retaining British paramountcy in Southern Africa.

The struggle was centred on two men, Cecil Rhodes, the Prime Minister of Cape Colony and also the head of the British South Africa Company which was developing Southern Rhodesia, and Paul Kruger, President of the independent Boer Republic. British settlers in the Transvaal the *uitlanders* – most of whom were prospecting for gold, felt alienated by lack of rights. Attempt at negotiation to settle the matter by Alfred Milner descended into threats and ultimata which eventually led to a declaration of war by the Boers on October 11th 1899. Their raison d'être was to pre-empt an expected British invasion. Typical reaction in Britain was that the conflict would be over by Christmas, a mirror for the euphoria to recur fifteen years later. Surely the conflict between a few scattered bands of ill-equipped farmers couldn't possibly withstand the might of the British Army. It proved, however, to be protracted, and very costly in lives and finance. The whole enterprise started disastrously with three major defeats in December at Colenso, Stormberg and Magersfontein in what became "Black Week". British garrisons, at Mafeking, Kimberley and, later, Ladysmith were sieged, and the general campaign was fraught. Until reinforcements arrived to turn the tide, fighting the boer *commando* guerrilla tactics were demoralising. The country was finally controlled by the construction of block-houses along the railways, from which a scorched earth policy was pursued. Kitchener's solution for the displaced population, mainly of women and children, was to create 'concentration camps' but these proved lethal for many thousands.

Kipling, a friend and confidante of Cecil Rhodes, supported him with his talent for communication. He had earlier been given the use of 'The Woolsack' an attractive residence on the grounds of Groote Schuur, and from thence he went towards the front. Lord Roberts, who Kipling greatly admired, asked him to set up a newspaper for the troops, the *Friend*, at Bloemfontein. Well known correspondents – Perceval Landon, Howell Gwynne, & Julian Ralph - gathered with him to produce something to raise morale. Wherever he travelled, in troop trains and hospital trains Kipling was received with enthusiasm. 'Tommy' who had always benefited from his verses of support, welcomed him as a hero. His *The Absent-Minded Beggar* had raised over a quarter of a million pounds in the currency of the day for their welfare and for those left back home, and they appreciated his effort. On one occasion he 'came under fire' at a skirmish at Karee Siding not far from Bloemfontein, but possibly slightly exaggerated the potential danger.

On his return home he set about recruiting a volunteer force and the wherewithal to train them in a drill-hall-cum-indoor range which he bought, and on the full scale range across Lustrell's Vale. His account in the letter to *The Spectator* was masterly. He also tried to campaign for more far-sighted and understanding in the high-command, but without notable success. He argued back in Rottingdean with 'little Englanders' especially Blaber, the Landlord of 'The Plough', who resented the presence of our troops in South Africa. At the news of the Treaty of Vereeniging in May 1902, he was forced to pacify an angry crowd who took exception to a banner put out by his own 'beloved-aunt' on North End House. *We have killed and also taken possession* – a quotation from the Book of Kings. (1 Kings 21, verse 19)

Appendix VIII

RAILWAY REFORM IN GREAT BRITAIN

Know, O my masters and noble persons, there was, in the days of the Caliph Haroun Alrashid, a certain Afrit of little sense and great power, named Beiman Be-uql [Faithless and Senseless], dwelling in the city of Bagdad, who had devised brazen engines that ran upon iron roads. These, by the perfection of their operations, dilated the heart with wonder and the eye with amazement, for they resembled, as it were, litters drawn by fire-breathing dragons. Now the Afrit did not make benefactions for the sake of the approbation of Allah, but for money. For such-and-such pieces of money the brazen engines of unexampled celerity accommodated themselves to the desires of the adventurous. They bore the lover to his beloved, the merchant to his market, the fisherman to his nets, and the weaver to his loom, as was permitted by the All-Merciful. The people of Bagdad, who are both amorous and adventurous, disported themselves by day and by night on these engines, and gave the Afrit gold as from a catapult; and some twelve merchants of the city entered into a partnership with the Afrit, for the gains that accrued. Accordingly the Afrit became slothful and of a negligent disposition, forgetting that which is written:-

'Except sword contend against sword in battle how shall a sword be sharpened?
Except his neighbour contend against him in the market-place even the Very Veracious would sell rotten figs at enormous profit.'

Allah (Whose Name be exalted!) caused the belly of the Afrit to expand with fatness, and his eyes to be darkened with over-much meat; and he dismounted from the steed of zeal and stretched himself upon the pillow of shamelessness, and ceased to concern himself at all with the comings and the goings of his brazen engines.

The rumour of these things reached the ears of the Prince of the Faithful (whose perspicacity be rewarded!), and he called Mesrour, chief of the Eunuchs, and Giaffar into his presence, and he said: `What is the complaint against the Afrit that his engines are lacking in celerity?' Upon which Mesrour kissed the ground, and said: `O my Lord, let the Prince of the Faithful go out into the city and make enquiry.' Then Mesrour fetched the clothes of three Frankish merchants, and they went out, all three, disguised as

Frankish merchants, to the place of the brazen engines, which is over against the chief quarter of Bagdad. And they met a young man with a pair of linen drawers upon his shoulder and a linen cloth under his arm-for he would bathe in the water-and as he walked he wept and recited the following verses:-

'May Allah preserve the pure-intentioned from the engines of the Afrit!
I am old in calamity, but expert in resignation. I enter the engines constrained only by stringent necessity:
They regard the efflux of time as a drunkard regards the fallen petals of his chaplet: and they attain their ends solely by the fortuitousness of unmitigated fatuity.'

Then they went into the caravanserai appointed for the coming and the departure, and it was as though a battle had passed that way; for the caravanserai was full of smoke, black and white, and the ground was piled with the baggage of the faithful-pots, and bundles, and food, and medicaments, and the implements of exercise and diversion, all in little heaps, and by each heap stood distressful women and children not a few, imploring guidance. Hereupon the Caliph enquired: `What have these done to merit extinction?' And Giaffar replied: `They go a journey in the brazen engines,' and he recited the following verses:
`The Mercy of Allah is upon all things created, whereby the ignorant emerge from vicissitude:
If it seem good in the eyes of the Fashioner of Events, doubt not that these, even these, shall ultimately arrive at their destination.'
Then came a servant of the Afrit clad in bluish raiment, and cried: `With thy permission!' and smote the legs of Giaffar from under him by means of a small wheeled cart which he wheeled in haste, and he recited the following verses:
`O True Believers! The first is behind the third, and the third is before the second. Advance boldly and turn to the right! Continue and turn to the left, for that brazen engine which departs for Lawaz and
Isbahan upon the hour of second prayer lacking one eighth of an hour.
Come hither, O true Believers, and behold the brazen engine which departs for Raidill: but go elsewhere if thou wouldst behold the towers of Harundill!
Ya Illah! Allah! Six is four and three is five; but the second and third are only little engines from Sha'ham.'
Then the Afrits of the engines shrieked with a lamentable shrieking, and the faithful were cast into turmoil.
Then came Mesrour with written bonds which he had purchased from the Afrit for money, and upon each bond was written the following verses:-

'By the merit of this white bond it is permitted to such an one, the son of such an one, to enter into such-and-such an one of my engines, and to sit in the place appointed for such as hold the white bonds, and to proceed to such-and-such a place.

But it is forbidden to such an one to linger more than a day after that he has purchased the bond: nor may he give away the bond even to his maternal uncle, but must strictly seat himself at the hour appointed.

Moreover, I take Allah to witness that I wash my hands thrice of all that may befall this person, either by the sloth and negligence of my Afrits, or by the sloth and negligence of any other Afrits, or by the errors of any of the creatures of Allah!'

And it was signed with the seal of the Afrit. And the Caliph said: `This is a notable bond. Whither go we?'

And Mesrour said: `To Isbahan by way of Lawaz. Come swiftly.' So through the Protection of Allah, Who protects whom He will, they entered the litter appointed for such as hold the white bonds of the Afrit-a room of six seats and no more, of a bluish colour, with windows upon either side, and in the roof a lamp. Now there followed upon their heels the wife of a fisherman, perfumed with new wine, a woman of scandalous aspect; and four children who had never known the baths; and two men, sons of a kabab-seller; and a gambler upon the swiftness of horses; and a maiden, whose hair was like brass wire, who leered with the leer of invitation; and the wet-nurse of a sickly one.

When the Caliph perceived that their bonds were written on blue or brown paper only, and not one upon white, he said: `This is the place appointed solely for such as have the white bonds. I conjure ye by Allah, remove elsewhere!' But they laughed, and the wife of the fisherman demanded of the maiden her opinion as to whether the Caliph resembled a water-bird of antiquity, and the two sons of the kabab-seller said: `Behold his hair!' which is the salutation of the unseemly. But the wet-nurse said: `Has Allah deprived thee of understanding, that thou hast forgotten the day is Saturday?'

At this the Caliph laughed and replied: `What is the merit of this one day which, by the ordinances of Allah, hath recurred once in the seven since the beginning?' And the wet-nurse recited the following verses:

`When the carpet of Opportunity is unrolled before thee, do not consider where thou shalt sit, but leap swiftly into the middle thereof, and take firm hold on all four comers.
Let the proud man be abashed, but consider thou thine own advancement.
What are the colours of bonds to the true believer, or the gradations of affluence to such as go in haste?'

So the Caliph said: `Of what good is the Afrit's bond?' And the maiden with the hair like brass wire laughed and said: `None to thee, O my beloved, but much to the Afrit,' and she spoke with laxity of the Caliph's wife (for she thought him to be a Frankish merchant) and of the legs and visage of Mesrour. So they abounded in impure talk and contention upon the way, and the wife of the fisherman vomited the wine from her stomach, and the Caliph's heart became contracted on account of the incommodiousness of the situation.

Thus they reached the city of Lawaz, and waited for a brazen engine to bear them to Isbahan. Now there are some eight alley-ways in that city for the entry and departure of the engines, but no man, not even the servants of the Afrit, knows by which alley-way any one engine will enter or depart. And lest men should by study attain enlightenment the place is without lamps, and the alley-ways are joined by magic bridges and corridors, and mazes that are each the work of Afrits. Therefore the adventurous must lay hold upon the bridle of courage and pursue the ball of his goal with the mallet of ferocity.

After a great while Mesrour said: `O Prince of the Faithful, there is no escape from this pestilent locality till the Afrit brings a new engine, and it is reported to me by the veracious, whose skins are wrinkled through long waiting, that that engine is not here.' Now upon the wall of the place was written: `At the hour of evening prayer a brazen engine will depart for Isbahan.' This was written in large characters, but beneath had the Afrit written the following verses:-

`O true believers, who can do more than set forth his holy intentions?
This is a heart-lifting verse to read-the verse of the engines arriving and departing.
Consider it no more than as a song sung in a rose-garden, or as the voice of the nightingale among roses.
I have bound roses round the rod of Inaccuracy, and wreathed Emptiness with a desirable wreath:
But of the coming and the going of the engines I have washed my hands thrice.'

And it was signed with the seal of the Afrit.

Then the Caliph's liver grew congested, and he said: `What are the promises of this impure Afrit?' And Mesrour said; `As a stake in bran! Behold his shamelessness, and the names of those whom he has afflicted.' And upon another wall was written that all might read:-

'Such an one, the son of such an one, was upon such-and-such a day beaten with **fifty** strokes of the ferash for that he tampered with a white bond of the Afrit. And such an one, the son of such another, was fined an hundred pieces of gold because he gave the half of a white bond to his maternal uncle.
O true believers, read and fear!'

And the Caliph said: `Not content with afflicting us by the means of his own idleness and uncleanliness, he afflicts the faithful by means of the law. Assuredly I will subject him to the operations of a law which he does not comprehend, and pursue him with a torment which he has not in the least anticipated.'

Then they leaped upon a brazen engine that came out of the darkness, and it bore them to a city called 'Alisham, and it ceased; and they waited in an extreme discomfort for yet other engines which came not. For three days and three nights the Caliph, and Mesrour, and Giaffar resigned the direction of their feet into the hands of the Afrit, but Allah (Whose Power is uplifting) maintained them alive. Throughout the length and the breadth of the Caliph's dominions there was not one brazen engine which arrived upon the hour appointed; nor within an hour of that hour; nor was there any shame or penitence among the servants of the Afrit. There was no dependence upon their veracity and no refuge under the shadow of their assertions. And the Caliph spoke with men anxious to see their sick who desired them; and with merchants hastening to the market; with lovers seeking their beloveds; with women purchasing commodities; with muleteers, and craftsmen, and butchers, and courtezans, and widows, and the pious, and the clean and the unclean who had confided themselves to the engines of the Afrit.

There was but one thing certain in all the machinations of the Afrit that he had taken the money of the true believers, and that he had cheated them all every one. Then the Caliph returned to his palace and bathed and refreshed himself, and repaired to the Lady Zobeide, his wife, and told her all that story. And she said: `O my Lord, I conjure thee to chastise the Afrit with a heavy chastisement.' And the Caliph said: `He is an Afrit. How may a creature of Allah chastise a son of fire?' Then the Lady Zobeide recited the following verses:

`At the end and the beginning of all events permitted upon the Footstool of God sits either a Man or a Woman.
Can a Woman be more than a Woman? No, or she would be in Paradise. Can a Man be more than a Man? No, or he would be elsewhere.
Allah be exalted, Who has decreed that we of flesh and blood, confident in integrity, meet with nothing in the world other than Men or Women!'
And the Caliph took counsel with the Lady Zobeide and together they devised an excellent device.
Know, O masters and noble persons, that the first of the twelve merchants of Bagdad who had associated themselves with the Afrit for the sake of gain was called Ali, son of Abu Bakr, and he was wealthy and he loaned money to the Afrit and took usury therefor. His stall was in the market, but his house where he received his friends was in the rich quarter of the city of Bagdad.

Upon a day appointed, when he was making merry with his friends, there came to Ali a messenger with a message, written upon pale paper, and the message said:

'Peace be unto thee, O Ali, son of Abu Bakr. I am a man with red hair, the father of three sons and two daughters. Also my income is sufficient for my needs. I am delayed an hour upon my journey by the faithlessness of one of thy brazen engines, and I tell thee this for the love I bear thee.'

And Ali said: `Whose is this shamelessness? I am no more than an overseer of the partnership with the Afrit. What have I to do with brazen engines?'

Then came a second messenger with a second message and it said:

'May we never be made sad by thy loss, O Ali, son of Abu Bakr. I am a widow lame of one leg, and I bear a little black bag. Moreover, it rains and I am cold. One of thy brazen engines has experienced a contraction of the interior, whereby it has ceased to proceed. Send hither an implement for its repair, if thou lovest me.'

And the skin of Ali's forehead wrinkled, and he cursed the widow and her forefathers, and said: `By Allah, am I the refuge of the destitute? Bring no more such messages to this house, O messengers, but take them to my stall in the market that the clerks may receive them. This house is the house of my rest.'

And the messengers said: `Little rest for thee, O son of Abu Bakr, for there walks an host behind us bearing messages which are not to thy clerks, but to thee! Doubtless thou hast relieved a city by stealth, which is only now known to the grateful.'

And there came a third messenger with a package, intricately corded, demanding a price and receipt, and in its heart was a huge stone delicately wrapped, and on the wrapping was this message:

'Allah preserve thee, O chief of the Directors of the brazen engines! I am the son of a barber newly affianced to be wed. It is reported to me in the city of Krahidin that one of thy brazen engines has not arrived upon the hour appointed. I myself use not thy brazen engines, preferring mules when there is any haste; but I have found upon the roadside this large stone which, it may be, falling upon the iron road, has delayed thy engine. I send it thee for a love-gift, worthy of acceptation.'

Then the moisture ceased in the mouth of Ali, son of Abu Bakr, and his eyes manifested anxiety, and he said: `What is this calamity which has come upon me from associating with Afrits? May Allah confound all red-haired men, with all lame widows and the affianced sons of barbers!'

Then entered Fatima his wife, and her countenance was dark, and she bit her lips and said: `What dost thou know of Cypress-Branch, O man of impure associates?' And he said: `I am in no humour to jest. Begone!' And she exhibited a message upon pale paper which the messengers had delivered to her, and she read it aloud, and it said:

'To the Lady Fatima, wife of Ali, Greeting! Kiss thy husband for me. I am slender as an Oriental willow-shoot, and of unequalled gait. Ali has caused me to be delayed in the city of Tabriziz because of the unveracity of his brazen engines. Wherefore I am unable to bestow upon him the kiss of affection, and supplicate thee to be my substitute.'

And the message was signed 'Cypress-Branch.'

Then Ali took off his turban and cast it upon the floor, and tore his hair, for his wife was old and of an unforgiving disposition, and she

ceased not to load him with reproaches for an hour; and she retired into her apartments and wept. Then Ali left her and went out, and he saw a multitude of messengers advancing in their stately procession, or sitting in the court and playing games of chance upon his doorstep, or winking upon his female slaves. In each man's hand was a message upon pale paper, or a packet intricately corded, demanding receipt, and to none might the messages be given except to Ali, son of Abu Bakr. So he dismissed his friends and forsook diversion, and he wrote receipts until evening, and he wept and said: `By Allah, this life is unendurable!'

Then there came a messenger to him and cried: `I conjure thee by thy ancestors to hasten to the hall of the merchants, O son of Abu Bakr, for they have called a council and thy attendance is requisite.' And Ali said: `It is the custom of those who are in partnership with the Afrit to meet but four times a year. Wherefore do they meet now?'

And the messenger said: `Inconvenience has overtaken them and they are afraid.'

Then Ali put on his turban and washed his face and went to the hall of the merchants, and the first that greeted him cried: `O son of Abu Bakr, hast thou seen the inscriptions by the roadside where our brazen engines go up and down?'

And Ali said: `No, I have sufficiency of sorrow in mine own house.' And they told him that within a night had sprung up intolerable inscriptions over against all the fields through which the brazen engines passed.

Then Ali laughed and said; `This is the work of a red-haired man and of a woman lame in one leg and of the newly affianced son of a barber.' And they said: `Allah preserve thy understanding, O Ali! Thou art mad.' And he laughed yet louder and said; `It is the work of Cypress-Branch.' Upon this the unmarried drew away from him, fearing the excess of his madness, but such as were married embraced him and said: `Is thy house also darkened by the machinations of Cypress-Branch and Jasmine, and Musk and Almond-Blossom? Verily this is an evil day for the upright.' So Ali's bosom expanded, for he said: `Fellowship in calamity diminishes the sharpness of sorrow. Shew me the inscriptions.'

The first inscription was white and blue, three-and-thirty times repeated upon high poles to the left and right hand of the iron road to Isbahan, and it said:

'There are no engines like the brazen engines of the Afrit. Let us therefore thank Allah!'

The second inscription was blue on white, an hundred times repeated upon painted wood to the left and right hand of the iron road to Krahidin and Tabriziz; and it said only:

`O True Believer, why dost thou not walk?'

And the third inscription was red upon black, an hundred and nineteen times repeated on the right and the left hand of the iron road, and it said:

'When the Artificer of all Things created Eternity He foresaw that the brazen engines of the Afrit would require a reasonable time to reach their destination. '

This was the nature of the three inscriptions, and they were offensive to all the twelve merchants. Then said Ali, son of Abu Bakr: `Let us issue a proclamation demanding the heads of those who have caused the intolerable inscriptions to be written, lest we become a mock to the people of Bagdad.' This they did, but there appeared forthwith an officer of the law, and cried: `I conjure ye by your pure forefathers to declare by what authority ye have issued the proclamation: for 1 am the servant of a great company of the oppressed, who have hired the ground in the fields whereon those inscriptions stand. May Allah render them salutary to you, O merchants!' And he haled them before the Caliph on account of their proclamation, and the people assembled in multitude like pelicans on a lake and waited on the judgment of the Caliph. Then the Prince of the Faithful took up the first inscription and said: `What is your complaint, O traffickers with the Afrit; for it is not said whether there be engines worse or better than the engines of the Afrit but only that there are no engines resembling them? This is no more than extreme laudation: yet if there be doubt, call thy witnesses.' And the twelve merchants scratched with the toe of distress upon the ankle of embarrassment and said nothing, and the Caliph spoke to the people: `O True Believers, are there any engines like to the engines of the Afrit? Then there came forward seven-and-fifty men, young and old, and thirty-four women, old and young, and said that were there no engines like to the engines of the Afrit. And he said: `Do ye thank Allah therefor?' And they said: `We thank Allah by day and by night.' So he fined the twelve merchants a thousand pieces of gold each. Then he took the second inscription and said: `Where was this found?' And the merchants said: `In a field.' And he said: `Do men walk in a field?' And they said: `Yes.' And he said: `Do the brazen engines walk in the field?' And they said: `No.' Then the Caliph said: `Where is the offence of this enquiry, seeing that those who go by the brazen engines are not walking, and that those who walk in the fields are not in the brazen engines?' And he fined the twelve merchants two thousand pieces of gold each.

And he took up the third inscription, and the veins of his forehead swelled, and he said: `Do ye deny that Allah created Eternity?' And they said: `We do not deny.' And he said: `Do ye deny that the brazen engines require a reasonable time wherein to reach their destination?' And they said: `We do not deny.' And he said: `Do ye know for what reason Allah created Eternity?' And they said: `Who are we to fathom the secrets of Allah?' Then he said: `What is your complaint?' and he fined them three thousand pieces of gold each, and the people extolled the justice of the Caliph (upon whom be blessing!), but the merchants wept.

When they had returned to their hall. Ali, son of Abu Bakr, said: `By Allah, O my masters, we have fallen into grievous calamity, and I see no method of delivery from the inscriptions wherewith we are tormented, except we expedite these accursed engines.' And the merchants said: `It is impossible, for it hath never been.' Then Ali recited the following verses:

'We are as those who have ascended a blossoming mulberry-tree, from which there is access neither to Heaven nor to Earth.

When the charioteer is Eblis, and the reins are held by the son of Eblis, who may talk of what is possible or impossible?'

So they took counsel with the Afrit, and by the Permission of Allah, to Whom nought is impossible of accomplishment, the merchants caused one brazen engine to arrive in the caravanserai upon the hour appointed. And they swooned with amazement. And when they were recovered they went, some to the baths, and some to the wine-sellers, and some to the inner apartments. About second cockcrow Ali, son of Abu Bakr, was washing himself in the baths and there came a messenger from the Caliph mounted upon a white camel, bearing a dress of honour, and he cast it upon Ali wet from the bath and constrained him by the wrist and said: `This is the reward of diligence.' And Ali said: `I conjure thee by Allah, O interpreter of the way, compliment me with no more compliments, for I am sick of compliments, but fetch me the towels.' And the messenger said: `I am but the mouth of the Prince of the Faithful, who hath need of thee!' And Ali groaned and wept and said: `Am I not already sufficiently afflicted?' And the messenger said; `Doubt not there are companions!' And he sat him upon a high white camel of unbridled disposition, and led him before the Caliph. And there were gathered in the courtyard of the palace the eleven his companions, each upon a white camel of a lofty nature, and each attired in a dress of honour; and they were speechless because of the honour that had been done them. At the hour that men can distinguish a black thread from a white, the Prince of the Faithful appeared at an upper window and he said: `O persons of integrity, it is reported to me that a brazen engine has arrived upon the hour appointed,' and he ceased not to extol their wisdom and diligence, their perspicacity and their zeal, until the hour of second prayer, in the presence of the city of Bagdad. And when the sun was high and men had eaten-all except Ali, son of Abu Bakr, and those eleven his mates upon the camels, he said: `O True Believers, I conjure ye by the benefits that ye have received from the Afrit that ye do not let these men of pure countenances at any time go unrewarded for their endeavours. If, therefore, one of their delectable brazen engines arrive upon the hour appointed, acquaint me of the circumstance that I may honour them in this fashion, and in others, upon whatever hour of the day or the night that that brazen engine may arrive.' And the people said: `Upon the head and the eye.'

Then he gave the merchants permission to depart and they returned to their houses. But the people of Bagdad sat by their doorsteps waiting for word of the arrival of yet another brazen engine upon the hour appointed. So the merchants within ate in haste and drank expeditiously and denied themselves to their wives, and remained far from their stalls in the market, and forsook the company of musicians. When a second brazen engine arrived upon the hour appointed, the people of Bagdad broke in upon them with salutations, and set them all upon tall camels of unbridled dispositions, and the messengers of the Caliph cast upon them dresses of honour, and they were borne to the very presence of the Caliph, who in all respects entreated them as before, for a very long while. But when that second engine arrived the Caliph (may his mercy be requited!) excused Ali, son of Abu Bakr, from the attendance; and when the third engine arrived he excused Hussein of the Fishmarkets from the attendance; and so with the other engines as they arrived, for he said: `If I make this honour common how shall it be prized? Verily punctuality is an unheard-of virtue, rarer than the egg of the Roc, but we must also remember the infirmities of mankind.'

The people of Bagdad delighted rapturously to do honour to the remnant of the twelve merchants. When the fifth brazen engine arrived upon the hour appointed, they beat drums and cymbals; and for the sixth engine they closed all the markets; for the seventh engine they lit torches and shouted; and for the eighth they burned fires, red, white, and blue, in all the wards; for the ninth they assembled the Army and exercised them in the exercises of war; for the tenth they invited their friends and acquaintances, in number like netted fish, who came drawn by brazen engines from Isbahan and Lawaz, from Krahidin and Tabriziz; for the eleventh they extended the arm of allurement to all the inhabitants of the earth as far as a brazen engine might travel, nor were the inhabitants undesirous to attend to assist and to admire; for the twelfth, when there was called but one merchant to the presence of the Caliph, they altogether abandoned gravity and delivered themselves in multitudes, together with vast assemblies from other cities, to the dominion of mirth and excess. On that day at one time they beat gongs and the instruments of music. they blew upon horns without ceasing; they burned coloured fires, and they exercised the Army, and they closed the markets, and they waved banners and recited verses in honour of the twelve merchants and their wives and their daughters and their sons unborn, so that for a day's journey round Bagdad the clouds quaked with tumult. And when the merchants had occasion to come forth the inhabitants of Bagdad pursued them with the steeds of unbitted praise, and buried them beneath the blossoms of importunate compliment, so that the merchants covered the face of humility with the hand of modesty.

And Ali, son of Abu Bakr, joined himself to a company of those rejoicing and said: `I conjure ye by your most remote ancestors, declare to me in what way ye have profited by the laudations wherewith ye have belauded us? For it is brought to my notice that through seven weeks the inhabitants of Bagdad have abandoned the pursuit of all trade and gain, that they may pursue me and my associates with an unmerited honour.'

And the merry-makers said: `May we never lose thy presence, O son of Abu Bakr!' and they recited the following verses:

'Have we wasted a day, or forty days, in unseemly revelry?

Still we have revelled, and the remembrances of our diversions will not soon depart from us.

But we assert that our merry-making was not flagitious, and that the echo of our laughter shall not perish out of men's hearts.

Give us an equal occasion, and we will disport ourselves anew, lest any should believe us incapable of more than a little mirth.

Truly our benevolence is inexhaustible, and our goodwill knows neither beginning nor end.

This is but a foretaste of our favours. We have unexpended a million million others.'

Then Ali said: `Is this of a truth your intention?' And the merrymakers said: `Have we not already proved it, or shall we set thee again upon the camel and delight thee with amazing caresses?'

Then he trembled excessively, and the sweat leaped out upon his forehead like seed-pearls, and he said: `I hear and I obey and I toil,' and he cast off his garments and bought a leathern apron and a porter's knot and went down to the caravanserai to oversee and to expedite the brazen engines.

But he found in the caravanserai, attired in leathern aprons, adorned with porters' knots, the eleven his companions, and the sweat stood out

upon their foreheads also like seed-pearls by reason of the vehemence with which they laboured both to oversee and to expedite the engines. And Ali said: `I am not alone in affliction.' And they said: `By Allah, dost thou call this affliction? It is altogether Paradise by the side of the honours to which we have been subjected, and we purpose to endure in it to our lives' end rather than to incur again the attentions of the inhabitants of Bagdad'... And they recited the following verses:

'Against all things, except Ridicule, hath Allah fortified the hearts of men; but even the most vicious desire not to be made a butt; and the brazen-faced preserve still a remnant of shame.

When sweet words are useless the fool speaks sourly; but the wise man maketh his speech yet sweeter, till the teeth of such as hear it ache from excess of sweetness.

Hast thou forgotten the red-headed man, or the widow lame of one leg, or the newly affianced son of the barber, or the inscriptions in colour like to the rainbow, or the lamentable chapter of the camels? Be sure that these are prepared against the day of Dereliction, and will inevitably return at the hour of Unpunctuality.

Allah hath applied a goad to the extremities of our reason.

He hath sent a remembrancer into our secret apartments, and an open shame about our feet going forth.

Alas for the days when, free and uncontrolled, we lived among the valleys of Bagdad, merrily, and in no very good fame!'

So, then, these twelve merchants, who were partners with the Afrit, laboured unremittingly for many years in honesty and sobriety and zeal and devotion to expedite the engines of the Afrit; and having, by the Permission of Allah, attained these ends, they were each at the appointed hour overtaken by Death, the separator of companions, the divider of real estate, the terminator of leases, the herdsman of heriots, and the completor of operations.

Extolled be the excellence of Allah-al-Bari Who alone is the contriver of wonderful things; the Artificer of the destinies of the Universe, and the Compeller of the hearts of men!

BIBLIOGRAPHY

General

Kipling has been the subject of a great number of biographies even from the early years of his fame. Some cover all aspects of his life and work, whilst others concentrate on specific aspects of his influence. This list is not intended to be comprehensive but it will provide a considerable choice. Where there is a significant subtitle, Rudyard's name is reduced to RK.

Autobiography

Rudyard Kipling	Something of Myself	Macmillan	1937
Rudyard Kipling Pinney, T. (Ed)	Something of Myself and other autobiographical writings	Cambridge U. P.	1990
	Exceptionally valuable because of the annotations		

Biography

Adams, J.	Kipling	Haus	2008
Birkenhead	Rudyard Kipling	Weidenfeld & Nicolson	1978
Brown, H.	RK – A New Appreciation	Hamish Hamilton	1945
Carrington, C. E.	RK – His life and work	Macmillan	1955
Fido, M.	RK – An illustrated biography	Bedrick	1986
Gilmour, D.	The Long Recessional	John Murray	2002
Hopkins, R. T.	RK – A Literary Appreciation	Simpkin Marshall	1915
Rewritten as	RK - A character study	Simpkin Marshall	1921
	RK -The Story of a Genius	Cecil Palmer	1930
Laski, M.	From Palm to Pine	Sidgwick & Jackson	1987
Lycett, A.	Rudard Kipling	Weidenfeld & Nicolson	1999
Mallet, P.	RK — A Literary Life	Palgrave Macmillan	2007
Nicolson, A.	The Hated Wife – Carrie Kipling	Short Books	2001
Palmer, J.	Rudyard Kipling	Nisbet	1915
Ricketts, H.	The Unforgiving Minute	Chatto & Windus	1999
Shanks, E.	Rudyard Kipling	Macmillan	1940

| Sutcliff, R. | Rudyard Kipling (A monograph) | Bodley Head | 1960 |
| Wilson, A. | The Strange Ride of Rudyard Kipling | Secker & Warburg | 1977 |

Introduction

Hopkins, R. T.	Kipling's Sussex	Simpkin, Marshall	1921
"	Kipling's Sussex Revisited	Herbert Jenkins	1929
"	The Kipling Country	Cecil Palmer	1924

Before Sussex

Allen, C.	Kipling Sahib	Little Brown	2007
Beresford, G. C.	Schooldays with Kipling	Gollancz	1936
Dunsterville, L. C.	"Stalky" Settles Down	Jarrold	1932
Ankers, A.	The Pater (1837 – 1911)	Pond View	1988
Baldwin, A. W.	The Macdonald Sisters	Peter Davies	1960
Flanders, J.	A Circle of Sisters	Penguin Viking	2001
Taylor, I.	Victorian Sisters	Adler	1987
Nicolson, A.	The Hated Wife	Short Books	2001
Munson, A.	Kipling's India	Doubleday	1915
Pinney, T. (Ed)	Kipling's India: Uncollected Sketches 1884 – 1888	Macmillan	1986
Cornell, L.	Kipling in India	Macmillan	1966
Allen, C.	Kipling's Kingdom	Michael Joseph	1987
McAveeney	Kipling in Gloucester	Curious Traveller Press	1996
	The Writing of Captains Courageous		
Murray, S.	Rudyard Kipling in Vermont Birthplace of The Jungle Books	Images from the Past	1997
Van de Water	Rudyard Kipling's Vermont Feud	Academy (Vt)	1981

The Sussex Landscape

| Brandon, P. | The Sussex Landscape | Hodder & Stoughton | 1974 |
| " | The South Downs | Phillimore | 1998 |

Gallois, R. W.	The Wealden District (British Regional Geology)	H.M.S.O.	1965
Gibbons, W.	The Weald (A geological field Guide)	Unwin Paperbacks	1981
Godfrey, J.	The South Downs Way (Aerofilms Guide)	Ian Allan	1992
Jebb, M.	A guide to the South Downs Way	Constable	1984
Jones, D. K. C.	Southeast and Southern England (Geofmorpholgy of the British isles)	Methuen	1981
Thompson W. H. & Clark, G.	The Sussex Landscape	A & C Black	1935
Steers, J. A.	The Coastline of England & Wales	Cambridge (UP)	1946
Wooldridge, S. W. & Goldring, F.	The Weald	Collins (NN)	1953

Downland Idyll

Copper, B.	Early to Rise	Heinemann	1976
Copper, B.	Bob Copper's Sussex	S. B. Publications	1997
Moens, S. M.	Rottingdean	John Beal	1953
Smith, M.	R.K. – The Rottingdean Years	Brownleaf	1989
Worster, W.	Merlin's Isle R-K's England	Gyldendal	1924

The Pioneer Motorist

Macdonald, M.	Kipling the Motoring Man	The National Trust	1983

The Very Own House

Goodwin, J.	Burwash and the Sussex Weald	Courier Publishing	undated
Lees-Milne, J.	Writers at Home Bateman's by Jonathan Keates	Trefoil Books	1985
Marsh, K. (Ed)	Writers and Their Houses Bateman's by Philip Mason	Hamish Hamilton	1993

Nicolson, A.	Bateman's (N.T. Guide)	The National Trust	1996
Ponton, D.	RK at Home and at Work	J. Looker	undated

Armageddon

Haig, D.	My Boy Jack (Play Text)	Nick Hern Books	1997
Holt, V & T.	My Boy Jack?	Leo Cooper	1998
Kipling, R.	The Irish Guards in the Great War	Macmillan (2 Vols)	1923
Kipling, R.	The Irish Guards in the Great War	Spellmount (2 Vols)	1997
	(with a fine Foreword by George Webb)		

Elite Motoring

Macdonald, M.	The Long Trail	Tideway House	1999

Kipling's Letters

The letters were collected and annotated by Professor Thomas Pinney in six volumes.

Pinney, T.	The Letters of Rudyard Kipling	Macmillan	
	Volume 1: 1872 – 89		1990
	Volume 2: 1890 – 99		1990
	Volume 3: 1900 –10		1996
	Volume 4: 1911 – 19		1999
	Volume 5: 1920 – 30		2004
	Volume 6: 1931 – 36		2004

The Kipling Archive

Parkinson, N.	Poets and Polymaths	University of Sussex	2002

Anthology

Mitchell, R.	Sussex – A Kipling Anthology	Padda Books	1990
& Vann, J.	(Illustrated by Leslie Benenson)		

Index

The index relates only to the main text and not to the Appendices